\CHANGING FATHERHOOD/

A MULTIDISCIPLINARY PERSPECTIVE

Edited by
Mirjam van Dongen
Gerard Frinking
Menno Jacobs

THESIS PUBLISHERS
AMSTERDAM 1995

CIP-DATA KONINKLIJKE BIBLIOTHEEK, DEN HAAG

Changing

Changing fatherhood : an interdisciplinary perspective /
ed. by Mirjam C.P. van Dongen, Gerard A.B. Frinking,
Menno J.G. Jacobs. — Amsterdam : Thesis Publishers
ISBN 90-5170-341-4
NUGI 651
Subject headings: fatherhood.

Cover: Mirjam Bode

ISBN 90-5170-341-4
NUGI 651

Contents

The authors

Frank van Balen
Institute for Pedagogical Science, University of Amsterdam
The Netherlands

Gijs Beets
Netherlands Interdisciplinary Demographic Institute
The Netherlands

Hélène Desrosiers & Céline le Bourdais
Institut National de la Recherche Scientifique
Canada

Mirjam van Dongen
Department of Demography, Tilburg University
The Netherlands

Tamara Hareven
Group for Family Research, University of Delaware
United States of Amerika

Arlie Hochschild
Department of Sociology, University of California
United States of Amerika

Menno Jacobs
Department of Demography, Tilburg University
The Netherlands

Yvonne Knibiehler
Em. Prof. Université de Provence
France

Trudie Knijn
Department of General Social Sciences, Utrecht University
The Netherlands

Anton Kuijsten
Department of Planning and Demography, University of Amsterdam
The Netherlands

Michael Lamb
National Institute of Child Health and Human Development
United States of Amerika

Charlie Lewis
Department of Psychology, Lancaster University
United Kingdom

William Marsiglio
Sociology Department, University of Florida
United States of Amerika

Marry Niphuis-Nell
Social and Cultural Planning Office
The Netherlands

Rossella Palomba
Institute for Population Research
Italy

François de Singly
Université de Sorbonne
France

Carol Smart
School of Sociology & Social Policy, University of Leeds
United Kingdom

Paul Vlaardingerbroek
Department of Civil Law, Tilburg University
The Netherlands

Tineke Willemsen
Department of Women's Studies, Tilburg University
The Netherlands

Preface

Changing Fatherhood was the subject of an international conference held at Tilburg University in May 1994. The initiators, Mirjam van Dongen, Gerard Frinking and Menno Jacobs, brought together prominent scientists from various disciplines to put forward their views on a number of aspects of changing fatherhood. The result was an inspiring three-day meeting with lectures, workshops and debates.

The conference on changing fatherhood was one of many important activities carried out by the research unit in the Work and Organisation Research Centre of the Faculty of Social and Behavioural Sciences of Tilburg University in 1994. In the previous year, a multidisciplinary team decided to start a research programme on developments in the division of paid and unpaid labour. The researchers participating in this programme come from various disciplines, such as sociology, demography, psychology and women's studies. The programme focuses on describing and explaining differences in the degree of participation in paid and unpaid labour by men and women. In this context, the position of men deserves special attention.

The aim of the conference was an exchange of knowledge about backgrounds and implications of changing fatherhood in a multidisciplinary and international perspective. Besides a scientific evaluation of research on fatherhood, attention was given to the policy implications of its changing nature.

The conference produced a large number of new, useful, interesting and stimulating ideas, represented in numerous papers and comments. Nineteen of these papers and comments have been selected for publication in this book. Since there is no societal change process that takes place in one discipline at a time, or in one country at a time, special attention in making the selection was given to the multidisciplinary and multinational nature of this subject. We tried to cover all the disciplines involved in fatherhood and in the conference, placing great emphasis on discussion and differences of opinion. The character of the book may therefore be labelled as broad-based or even fragmented, but this diversity and fragmentation may be seen as a metaphor of changing fatherhood itself. We hope that the dialectical set-up of the book will provide a receptive ground for further discussion and political debate about fatherhood.

This book could not have been published without the help of many people. First of all we would like to thank the participants of the conference for their social and intellectual efforts. Special thanks goes to the authors of the articles in this book, who were so kind to prepare their lectures for publication. Financial support was obtained from the Netherlands Graduate School of Research in Demography (PDOD), the Faculty of Social Sciences of Tilburg University, the Ministry of Social Affairs (SZW-DCE), the Royal Dutch Academy of Sciences (KNAW), the Work and Organisation Research Centre (WORC), and Akzo Organon.

The conference was bilingual: English and French. As a result, translations and corrections had to be made in order to be able to publish this book in the English language. Translations were done by W. Coffey (chapter 2) and Michael O'Loughlin (chapter 9). Willemien Kneppelhout made corrections to chapters 1, 3, 4, 5, and 8, with great accuracy.

Mirjam C.P. van Dongen
Gerard A.B. Frinking
Menno J.G. Jacobs

Tilburg University
June 1995

Introduction

Menno Jacobs

The state of the art of fatherhood

Fatherhood is in a state of crisis. It is with this sentence that Trudie Knijn opens her article on the first page of this book. There seems to be an ongoing process which is undermining many of the old pillars of fatherhood. In all Western countries almost every aspect of fatherhood is changing very quickly, or has already changed. We see sociological, psychological, bio-medical and legal changes, all intricately linked. Developments in one field almost certainly lead to changes in another. New biomedical techniques, for example, lead to legal obscurities. Now that it has become possible to fertilise ova with donorsperm, a clear distinction has to be made between a biological, a social and a legal father. This means that there are several kinds of fatherhood, each of them leading to a different experience of fatherhood by the individual and a different concept of fatherhood in society. This example illustrates the interdependency of multiple changes in various disciplines. Developments in medical science have an impact on law, psychology and sociology, which in turn influence medical science.

Suppose we follow the circle the other way around. Structural societal changes, such as the growing popularity of cohabitation and the increasing labour force participation of women, place different demands on individual fatherhood, and create a need for a more differentiated system of paternal rights and duties and to more sophisticated biomedical techniques which give ultimate control of parenthood. Here again a great variety of changes are taking place at several levels.

Looking at the changes in fatherhood described by Knijn, it would not be too much to speak of a crisis in fatherhood. The main characteristic of the crisis is a decreasing emphasis on male gender identity, which is one — if not the most important — 'old pillar of fatherhood'. However, crisis means more than just an awkward situation. It also means a turning point: the beginning of the emergence of a 'new father', although it is still far from clear how the new identity of the father will develop. In his comment on Knijn's article François de Singly critically examines the identity of the male. He states that this new identity may not be as new as we are inclined to think. Whatever ideological changes may be taking place, in day-to-day practice we see relatively little difference with, say, some twenty years ago. Therefore, according to his opinion, there would be no awkward situation, no turning point, no crisis.

The article by Hélène Desrosiers and Céline le Bourdais provides some empirical support for Trudie Knijn's opening statement. The 'New forms of male family life in Canada' refer mainly to single parenthood and step-families. Using the Survey on Family and Friends held in 1990, the authors first give an estimation of these family types observed in Canada and present some of their demographic characteristics. They also examine the processes of formation and dissolution of the first episodes of single-parent families and step-families. Many marriages end in divorce, some men experience some form of single parenthood and most of these men remarry after a short period of time. The exact figures of these transitions differ per country, but the trend is the same in all Western countries. Whatever their magnitude, they illustrate the decline of the traditional long-lasting family.

An important aspect of the article by Desrosiers and Le Bourdais is their focus on the male from a demographic point of view. This aspect is welcomed by Anton Kuijsten in his comment on the article. He argues that the study by Desrosiers and Le Bourdais could have been improved by looking at the subject from a life-course perspective. As a result, Kuijsten misses "the very first beginning, in the sense of entering fatherhood for the first time". The contribution by Menno Jacobs focuses on this subject: the wish to become a father. Although the life-course perspective that Kuijsten pleas for can not be accomplished in this study either (this would require a much larger data set), Jacobs offers insight into the way men decide in favour of parenthood.

The transition to parenthood is no longer a fact of life, or, to be more precise, of marriage. Couples make careful and deliberate considerations before entering the new phase of life called parenthood. Many sociological and societal changes make it more than justifiable that individual motives with regard to having children are examined separately for women and men. For men, the wish to have children, ideas on fatherhood and career ambitions and perspectives all play a significant role in their choice process. Data taken from a relatively small survey suggest that altruistic, affective motives seem to be stronger than, or even replace the individualistic, freedom-curtailing drawbacks in coming to a positive decision. Naturally, the role of the woman and the role which age plays, should not be neglected in this respect, as Van Balen clearly points out.

Men are now more aware of the impact and consequences of their possible fatherhood than they were before the free availability of contraceptives; that is to say, since having children is no longer 'the order of things'. This means that they (should) also feel more responsible for the consequences, one of which is child care.

Mirjam van Dongen addresses the interesting question of men's aspirations concerning child care and the extent to which they are realised. However, in order to be able to make statements about this question we must have an accurate and differentiated view on child care itself. Contemporary theories which are based on resources, ideology and time are not entirely satisfactory, according to Van Dongen. She offers a more sophisticated concept of care, through which the often demonstrated gap between aspirations and practices, or thoughts and deeds, can be better understood. But what about the lorry driver, caring about his family, waking up at five a.m. and working all day? Even if he would want to take care of his children, the family cannot afford it. Charlie Lewis, using this example, leaves room for an explanation of the father's involvement in child care in terms of resources, ideology and time. Whereas Van Dongen is optimistic about an ongoing phased redivision of paid and unpaid labour between the sexes, Lewis has a more pessimistic view.

Implications of changing fatherhood

The implications of changing fatherhood are too numerous to be explored in one volume about fatherhood. Four important areas are examined. First we look at legislation and law, from the point of view of a Dutch lawyer and an English sociologist. Then we move on to a thorough investigation of the paternal role in child development, and of fathers themselves. Finally, we take a close look at some emerging policy issues.

One field on which the changing role of the father clearly has an influence is legislation and law. Paul Vlaardingerbroek sketches the legal situation for Dutch fathers. The legal rights of the married father have diminished in favour of those of the married mother, and in favour of those of the unmarried father. A shift has taken place from paternal authority to parental authority. However, since sexual intercourse is no longer a necessary aspect of conception, many forms of fatherhood have emerged. A man may become a genetic father, or a social father, or a legal father, or a combination of these. A clear distinction between genetic, social and legal fatherhood is, from a lawyer's point of view at least, difficult to make. DNA-techniques enable the identification of a genetic father, but it remains problematic to demonstrate the existence of a social father by proving that there was such a thing as 'family life'. Besides, it was only quite recently that the Dutch court accepted DNA-fingerprinting as proof of affiliation. Jurisprudence has slightly updated outdated laws, but, according to Vlaardingerbroek, it is time for the practitioners, lawyers, administrators and legislators to make their move in order to find solutions to these complex problems.

Carol Smart explores contemporary legal and policy responses to fatherhood in the United Kingdom. The main concern of legislation about fatherhood in the UK seems to be the welfare of the child. It stresses the importance of being a 'good father'. However, the effects of these laws are not always in favour of the child. Smart poses the question whether there are any 'solutions' to these problems. Law itself should be regarded as part of the social process, and thus as part of the problem.

Still, the best conditions for the welfare of the child are the conditions at home. For that, no laws can be written. Social scientific studies seem to be often shortsighted in their views about what a 'good father' or a 'good mother' should be. It is even questionable whether one should speak in such moral terms as 'should be'. Michael Lamb looks at five Anglo-American research paradigms and five views on the relationship between the father and his child(ren). Research seems to be rather traditional in its assumptions and hypotheses: The role of the father is that of a gender-role model in the first place; more time spent with the children would 'automatically' lead to better social adjustment. Lamb's conclusion is that much research that is being done on the father-child relationship should be qualified. It is the quality of the relationship of the parent with the child, and among the parents themselves, that may enhance the psychological well-being of the child. Differences between the father and the mother are much less important than the similarities. These findings lead to the conclusion that there is no prescription for 'the best father's role'. Besides, the findings place the often heard plea for 'more paternal involvement' in a different light, because 'more' does not necessarily mean 'better'.

Mater semper certem est — the mother is always certain — goes a Latin saying. In earlier days the presumed father could not be a hundred percent sure that he was the real father. Only the mother was certain, because she gives birth to the child. Nowadays a social father can be a hundred percent sure that he is also the real, i.e. biological, father, thanks to DNA-identification, or in the case of in vitro fertilisation with his donor sperm. These days, however, it is possible that the mother is *not* certain. This is the case, for example, when an anonymous donor's ovum is used for in vitro fertilisation. William Marsiglio sketches the possible implications of the 'eight permuta-tions of noncoital reproduction among heterosexual couples' for (presumed) fathers. Due to present-day artificial fertilisation techniques the meaning of the reproductive realm has altered. Unfortunately, no data are available to assess the extent to which and the way in which it has changed, although Marsiglio's theoretical framework of procreative consciousness and procrea-tive responsibility provides some indication. However, according to Gijs Beets Marsiglio's contribution is too much of a theoretical exercise. In order to study the impact of artificial fertility techniques a more realistic and dynamic frame of reference would be preferable. Beets emphasises the role of the woman, since many men would admit that the ultimate decision in favour of parenthood is made by their wives. Although the last word has not yet been said about this, it illustrates the huge methodological problems that occur when investigating complex psychosocial phenomena such as these.

Expectations about changing fatherhood

Many people cherish high hopes for the changing nature of fatherhood. In their view it is only a matter of time before an equal division of paid and unpaid labour in households will become reality. At last, men are allowed to express aspects of female gender identity that were hidden in them for too long. The process of change has begun, so we simply have to wait for it to be completed.

Unfortunately, it cannot be denied that it might be too soon to start cheering. The change in fatherhood is not uni-directional, it has different starting points, and it differs per country. Although there is a growing consensus about the existence of some sort of a 'new father', it is very difficult to predict a future of fatherhood or to work out a consistent and adequate policy.

The contributions by Rosella Palomba and Marry Niphuis-Nell may serve as an example of this incoherent situation. It is striking, and revealing, how strongly two interpretations about 'new fathers' may differ from each other. Whereas Palomba states that the social and political image of motherhood has improved, more or less at the expense of fatherhood, Niphuis-Nell states the opposite.

A state, or government, may strive for one of three policies with regard to fatherhood: It may recognise the existence of a new father, it may adopt a favourable policy towards changing fatherhood, or it may be more regulative. Which policy is best differs per country. In countries that are somewhat behind on 'the road to egalitarianism', a policy of recognition and regulation might be appropriate. In other countries a favourable policy might be appropriate, gently steering the change process in the 'right' direction. Palomba puts forward the view that authorities should recognise the fact that either parent is able to raise children and that they should apply 'policy measures explicitly and exclusively designed for fathers' to 'encourage men to find a new identity as males and fathers based on companionship rather than authority'. This means recognition and regulation. Niphuis-Nell states that new fathers are already recognised, and seems to argue in favour of a favourable policy. It is not clear, however, which countries exactly Niphuis-Nell or Palomba have in mind. What is clear, is that countries and their governments differ substantially in their views on the concept of a new father.

Before exploring the future for this new father more closely it is useful to consider the past. Yvonne Knibiehler goes way back to the concept of patriarchy in the Roman period and describes some dramatic changes in fatherhood from that period until the present day, compared to which 'our' change in fatherhood may turn pale. Although it is precarious to draw simplistic conclusions from the past, it may be stated that the course that the father has gone through, has been one of a reduction in paternal authority. The role of the father has changed from a mighty one (the Roman omnipotent Pater Familias) into an obliging one (the involved father of today). Moreover, the public authorities have taken over many of the old paternal tasks.

In her comment on Knibiehler Tamara Hareven focuses on the period from the early nineteenth century until the present. According to Hareven, Knibiehler could have paid more attention to 'three additional significant developments that may have contributed to the changing role of the mother and the father', namely (demographic) changes in marriage, fertility and mortality, the increase in female labour force participation and the increase in divorce rates.

There have, no doubt, been more historical events that have contributed to the emergence of the image of a new father. However, we still do not know what this new father looks like exactly. We know that fatherhood is changing. We could conclude that fatherhood is in a state of crisis, but we do not know to what kind of new father this will lead. In order to know more about that, we have to tread on shaky ground by looking into the future.

Arlie Hochschild would certainly subscribe to the difficulties of predicting possible directions in which future fatherhood may go. Despite this she is able to sketch three scenarios: The new father may become a reality due to the increasing labour force participation of women and 'the appeal of the ideal'; the new father may move himself away from reality through an ongoing loosening of family ties; or, for the same reason, the ideal of the new father may be undermined altogether. In Western societies there are several forces which are pushing and pulling at fatherhood in different directions, leading to diversity and fragmentation; or even to crisis.

Hochschild (and many other authors) writes about this 'new father', as a given. Tineke Willemsen also recognises his existence, but she poses some questions as to how he should be studied. The new father as well as the new mother should be studied in their own right. A categorisation of forms of parenthood could easily lead to oversimplification. It may lead to a hierarchy of categories therefore maintaining the established order. Maybe it would be better to speak of the emergence of a new parent instead of a new father.

So, what is fatherhood? Is it a profession, an art, or a vocation? And what will the new father look like? Will he be a 'new' father or a 'new father'? Although we may not have the answers, posing these questions is in itself a useful exercise, as this volume on fatherhood will undoubtedly show.

1
Towards post-paternalism?
Social and theoretical changes in fatherhood

Trudie Knijn

Fatherhood is in a state of crisis. There are two reasons why I have opted for the term 'crisis'. The first is that what we used to mean by fatherhood is being disputed. The foundations of fatherhood — the father's status and position and male gender identity — are no longer indisputable (see also Kimmel, 1987; Morgan, 1992). The second reason for using the term crisis is that — since the foundations of fatherhood are being challenged — many fathers have lost sight of what fatherhood could or should entail, and of what is expected of them. Changes in the nature and identity of what seemed to be an institutionalised role — the role of the father — could lead to much confusion (see also Meuffels, 1993).

This does not mean that changing fatherhood has negative repercussions only. On the contrary, the crisis could be very fruitful. It could give rise to new experiences and have a favourable impact, provided that fathers experience it as a challenge for the development of new forms and structures and for the establishment of new relationships with their children. However, like all crises, the crisis in fatherhood is sadly accompanied by anxieties, opposition to change, violence and personal vindictiveness. These reactions all form part of a process of change to what used to be one of the most stable social positions: that of the father.

This twofold nature of the crisis in fatherhood — its comprehensiveness and its ambiguity — are a source of both inspiration and concern for anyone involved in the development of fatherhood. Which changes lie ahead? Will fathers disappear from their children's lives, will they become superfluous in the process of reproduction, will they try to protect what remains of their traditional role by force or through legal action, or will they develop new forms of true co-parenthood and begin to actively take part in child care and in the upbringing of their children?

In this article I shall explore the complicated and comprehensive character of the current crisis in fatherhood, I shall summarise some of its social and theoretical implications and present a number of interpretations.

The crisis in fatherhood

The current transformation in fatherhood is multifaceted. It affects not only the representation of fatherhood but also the father's position as the breadwinner, his pedagogical contribution to the socialisation of his children, his legal rights and duties, his biological parenthood and his emotional habitus, his attitude towards his children and his social identity as a father. It is not yet clear which direction any of these transformations will take. Nor can we predict how fathers will deal with them.

How is the father represented?
The changing representation of fatherhood betrays the first traces of a crisis. Its *symbolic representation* has changed considerably. During the past ten years or so the visualisation of fatherhood has become a world-wide phenomenon. Young fathers record their image of fatherhood on videos and photographs, inspired by picture postcards and the world of advertising. The image of man-with-baby, usually bare-chested and wearing jeans — the symbol of freedom — is becoming increasingly fashionable. This kind of image is very popular among pop artists and football players and is an acknowledged success in advertising. Lately, non-celebrities of all walks of life have begun circulating such photographs at parties, showing their friends and acquaintances that they also perform a role as a father.

This personal and public representation of fatherhood can be interpreted in several different ways. The first interpretation is that this new image expresses a desire to 'be known and recognised' as a father. This recent image is the strongest clear-cut representation of fatherhood since the traditional family photograph — in which the mother and children were invariably placed on either side of the paterfamilias — fell from grace. It is as if the 'new' father would like to say: "I am not just the tough football player, I am not just the rough pop star who likes to live dangerously, I am not only the provider of my family, I am also a good father and I'd like the world to know that". In fact, young fathers are 'going public' with their children; they are 'coming out' as fathers. But there is more. Their open declaration also shows that fathers like to present themselves as being involved, committed and concerned about their children. The photographs reveal personal intimacy, trust, and bonding. Fathers present their children as a part of themselves, as children they care about, and they take pride in doing so.

There is, however, another interpretation which says that fathers do not really care for their children but that they realise that their female friends and relatives are charmed by such sensitive pictures. The men want their photographs to impress their female audience who are increasingly in search of dedicated fathers. This interpretation assumes that fathers know that this image increases their sex-appeal and that this is how women would ideally like fathers to be. Fathers can keep control over their families by showing affection towards their children and by recognising that fatherhood forms part of their identity because it meets with the approval of the mothers (Segal, 1990). This explanation may sound rather cynical, yet it can not deny or negate the changes which are taking place. Whatever the interpretation, fathers are rethinking their relationships with their children. Caring fatherhood is — at the very least — becoming a part of male gender identity, however superficial it may be at the present moment.

A second kind of representation of fatherhood is gaining ground. During the past few years the public expression of needs, desires, emotions and feelings by fathers in the mass media, especially in TV talk shows, is drawing widespread interest. Every possible aspect of fatherhood is subjected to public debate; every day of the week a new, usually problematic, aspect of fatherhood is discovered and debated in the public arena which gives meaning to our daily lives: television. For our entertainment, fathers defend their long working weeks, they puzzle with the reasons why their child became a junkie or committed suicide, they mourn the loss of their children after divorce, and they explain why they sexually abused their daughters. On a more positive note, there are fathers who explain why they are enjoying their parental leave and how they discovered the pleasures of caretaking, fathers who like to combine fatherhood with a part-time job, and fathers who are reevaluating their views on life now that they have a child.

If Foucault (1976) is right, this public expression of personal feelings and desires forms part of a universal process whereby personal control and power are lost. Personal control is passed onto others, namely one's audience, by way of such public confessions. The confessant relinquishes all control over his actions and emotions, and becomes dependent on the priest, the scientist or — in the case of television — the viewers who are given the power to interpret and judge his ideas, behaviour and intentions. These public debates on fatherhood can be interpreted as a public defence of fatherhood, of how fathers think and (want to) act. They seem to indicate that the traditional institute of fatherhood is crumbling. By watching television, we are all involved in an effort to develop a new 'communis opinio' on fatherhood; in this process men and women try to discover what can and should be expected of fathers. It is the process and to a lesser extent its outcome which is of importance to the transformation of fatherhood. The identity, status and even the feelings of fathers are being challenged, but viable alternatives have not yet taken their place. In the visualisation of the new father and in the ongoing public television debates on all aspects of fatherhood we recognise a crisis in the image of fatherhood, a crisis which paves the way for democratic communicative processes of change.

The role of the father as an educator
The specific contribution which the father can make to the upbringing of his children is currently being discussed. In the old days the pedagogical role of the father was twofold. Firstly, he was the one who introduced his child into the outside world; and secondly he was the one who personified ultimate authority. His influence was indirect. It was mediated by the mother who tried to find a balance between his opinions on the education of their children and her own views on their well-being. This twofold pedagogical function now sounds like a vestige of the past. Professionals and mothers alike are demanding that the father be more directly involved in the upbringing of his children. However, fathers feel uncertain and ill-equipped to perform these tasks, they have not been prepared to carry out these activities and they feel that they have no control over the situation. Those who have the courage to enter this domain feel dependent and anxious, feelings which are not popular among men (Jackson, 1983; Lewis, 1986). Moreover, we often forget that it is the mothers who receive guidance from experts and health clinics, who read special tips for mothering in women's magazines and who receive the assistance of girlfriends and female kins. Despite the fact that many young mothers no longer raise their younger brothers, sisters, nephews and nieces, they still receive more information than fathers do. Over the past decades new ideas about how to raise and socialise a young child have been passed on to mothers; fathers were only incidentally informed about these changes (Knijn & Verheijen, 1988; Kaplan, 1992; Van Lieshout, 1993). Differences of opinion between mothers and fathers regarding the upbringing of their children should therefore not only be seen as a struggle between the sexes, but also as a historical struggle between 'old' (hierarchical, instrumental and value-laden) an 'new' (sensitive, democratic and person-oriented) pedagogical points of view.

Fathers have always been involved in the upbringing of their children in adolescence and in their teens, a situation often characterised by conflict. In this age group, the authority of the father seems to have lost ground. Since virtues, morals and respect have been replaced by communicative norms, since socialisation at school has become more important than socialisation within the family, since it is becoming harder to explain to one's children what the father's job entails, and since many fathers only have time for their children on Saturdays, mothers have to tell their husbands how to deal with their teenage children. Or else the teenagers themselves will tell them. If he still thinks he knows best, his children look at him pityingly: he is seen as an 'old-fashioned' man, not only in the eyes of his children, but also in the eyes of his peers. 'Haven't you ever been young?' they ask him.

The question is: How do fathers deal with this crisis in their pedagogical role? The first reaction is, and this is confirmed by many studies into the father-child relationship, that those fathers who are involved in child care prefer to play with their children, engage in sports, fool around, go for walks and bicycle rides; indoors fathers play with their children while the mother does the housework. Fathers are increasingly involved in the enjoyable and relational aspects of child care. In this respect fathers are fleshing out their own specific domain within family life: 'For him the play, for her the rest' Carla Verheijen concluded some years ago (Verheijen, 1987).

The second reaction is that some fathers are trying — by trial and error — to be involved in all aspects of child care. They do not shirk from changing a nappy, they want to know more about a child's diet, and they take their children to the health clinic. Their pedagogical role is to raise their children and to care for them. Such fathers are few and far between and many studies show that fathers who try to take on this caring role suffer from ambivalence and insecurity (Lamb, 1976/1981; Parke, 1981; Russell, 1983; Jackson, 1983; Lewis, 1986). Such feelings of ambivalence and insecurity may be rooted in the fact that they are ill-equipped for the job, or simply in the fact that caring fatherhood is still not fully accepted by society. It seems to be incompatible with real masculinity. Moreover, even in situations where both the mother and the father suffer from feelings of insecurity regarding the upbringing of their young children, the expression of these feelings is interpreted in different ways. Nowadays 'insecure' motherhood is accepted; insecure fatherhood, on the other hand, not only shatters the image of the good parent but also the image of the man who has everything under control.

Both reactions — the father who likes to explore the playful, relational ties with his children and the father who wants to be involved with child care — are indications that the pedagogical aspects of fatherhood are changing. The father is no longer the unapproachable educator. He is no longer the one who gives direction to his children as a representative of the outside world and as the head of the family. He now wants to become a child amongst the children and a co-parent. This change has been well-received by teenagers (Van Wel, 1994). However, this transformation is likely to spark another crisis in fatherhood: a crisis in the moral aspects of a child's upbringing. Until now social scientists have attributed the impending crisis primarily to a decline in paternal authority. Donzelot (1979), Lasch (1979) and Popenoe (1988) strongly stressed the relationship between a loss of paternal authority and moral values in a child's upbringing. It should be possible to rethink the moral and socio-cultural aspects in a more gender-neutral, or 'parental' way. For we can not neglect the fact that many parents — both mothers and fathers — no longer seem to know what raising children entails. Many parents have expressed or experienced ambivalence with respect to the norms and values which they could, or should impart to their children. Many parents are finding it hard to teach them what is right and wrong, what is social and anti-social behaviour, commitment and egotism. Singer (1993) has called this a declining 'security in upbringing'. Parents are increasingly trying to meet the 'fun needs' of their children, and if they fail to do so they call in the assistance of professionals. Both these alternatives can be seen as an escape from the parent's own responsibility in the upbringing of their children (see also de Winter, 1990). This pedagogical escapism can quite easily be explained if we take the ideas on education spread by the mass media seriously. On the one hand we can hardly resist the temptations of consumerism; on the other hand special magazines for parents propagate the importance of a communicative, sensitive and non-authoritarian upbringing. Well-informed parents will take care not to educate their children. And so we have been plunged into a pedagogical crisis in parenthood which — according to Lasch, Donzelot and Popenoe — can not be resolved, by restoring paternal authoritarism. Both parents — not only the father — have to find a solution to this problem. The stereotypes of an authoritarian father and a moral mother can not survive in an environment which entrusts both parents with equal responsibility. Now that these two stereotypes are crumbling, we shall have to review the situation. One of the challenges we face in the crisis in fatherhood is to fill the moral and socio-cultural void which has been created by the disappearance of the Father (authority) and the Mother (morality).

The psychology of fatherhood
The fathers' psychological contribution to the child's development has probably been one of the most heavily debated aspects of fatherhood during the past decades. Contrary to the pedagogical aspects of fatherhood, the psychological debate has taken on the characteristics of trench warfare. We all know who is attacking and who is on the defensive. The struggle is rather static and no one likes to gamble on future winners or losers (Knijn & Mulder, 1987; Knijn, 1990; Duindam, 1991). Some bet on universal laws that state that the identification with a caring father in the early years of childhood has a lasting influence on the gender identity of the children (Chodorow, 1978; Jalmert, 1993). Others place more emphasis on environmental factors and state that the nature of the father's involvement

during the early years of childhood has a minor impact (Singly, 1993). The most striking aspect of this trench warfare is its academic nature. Neither fathers nor mothers seem to worry about the relationship between their contribution to their son's or daughter's upbringing and his or her personality. Parents, men and women alike, do not seem to worry about whether their masculine or feminine behaviour will hamper or help their child's gender identity. Nevertheless, the psychological debate about the gender identity of the parents is an important one because it poses theoretical questions about what is masculine and what is feminine parental behaviour. If we acknowledge the fact that almost all empirical research leads to the conclusion that neither feminine behaviour by fathers nor masculine behaviour by mothers confuses the children's gender identity, if we admit that children of homosexuals can become just as heterosexual as the children of the average population, and vice versa, if we agree that one's sexual preference is a personal matter, if we know that sons of authoritarian fathers can become caring fathers, and vice versa, and that daughters of caring fathers sometimes marry authoritarian men, then we can draw only one conclusion: the central assumptions of psychological theories of the twentieth century need to be revised. This is also the reason why eminent scholars of fatherhood have adjusted their paradigm in recent years. Researchers such as Lamb (1975/1976) and Pleck (1981) no longer pose the question: 'What is the influence of a male-specific parental role on children?'. Instead, they are now asking: 'Which aspects of male gender identity are preventing men from taking care of their children'? They are contextualising developmental psychology. The focus of their research is not the development of the child but the development of the father. In fact, the determinants of developmental psychology are being linked to cultural, social and institutional factors. The academic discussion is put into the context of the cultural values which shape everyday life.

The legal position of the father
The crisis in fatherhood is also reflected in their legal position. Where there is a crisis in fatherhood, fathers establish organisations that strive to secure their traditional rights. Such 'father organisations' demand that fathers are granted the custody of their children following divorce, they claim the right to introduce their children into their new families, they oppose the obligation to pay alimony, and they want a say in decisions concerning abortion. It is rather ironic that you often need a divorce for fathers to join forces. One explanation could be that fathers do not realise how important their children are to them until they get divorced. It is equally plausible that fathers oppose the loss of what they see as their 'legal right to their children'. This sense of justice often appears to be stronger than their sense of duty, among both married and unmarried couples.

While former research, in the tradition of the theory of paternal deprivation, focused on the harmful effects of the absence of the father on the development of the child (Biller, 1971), recent studies devote more attention to the 'best interest' of the child. The latter studies show that the interests of the child are only indirectly related to the presence of both a male and a female parent. On the one hand researchers such as Thompson (1983) conclude that "fathers can be adequate and competent in the primary caretaking role... if they choose to do so." (p. 91). On the other hand the study shows that the division of caretaking tasks among the parents prior to divorce gives a better guarantee for successful custody than their gender does. The primary caretaker before divorce will most likely be the best caretaker after divorce.

If we relate these conclusions to research on the legal criteria which apply when granting custody following divorce, some ambiguities remain. From these studies we know that judges tend to grant custody on the basis of arguments which are only indirectly related to the former caretaking roles of the parents: the parent's income (this is almost always to the advantage of the father), whether the parent has a new family (in which case the father can offer the child a 'second mother'), or the absence of a parent prior to divorce. Because of this discrepancy between the legal criteria for custody and the results of research into the 'best interest' of the child, some feminist lawyers have lodged a plea for the integration of concepts of care, needs and responsibilities into the legal language of interests, obligations and rights in custodial matters (Brown, 1980; Bönnekamp, 1988; Sevenhuijsen, 1992; Thompson, 1983; Holtrust, 1993).

The crisis in the legal aspects of fatherhood may therefore be attributed to the rising divorce rate and to the changing sexual division of labour within marriages. According to current research, the best caretaker before divorce is the best parent following divorce. However, recent legal claims filed by fathers and the settlement of these claims by judges do not often tally with the research results. Will fathers begin to realise the importance of child care while they are still happily married, or will fathers increasingly manage to be granted custody of their children on the basis of other than the above-mentioned reasons?

The biological contribution of the father
The biological crisis in fatherhood is primarily reflected in the fact that women are gaining more and more control over reproduction. The World Population Conference in Cairo drew three conclusions in this area. First of all, the conference once again underlined that there are significant cultural, religious and ethnic differences between countries.

Secondly, the conference showed that there is a growing global consciousness that decisions regarding reproduction should be made by women, and thirdly that an increasing number of women are actually claiming their rights, and are demanding — and this is a new development — that their governments protect their rights to reproductive freedom. More and more women are making their own reproductive decisions thanks to such developments as the availability of contraceptives, abortion, protection against rape within marriage and outside of marriage, the postponement of the birth of the first child giving women more socio-economic independence, and the option of single motherhood thanks to artificial insemination or self-insemination with the aid of a male friend or an unknown man under contract. Although we can assume that married and cohabiting men still have some say in whether or not they want children, the relationship between sexuality and reproduction is no longer automatic. As a result, the paternal control over women's reproductivity has declined considerably. The Cairo Conference clearly showed that some governments and church institutions are again trying to turn the tides. National governments are implementing population policies based on the trend towards greater reproductive freedom of women. These policies are designed to stimulate women to have children by making it easier for them to combine children with a job. They include measures such as maternity leave and other forms of parental leave, and child care. At the same time, governments are trying to cut back single motherhood. One of the measures used is to restrict the rights of single mothers to social welfare. Another measure is to prohibit anonymous donor-insemination (which creates the illusion that female reproductive behaviour can even be controlled without the personal authority of men). A third measure is to reinforce the financial responsibilities of fathers following divorce. By tightening their obligation to pay alimony as providers of the family, the relationship between fathers and their offspring is strengthened — at least financially.

The crisis in biological fatherhood expresses the bankruptcy of the relationship between sexuality and reproductivity which was the cornerstone of a male-dominated marriage and of the father's undisputed relationship with his children born in marriage.

However, the biological crisis in fatherhood also has advantages for men. For the first time in history the media and scientists are paying heed to the fact that men want to have children too. It is no longer an automatic assumption that men have children as a result of a sexual relationship with a woman and that women are the only ones who really want children. Men's motivation to have children is drawing increasing interest, as are the consequences of the decision to have a child for the men concerned: their psyche, responsibilities, position and status (Van Dongen, 1994; Jacobs, 1994). A second advantage of this trend is that the taboo on male infertility is decreasing as a result of the growing application of artificial insemination. Physicians and psychologists are paying more attention to the medical and psychological causes of male infertility and they are developing successful therapies and cures.

The social position of fathers

Last but not least the social position of the father in his capacity as breadwinner and head of the family is an important aspect of the crisis in fatherhood. Traditionally, the father was seen as the representative of 'his' family in the outside world. He was formally and informally seen as the head of the family and was thus considered to be ultimately responsible for the behaviour of 'his' wife and children. This position is now being undermined as a result of the democratisation of family relations and the growing participation of women on the labour market and in public life in general. This is changing the social and financial relations between husband and wife and between father and children. In many families fathers are indeed still the primary breadwinners, but they are no longer the sole breadwinner. Like male employment, female employment is putting a strain on family life, women are increasingly representing their families outside the home, and many now have a social life of their own, alongside that of their husbands.

Needless to say such developments are undermining the (power) position of the father within the family. The changing social and economic position of the father and the consequences of this development for paid employment outside the home and the division of labour within households is perhaps the most widely studied aspect of the crisis in fatherhood (see, among others, Rapoport and Rapoport, 1971; Pleck, 1977; Backett, 1982; Russell, 1983; Komter, 1985; Gerstel & Gross, 1987; Hunt & Hunt, 1987; Knijn & Verheijen, 1988; Hochschild, 1989; Wheelock, 1990; Brannen & Moss, 1991; Stacey, 1991; Knijn, Van Nunen & Van der Avort, 1994; Mozes & Wester, 1993).

Most studies conclude that although some fathers are willing to change from breadwinner into co-parent, most fathers are facing emotional and social problems because of these changes. Some studies show that these problems are primarily caused by the structure of the labour market, the culture of the workplace and government income policies which form an impediment to co-parenthood. Other studies state that the problems are caused by the fact that many fathers do not want to let go of traditional views and the traditional male gender identity. Still, we can say that the position of the father as the sole provider of his family is being challenged in most cultures.

Explanations of the crisis in fatherhood

All the aforementioned aspects of the crisis in fatherhood may be attributed to a combination of changes in family life: a shift in pedagogical norms, women's desires and needs for the greater involvement of their husbands in child care, the undesirability of authoritarian behaviour in the democratic times we live in, the widespread use of contraceptives, increased sexual freedom, the rising divorce rate, an increase in the level of education among women and growing career opportunities for women, a decline in men's withdrawal from family life as a result of workaholism, extra-marital relationships and divorce. These fragmented developments have one thing in common: a decreasing emphasis on male gender identity in fatherhood. Both in the relationship between husband and wife and in the relationship between the father and his children the qualities of the father as a parent are now more important than his qualities as a man. This trend has not, however, been unanimously welcomed.

The diversity in the aforementioned explanations could give the impression that the crisis in fatherhood is the result of a contingent and amorphous process of transformation, a development in bits and pieces lacking a clear pattern. The contrary seems to be the case. The crisis in fatherhood is more than a voluntaristic development in which 'progressive' fathers set the train in motion and 'conservative' fathers put on the brakes. In the following I shall review more comprehensive patterns which form the fundamental structures underlying the crisis in fatherhood.

The feminist explanation
The powerful attack on the authority and absence of the father by the feminist movement is one of the explanations for the crisis in fatherhood. In classic feminist works the biological role of the father (Firestone, 1971), his authoritarian pedagogical style (Rich, 1978), his absence (Friedan, 1963) and his symbolisation as the almighty (Millet, 1970) were viciously attacked and devaluated. Since then the father has been the target of many feminist campaigns, books, legal fights and personal struggles. The feminist movement thrust fathers and fatherhood into a 'patriarchal system' only to subsequently dismantle every aspect of that system. Feminists, and at a later stage women who claimed they were not feminists, tried to drag fathers out of their position as absent authorities by claiming and opting for voluntary single parenthood, reproductive freedom, (sexual) equality within relationships, rights on the basis of motherhood, and shared responsibility

for housekeeping and child care. They did so not only for democratic reasons or to achieve equal rights but also for the sake of the fathers themselves. In the post-war years fathers had become so estranged from their families, relations and other personal acquaintances and so involved with their jobs, their colleagues and their status in the world at large, that women had to make a lot of noise in order to wake men up. It was the female half of the population who discovered that men had lost all ties with their families, that they had individualised to such an extent that they were left out there on their own and had become strangers in their own personal environments (see in particular Stacey, 1991). And even now, twenty-five years later, only a small number of fathers are beginning to realise that they have something to gain by investing in personal relationships in a caring environment.

This explanation, which says that the feminist movement is responsible for the current crisis in fatherhood, has not only been put forward by those who are in favour of the current turnabout (Lamb & Sagi, 1983; Hodson, 1984; Seidler, 1989; Morgan, 1992). Strong opponents of the current changes — both laymen and scholars — also support this point of view. "Nothing will change until the feminist movement disintegrates", they say. So, as long as the development of new forms of fatherhood is believed to be generated by female pressure, changes in fatherhood are likely to be retarded and the current crisis will persist. As long as this belief holds sway, both fathers and scholars will persist in trying to oppose or deny these changes.

The problem with this explanation, however, is mainly a theoretical one. Social scientists know that dramatic transformations in family life or other social and personal relations are not caused by social movements only, not even by a very powerful one such as the feminist movement. Such movements could, at most, give direction to an ongoing social process.

They can act as catalysts in the sense that they draw attention to new, as yet barely visible developments and incorporate them in programmes, activities and objectives which may subsequently play a major role in keeping these developments on the public agenda. So, besides the contribution made by the feminist movement we have to look for other explanations for the current crisis in fatherhood.

Structuralist employment explanations

A second possible explanation for the crisis in fatherhood is a structuralist one, either neo-marxist or sociological. In this case they represent the two sides of the coin. This explanation stresses that changes in economic and industrial structures instigate changes in family life, motherhood and fatherhood. Since historians tend to support this paradigm, we shall deal with an earlier transformation in fatherhood which took place during the industrial revolution (see, amongst others, Hareven, 1976/1987; Stearns, 1991). I shall briefly summarise this explanation. In the 18th and 19th centuries, the formal patriarchal dominance disintegrated following the introduction of a free market economy and concomitant individual wage labour. Like their teenage daughters and sons, and often their wives as well, fathers became dependent on market mechanisms in the labour market. As a result, they lost a great deal of economic control over the members of their families. The introduction of child welfare legislation paved the way for the protection of wives and children by the authorities. Husbands no longer had authority over the labour of their wives and children who were now able to earn an income of their own. At the same time the gap between public and private life was widened. Factory workers in particular started a career as absent fathers. This trend was soon followed by most men. Until this very day historians disagree about the consequences that this industrialisation process has had for the role and status of fathers in family life. Some scholars state that fathers tried to make good their lost authority by being extra authoritarian in the home; others stress the growing search by fathers for intimacy in their private lives. All agree, though, that this period heralded the end of private patriarchies, as witnessed, for example, by the fact that more and more children were abandoned by their fathers towards the end of the 19th century. What's more, for the first time in history the phenomenon of 'bad fathers' was a matter of public debate, triggered by an increase in criminal and abusive behaviour by fathers.

Lastly, the reappraisal of motherhood during this period is indicative of the waning influence of the father on the family in general and on the upbringing of the children in particular. In paintings, literature, textbooks and pedagogical theories the importance of good motherhood was stressed whereas the educational role of the father was hardly mentioned (Note that 'moral motherhood' was an important topic of discussion in the first feminist movement). What remained for fathers was simply to become the major provider, a position which offered status and financial compensation for the prolonged absences from the family and the long working weeks they had to spend in a hierarchical environment. The reward for being the major breadwinner was a comfortable home in which the father was looked after and respected (Hunt & Hunt, 1987). In most countries, men won the struggle and became breadwinners, thanks to the efforts of the trade unions and a belief that took root among employers, namely that workers were more productive if they could fall back on a stable family life. At the beginning of the twentieth century, the provider role was institutionalised and assumed by fathers; it was to become the most important aspect of male gender identity.

Back to present times. Since similar analyses about recent trends in fatherhood are sadly lacking, I shall continue along the former line of reasoning and apply it to the current crisis in fatherhood. Two processes merit attention. First of all the transition from an industrial to a postindustrial economy, and secondly the development of the welfare state. The postindustrial economy had, and still has, a strong impact on the composition of the labour market. Comparative research shows that the more postindustrial an economy is, the higher the female labour force rate and the more women are working fulltime (Esping Andersen, 1990). Moreover, the demise of traditional industrial sectors gives rise to high unemployment among unskilled and semi-skilled men, while at the same time their female partners are increasingly successful in finding employment in the service sector (Wheelock, 1990; Stacey, 1991). The improved level of education among women also leads to changes in the labour market; both national governments and private enterprises are becoming aware of the fact that investments in female human capital are not to be wasted. Resistance to labour participation by mothers is diminishing and active attempts are being made to keep mothers in the labour force. The postindustrial economy has, after all, drastically changed the type of jobs on offer. Flexibility is now the name of the game. This has changed family life and the division of labour between fathers and mothers, albeit to differing degrees and in different ways. Such changes in the labour market have meant that women increasingly need their male partners in order to be able to run the household, that they have begun making demands on their partners, and that the father's job is no longer the only outside influence on the family.

A second structural explanation for the crisis in fatherhood can be found in the post-war development of the welfare state. Despite a global diversity in underlying principles and manifestations, the welfare state has paved the way for the individualisation of women and for their increased social participation and autonomy. It has generated the improvement of women's level of education and the introduction of individualised social security benefits, insurances and pensions which in their turn have undermined the mediating role of the family and strengthened the direct contact between the state and its female citizens. And although many welfare states are now rethinking their responsibilities, it is highly unlikely that this will lead to a restoration of the traditional family as an institute between the state and its citizens. On the contrary, the reassessment of the welfare state seems to be moving in the direction of neo-liberalism. This will place higher demands on the flexibility and creativity of its citizens as well as on personal relationships. At the same time men and women will have to align their parental responsibilities as providers and carers. It remains to be seen whether new fatherhood is ready to allow this to happen in a synchronised fashion. The crisis in fatherhood may not yet be serious enough for men and women — fathers and mothers — to react to market pressure by sharing the joys and burdens of family life. The displacement of women — without providing them with viable alternatives — may well be one of the paradoxes of the increasing interrelatedness of the economy and the family at the turn of the 20th century.

This explanation sees the crisis in fatherhood as a reaction to industrial and socio-economic developments which demand more flexibility from fathers and mothers whilst at the same time providing the conditions for more symmetrical and reciprocal familial relationships. This explanation sees changing fatherhood as an inevitable structural process, which is expressed in its fragmentation. Each in their own way, individual fathers are searching for a form of fatherhood that best fits their own specific situation, that is to say their own — and their partner's — opportunities on the labour market. It is in this perspective that studies are currently being conducted into the question as to how and why fathers and mothers 'choose' to do the work they do. However, rational choice theories (also called new home economics), which are beginning to dominate these kinds of studies, hardly pay attention to the broader historical context of such negotiation processes. Neither do they pay much heed to the emotional and social ambivalences which men could face when they have to relinquish their role as major providers (Knijn, Van Nunen & Van der Avort, 1994).

Cultural explanations

A third explanation for the transformations in fatherhood focuses on the cultural processes which go hand in hand with modernisation; the continuous trend towards emancipation and the politicisation of everyday life. This explanation offers an optimistic view on personal relationships and human behaviour. It assumes that modernisation leads to a breakthrough in set practices and it challenges the power of religion and morality over every aspect of life. In this process life politics becomes lifestyle politics, the politics of making conscious choices, in which individuals no longer feel bound by fixed patterns and actually start contesting these patterns. That is why men and women expect greater equality, emotionalism and reciprocity in personal relations, including marriage (see also Van der Avort, 1987). As a result of this process, communication and negotiation have become the major characteristics of modern partner relations, and fathers and mothers expect a more personal, rather than gender-specific, investment in their duties and responsibilities as parents.

From this point of view, changes in fatherhood are in line with the growing awareness of, or belief in, personal identity as a reflexive identity. Gender identity is a central issue in this reflexive activity. "The more we reflexively 'make ourselves' as persons, the more the very category of what 'a person' or 'human being' is comes to the fore" (Giddens, 1991, p. 217). And the less we assume a pre-fixed gender identity, the less we know about fatherhood is meant to be and about how men have to behave in their role as fathers.

Self-reflexivity may seem like a neurotic hobby for those who have no more useful things to do, yet in parenthood it is highly functional. After all, these days nothing demands as much personal investment as raising children. Educating and socialising one's children requires that both their reflexive and their cognitive talents are developed. Preparing children for a job in the bureaucracy of welfare states, for technical jobs or for social service professions entails inspiring self-confidence in them, and instilling in them a sense of loyalty, flexibility and integrity. These qualities are needed when working in an anonymous organisation. Such an upbringing demands a supportive attitude from both fathers and mothers. Communicative, sensitive and relational pedagogical styles have proven to be more successful than hierarchical, moralistic and authoritarian styles (Miller & Swanson, 1958). The integration of moral values could be the next step in democratic parenthood.

This explanation sees the crisis in fatherhood as the implicit result of processes of modernisation in which self-reflexive personalities, supportive and sensitive parents and sexual and generational equality are inevitable. An authoritarian and/or absent father is not in keeping with the assumption of the 'ongoing growth' of the child, the father and the relationship between them.

Conclusion and discussion

Summarising, I would like to say that long-term processes underlie the multifaceted crisis in fatherhood, as well as the symbolic, pedagogical, psychological, legal, biological and social transformations in fatherhood. The crisis in fatherhood should be seen in the context of processes of modernisation and their repercussions for prevailing views on personal identities, socio-economic processes and their impact on the sexual division of labour, the development of the welfare state and the concomitant individualisation of women, and lastly the powerful feminist movement — and the less powerful male movement.

Changes in fatherhood should not be seen as a temporary choice made by a number of individual fathers. They form part of a historical process aimed at finding a new balance between and within all the aforementioned elements of fatherhood.

The problem is, of course, that we can no longer speak of a convergence in fatherhood because of the multifaceted character of the crisis and because the underlying processes are proceeding at different speeds. In fact, we now see a divergence in fatherhood, in family life and in lifestyles in general. The process of change has different repercussions for different types of fathers, depending on their social and economic position, their ability to change, their resistance to the loss of certainties, their capacity to change set habits, and their emotional stability. The crucial factor, however, is masculine gender identity. This also constitutes the major impediment to change. Only when fathers attach importance to parenthood rather than fatherhood will we get a society in which fathers without a capital F play a central role.

References

Akker, P. van den (1986). Eenouderschap na echtscheiding. In P. van Engelen (Eds.), *Ouderschap in verandering* (pp. 168-179). Lisse: Swets & Zeitlinger.

Backett, K. (1982). *Mothers and fathers. A study of the development and negotiation of parental behaviour.* London: Macmillan.

Biller, H.B. (1971). *Father, child and sex role.* Lexington: Heath Lexington Books.

Bozett, F.W. & Hanson, S.M.H. (Eds.) (1991). *Fatherhood and families in cultural context.* New York: Springer Publishing Company.

Brannen, J. & Moss, P. (1991). *Managing mothers. Dual earner households after maternity leave.* London: Unwin Hyman Ltd.

Brown, C. (1980). Mothers, fathers and children: From private to public patriarchy. In Lydia Sargent (Ed.), *Women and revolution: A discussion of the unhappy marriage between marxism and feminism.* Boston: South End Press.

Cheal, D. (1991). *Family and the state of theory.* Hemel Hempstead: Harverster Wheatsheaf.

Duindam, V. (1991). *Ouderschapsarrangementen en geslachtsidentiteit.* Utrecht: Lemma.

Ehrensaft, D. (1987). *Parenting together: Men and women sharing the care of their children.* New York: Free Press.

Firestone, S. (1971). *The dialectics of sex.* New York: Bantam.

Foucault, M. (1976). *Histoire de sexualite 1, La volonte de savoir,* Parijs, Gallimard.

Friedan, B. (1963). *The feminine mystique.* New York: Norton.

Gelder, K. van (1987). *Alleen zorgen. Een onderzoek naar het functioneren van eenoudergezinnen.* Den Haag: Nimawo.

Gerstel, N. & Gross, H.E. (Eds.) (1987). *Family and work.* Philadelphia: Temple University Press.

Giddens, A. (1991). *Modernity and self-identity.* Cambridge: Polity Press.

Giddens, A. (1992). *The transformation of intimacy.* Cambridge: Polity Press.

Folbre, N. (1987). *The pauperization of motherhood: Patriarchy and public policy in the United States.* In N. Gerstel & H.E. Gross (Eds.), *Family and work* (pp. 491-511). Philadelphia: Temple University Press.

Hareven, T.K. (1976). Modernisation and family history: Perspectives on social change. *Signs, 2,* 1, 190-206.

Hareven, T.K. (1987). *The dynamics of kin in an industrial community.* In N. Gerstel & H.E. Gross (Eds.), *Family and work* (pp. pp 55-83). Philadelphia: Temple University Press.

Hochschild, A. (1989). *The second shift.* New York: Penguin Books Inc.

Hodson, P. (1984). *Men, an investigation to the emotional male.* London: BBC/Ariel Books.

Holtrust, N. (1993). *Aan moeders knie.* Nijmegen: Ars Aequi Libri.

Hunt, J.G. & Hunt, L.L. (1987). *Male resistance to role symmetry in dual-earner households: Three alternative explanations.* In N. Gerstel & H.E. Gross (Eds.), *Family and work* (pp. 192-203). Philadelphia: Temple University Press.

Jackson, B. (1983). *Fatherhood.* London: Allen & Unwin.

Jacobs, M.J.G. (1994). *The wish to become a father: How do men decide?* Paper prepared for the Conference on Changing Fatherhood, WORC, Tilburg University.

Jalmert, L. (1993). The father's role in child development. In *Father and families of tomorrow.* Report from the Conference, The Danish Ministry of Social Affairs/The European Commission, pp. 76-86.

Kamerman, S.B. (1983). *Fatherhood and social policy: Some insights from a comparative perspective.* In M.E. Lamb & A. Sagi (Eds.), *Fatherhood and family policy* (pp. 23-34). Hillsdale, NJ: Lawrence Erlbaum Associates Inc.

Kaplan, A.E. (1992). *Motherhood and representation.* London: Routledge.

Kimmel, M.S. (1987). The contemporary 'crisi' in masculinity in historical perspective. In H. Brod (Ed.), *The making of masculinities* (pp. 121-154). Boston, MA: Allen & Unwin.

Knijn, T. & Mulder, A-C. (Eds.) (1987). *Unravelling fatherhood.* Dordrecht: Foris Publications.

Knijn, T. & Verheijen, C. (1988). *Tussen plicht en ontplooiing.* Nijmegen: ITS.

Knijn, T. (1991). Hij wil wel maar hij kan niet. *Psychologie en Maatschappij, 14,* 2, 99-111.

Knijn, T., Nunen, A. van & Avort, A. van der (1994). Zorgend vaderschap. *Amsterdams Sociologisch Tijdschrift, 4,* 70-97.

Lamb, M. (1975). Fathers, forgotten contributors to child care. *Human Development, 18*

Lamb, M. (Ed.) (1981). *The role of the father in child-development.* New York: Wiley.

Lamb, M.E. & Sagi, A. (Eds.) (1983). *Fatherhood and family policy.* Hillsdale, NJ: Lawrence Erlbaum Associates Inc.

Lasch, C. (1977). *Haven in a heartless world.* New York: Basic Books.

Lewis, C. (1986). *Becoming a father.* Milton Keynes: Open University Press.

Lewis, C. & O'Brien, M. (Eds.) (1987). *Reassessing fatherhood. New observations on fathers and the modern family.* London: SAGE.

Lieshout, I. van (1993). *Deskundigen en ouders van nu.* Utrecht: De Tijdstroom.

Morgan, D.H.J. (1992). *Discovering Men.* London: Routledge.

Morrissey, M. (1987). *Female-headed families: Poor women and choice.* In N. Gerstel & H.E. Gross (Eds.), *Family and work* (pp. 302-315). Philadelphia: Temple University Press.

Meuffels, W.H.F. (1993). Aanstaande vaders in crisis. *Maandblad Geestelijke volksgezondheid, 48,* 4, 376

Parke, R. (1981). *Fathering.* London: Fontana Paperbacks.

Pleck, J. (1981). *The myth of masculinity.* Boston: MIT Press.

Pleck, J. (1985). *Working wives/working husbands.* Beverly Hills: SAGE.

Rapoport, R. & Rapoport, R.N. (1971). *Dual career families.* Harmondsworth: Penguin.

Rich, A. (1978). *Of woman born.* New York: W.W. Norton & Company Inc.

Russell, G. (1983). *The changing role of fathers.* London: University of Queensland Press.

Segal, L. (1990). *Slow motion, changing masculinities, changing men.* London: Virago Press Ltd.

Seidler, V.J. (1989). *Rediscovering masculinity, reason, language and sexuality.* London: Routledge.

Singer, E. (1993). Shared care for children. *Theory & Psychology, 3,* 4, 429-449.

Singly, F. (1993). The social construction of a new paternal identity. *Fathers in families of tomorrow,* Report from the Conference, The Danish Ministry of Social Affairs/The European Commission, pp. 42-75.

Stearns, P.N. (1991). Fatherhood in historical perspective: The role of social change. In F.W. Bozett & S.M.H. Hanson (Eds.), *Fatherhood and families in cultural context* (pp. 28-52). New York: Springer Publishing Company.

Thompson, R.A. (1983). The father's case in child custody disputes: the contributions of psychological research. In M.E. Lamb & A. Sagi (Eds.),

Fatherhood and family policy (pp. 53-100). Hillsdale, NJ: Lawrence Erlbaum Associates Inc.

Verheijen, C. (1987). Mother knows best: For him the play, for her the rest. In T. Knijn & A-C. Mulder (Eds.), *Unravelling fatherhood* (pp. 37-47). Dordrecht: Foris Publications.

Wheelock, J. (1990). *Husbands at home, the domestic economy in a post-industrial society*. London: Routledge.

François de Singly

Implementing a new model of paternity

I will explain the feeling I got from the very rich piece by Trudie Knijn, by quoting Peter Handke: 'I sometimes feel I am living in a sad, beautiful period of transition.' It is in fact a very restrained text, somewhat anxious, but not reactionary, not conservative. It is so to speak a landscape in the rain, but with the sun rising for all that, perhaps even a rainbow for the conclusion. According to Trudie Knijn we are living in a difficult period of transition when men have to abandon their old habits as fathers and adopt or have to adopt, new habits. Now sometimes they are under the impression that these new habits are not yet ready, sometimes they think that these new habits they have taken on do not entirely suit them. Trudie Knijn's text is doubly interesting. On the one hand it covers the whole, or at least a vast field of dimensions which define the father, which allows us to understand the entirety of the procedures of transformation of paternity. On the other hand, it articulates a strong hypothesis, an articulation between the role of the father and masculine identity.

To open the discussion, I would like to ask some questions and put forward some contentious propositions.

1. My first point refers to the period of transition we assume we are currently living through in contemporary societies (Western ones). I agree with Trudie Knijn that this period does exist, but I think its definition does not lie in the search for a model of paternity. On the contrary I think that this model exists, that it is not only formed in the imagination but that it has been internalised by a large number of social actors. The problem raised by this period of transition is different, it is that of the progressive placing of the social and psychological conditions for the realisation of this model.

The model therefore exists (that is my thesis): it is that of a physical and emotional proximity (de Singly, 1993a) of the man to his children. This physical and emotional proximity includes in itself a devaluation of authority on the one hand and the demand of a greater presence on the other hand. At the beginning of her text Trudie Knijn provides an image which you can find on postcards, of a father with a naked torso and jeans holding a baby to him. This image translates well this movement of proximity, of bodily contact through the jeans and naked torso, and hence the renunciation of the father's superior position. The absence of uniform (symbolised by the jeans) allows contact between two human beings, abolishing the symbolic barrier of the roles. Nevertheless Trudie Knijn does not insist enough on the other contents of the image. The man is muscular, he is not puny. He displays a certain virility. And his gesture is a protective one. The father holds the child against himself, with a specific position of the hand which again protects the child's head. On the whole this reflects something of the father's old role. This image allows us to understand the extent to which the new model of the father is not revolutionary, contrary to what Trudie Knijn perhaps believes too strongly. In fact if one mentions a crisis, there is a revolution. For the sake of argument I think it is also necessary to think about the presence of continuity in discontinuity. Masculine identity is being recomposed, but not abandoned.

To support my claim with regard to the internalisation of this model of proximity, the personal involvement in the relationship with the children, I will give a single example, taken from an opinion poll conducted among a representative sample of French people (published by the newspaper *La Croix*, January 1994, on the occasion of the International Year of the Family). To the question of what are the qualities of the good father and the good mother, the answers revealed very slight differences. The picture of the ideal mother and that of the ideal father differ very little, in such an approach. The paternal attribute par excellence in the traditional model — authority — came seventh in twelve suggested qualities, with a much lower score than availability, listening capacity, tolerance, patience. The score of the sense of authority is equivalent to that obtained by the qualities openness of spirit and humour. Also significant is that the quality occupying last place in the classification of men and women of the idea of the father is exigency. Demanding something of children lags very far behind. The father is not supposed to be rigid, thinking only of imposing and demanding; he should listen to the younger generations from who he too can learn.

It is apparent that this model of proximity contains the critique of the old model. One can think of the shibboleth of the International year of the Child: 'The family, a small unit, the smallest unit of democracy'. This slogan shows, intentionally or not — that is a different question — , a break with the image of the family in which the father has authority as a matter of course, because every group needs a leader and it is normal for men to be this. When the family is nowadays associated with the term democracy, this means that the valued kind of organisation is not that of organisation from above, but that of an organisation which if not egalitarian is at least negotiated.

I said at the beginning that the problems of the transition lay in the conditions for applying the model, conditions which have not all been met. I will here state some of those difficulties.

In the first place, this model which I call that of personal involvement is in competition with the maintaining of certain dimensions of the former role of the father. One which has noticeably not disappeared is the dimension often designated by the term 'breadwinner function' associated with the function of ensuring the family's survival. This function, contrary to what Trudie Knijn claims, still exists. The extension of salaried work to women has modified the landscape of the family, it has resulted in the movement from a model of strict division of labour between the partners to a model of a more supple division (certain mechanisms of which can be found in Jean-Clause Kaufmann in the version 'domestic labour'; 1992). But a transformation is taking place of such a sort that the man's professional labour is most frequently considered to be the labour of reference within the family, and that the woman's professional labour, even when full-time, occupies an inferior position. When a child falls ill, in the couples where both parents have leave for a sick child, one sees that it is almost always the mother who stops work and who justifies it by thinking that her husband's work is more important (de Singly, 1993b).

To illustrate this hierarchy of professional constraints according to the types and the maintenance of the place of work in the construction of the masculine identity, one can quote a father from Quebec which shows how a tension is born between that place and the demands of the proximity model: "If I did not have so many professional matters to attend to, there would be no limitations and I would like to spend time with my children. It is always heart-rending. If you work then you feel guilty because you are not concerned with the children, if you are with the children you feel guilty because you are not working." One of the problems of implementing the new model of paternity is thus that of reconciling professional and family life, which is not exclusive to women.

The second difficulty for fathers lies in the practical translation of this emotional and physical proximity. Men do not know how to do it. They have never been socialised with regard to the body. And they lack the imagination (perhaps the will too) to transcribe this need into activity. The woman — it is simultaneously a constraint and an opportunity — does not ask such questions, she has so much to do with her children that this proximity is inscribed 'naturally' through practice. The father looks desperately for a solution. The example of photography, quoted by Trudie Knijn, well illustrates this form of creative impotence which does not concern the upright man who embraces his child tightly to him. It lasts the length of a cuddle, the time for a photograph, it is not long enough to create strong bonds. The everyday life of men is too lacking in practice with children for proximity to become a true reality. The division of labour at home is not only a demand in terms of justice between types, it allows or will allow the realisation of a model which too often remains imaginary. In the case of divorce or separation, there is even more wavering. The transcription of the proximity model will again become more problematic, how is it possible to be close when objectively the father is far removed from the child?

There are other difficulties limiting the personal involvement of the father. On the one hand, certain specialists, notably in psychology and psychoanalysis, criticise this new model on the basis of the specificity of the father's role (as they see it in the context of their theories). They think that the father risks becoming too close when on the contrary he should be the one who breaks up the collusion between mother and child, which creates distance. The father is subject to a double bind, he needs to be simultaneously near and far! On the other hand, and Trudie Knijn did not have the time to look at this, there are also social differences which contribute to making the realisation of the model occasionally more uncertain. In this manner, the model of proximity can contradict the maintaining of an image of virility in popular environments, with the demand for a tough man who is not supposed to show his feelings (so as not to become effeminate). The tension between the old and the new varies socially.

2. My second point bears upon the analysis of the central hypothesis of Trudie Knijn's text, which articulates the model of the father and masculine identity. Trudie Knijn affirms again and again that there is a 'de-emphasis' of masculine identity, that this identity is dissolving as authority and the breadwinner function — decisive dimensions of the old model — have lost their superiority, are devalued. I accept the statement with regard to the dimension of authority. With regard to the breadwinner dimension, this seems to me less evident. I have already tackled it in the previous sections, but let us resume the discussion.

The professional labour of the woman, due to its success, has directly emphasised the evidence of this form of self-realisation, and the relative devaluation of the other mode of self-realisation, indirectly or through mediation (de Singly 1993a; 1993c). The professional dimension has thus not been destabilised by the rise of salaried work among women. On the contrary, there is a social recognition of the good basis of such a construction, and at that level there is an alignment of feminine values to masculine values rather than the inverse movement. Professional labour has become a normative principle for everyone (in France at least) and the man's professional work has remained the principal work.

This double movement — the alignment of women to the values of paid work, values formerly masculine and the translation of the division of labour between the partner (see 1) — has not had much effect if one measures it by the variations of equality of opportunity between the types. In the reprint of *Fortune et infortune de la femme mariée* (de Singly, 1994a), I revised the calculations of returns on qualifications according to the family status and type on the labour market. Between the 1970s and the 1990s, during the period of the extension of salaried work for women, the cost of marriage and family life has varied little for women, The masculine investments remain clearly superior to the female investments when both embarked on the parental career.

The definition of the new role of the father is not blurred, it is more a question of making this role compatible with the function of breadwinner. That is, the revolution has not taken place! The old regime is still there, it coexists more or less peaceably with the new one. The function as indicator of personal and familial success, the reference of the social position of the family group, is still more the social position through the man's work than the social position through the woman's work Division of paid labour between the partners has not brought with it equality between these two labours.

3. To conclude, it is necessary to return to the theoretical construction of the masculine identity. The model proposed by Trudie Knijn is that of coherence between the coded paternal dimensions and the other masculine coded dimensions. It seems possible to me to propose another theoretical model (which is not necessarily more verified in the social world than the other, it is for the sake of discussion). It is a model of the masculine type according to which the strictly paternal dimensions (in the sense of the ancient models) will have lost their value, but without the other masculine dimensions having been devalued in the same way. It is a model of incoherence.

In fact, it is not because a dimension in this structure which constitutes an identity of type loses its social value that the ensemble of the model collapses, the latter can recombine in a new structure in such a way that the new dimensions can coexist with the other, older dimensions (Japan is an example, in another register). Compromise between the types and between the generations during the last twenty years in the West operates with regard to the most emblematic dimension of masculine identity, that of the father in his authoritarian expression. As it is a compromise, this also means that men have not surrendered to the pressure of women, the women's movements notably, above all; they have kept in reserve other dimensions of their identity. On the level of feminine identity, a comparable movement can be reconstructed.

The question posed by these encounters on the father also deserve to be examined from the point of view of the child. According to the current norms (de Singly, 1994b) the child needs the two parents, his two parents. If it is true that the model of the father's personal involvement resembles that of the personal involvement of the mother, that does not mean that the images of the father and the mother are intermingled for the child. For the latter it is actually the totality of the identity of his parents of reference which counts, and not only, as opposed to the words, the paternal and maternal dimensions. Close to its parents, to its mother, to its father, the child learns not only the coded paternal dimension and the coded maternal dimension; it learns by looking, by living with the other dimensions of the type (to become itself, whether a boy or a girl). If my model is right, that of the recombination of masculine and feminine identities without revolution, the child does not have confused images before him, he can recognise his father and his mother, because that cannot be reduced to the fact of being close to him.

The post-paternalism as sketched by Trudie Knijn is simultaneously right and wrong. The transition from a capital letter Father and a small letter mother to a period when the two parents will be small letters corresponds to certain transformations. But at the same time, men and women keep the colours rather separate in the public realm, colours of identity which run together in the bosom of the family. Small letters, no doubt, both of them, but the alphabet includes a certain number of small letters. The child no longer has a big A and little b before him, this does not imply that he lives with two little c's; he can develop thanks to the active support of a little d and a little e, or if one prefers, of a little x and a little y!

References

Kaufmann, J-C. (1992). *La trame conjugale*. Paris: Editions Nathan.

Singly, F. de (1993a). *The social construction of a new paternal identity*. Conférence introductive à la conférence Fathers in Families to Tomorrow, Copenhague, 17-18 juin, Report Social Ministeriet, Danish Ministry of Social Affairs — European Commission, pp. 42-75.

Singly, F. de (1993b). *Parents salariés et petite maladie d'enfant*. La Documentation Française, Paris.

Singly, F. de (1993c). Les rivalités entre les genres dans la France contemporaine. In G. Duby & M. Perrot (Eds.). *Femmes et histoire*. Editions Plon.

Singly, F. de (1994a). *Fortune et infortune de la femme mariée*. Paris: Presses Universitaires de France (3ème éd. remaniée).

Singly, F. de (1994b). Les repères normatifs supportant l'enfance contemporaine, conférence introductive, Colloque L'enfant, savoirs, valeurs et normes, Congrès de l'association canadienne-française pour l'avancement des sciences, mai.

2

New forms of male family life in Canada

Hélène Desrosiers
Céline le Bourdais[1]

Introduction

The changes observed in the marital and reproductive behaviour of individuals over the past twenty-five years has significantly modified the formation, dissolution and recomposition of families in most Western societies. These changes have led to an increase in single-parent and step-families, and have led to important modifications in the nature of fatherhood. Due to increases in the dissolution of unions, a growing number of fathers must henceforth assume alone, or jointly with their ex-spouse, the custody of their children. Others will play the role of step-father while sometimes being deprived, whether voluntarily or involuntarily, of daily contact with their own children.

While certain studies have described various facets of fatherhood and have emphasised the multiple responsibilities (e.g., social, legal) that are attached to them, very few studies have sought to measure from a demographic perspective the importance of new family configurations in males' lives. For various reasons, both theoretical and methodological, most demographic research on families in Canada and in other countries has focused exclusively on women, neglecting to examine the role of men as social actors involved in the process of increased conjugal and familial mobility. In order to explore the future evolution of fatherhood, however, it is first necessary to sketch a general portrait of family mobility from the male viewpoint.

How many men are likely to become single parents at one time or another in their lives? How many will experience life in a step-family? What will be the duration of these episodes? These are among the questions that

1   This research was made possible thanks to the financial support of the Canadian Donner Foundation and the Quebec government's *Fonds pour la formation de chercheurs et l'aide à la recherche (FCAR - Équipes)*. The authors are grateful to Nathalie Vachon for the computer programming related to the reconstitution of family episodes, to Karen Lehrhaupt for a preliminary analysis of the data, and to Julie Archambault for producing the figures.

will be examined in this chapter, using a retrospective survey conducted in
Canada in 1990. In order to better identify the specific nature of family
situations experienced by men, some comparisons with women will also be
made during the analysis. We will also emphasise the limits of the available
data and identify certain promising research directions.

Current male family configurations: a little-known reality

Fatherhood represents a relatively new area of social science research. In the
US it was not until the 1970s that researchers emphasised the necessity of
shifting from a mother-centred paradigm to one putting greater emphasis
upon the role of fathers within the family (O'Brien, 1991). This new interest
in the father-child relationship is closely associated with the entire set of
demographic and social changes that most Western countries have
undergone over the past quarter-century: increased labour force participation
of mothers, the growing fragility of unions, rising male unemployment rates,
the emergence of the feminist movement. The rise of 'masculinist' groups,
especially in the US, also helped to emphasise the importance of the role of
fathers within contemporary families (O'Brien, 1991). Currently the focus
of much attention, the study of father-child relationships interests not only
researchers but also the media and the general public (Dulac, 1992; Gauthier,
1987; Furstenberg, 1988).

In Canada, male single-parenthood has been the object of several
demographic studies. Data from the 1991 Census reveal that single-parent
families, which represent 13% of all Canadian families, were headed by
males in nearly one out of five cases (18%). This percentage is similar to that
observed in 1981 (17%), but significantly lower than the figure of 26%
observed in 1941 (Oderkirk and Lochhead, 1992). The decline in the
proportion of single-parent families headed by males must be seen in the
context of the femininisation of single-parenthood observed over this period
(Dandurand and Saint-Jean, 1988). In fact, the circumstances surrounding the
formation of a single-parent family have significantly changed since 1941.
Formerly associated with the death of a spouse, single-parenthood is today
most often the result of the dissolution of a union, after which the custody
of the children is generally awarded to the mother. In 1990, for example,
after a divorce, women obtained the sole custody of 73% of all children
involved; 12% of all children were placed in the custody of their father,
while 14% lived in a situation of joint custody (Statistics Canada, 1993)[2]. In
spite of this decline in *relative* importance, the number of single-parent
families headed by males increased from 124,200 to 168,200 in Canada

---

2   The figures in several European countries are comparable (see Bawin-Legros, 1991).

between 1981 and 1991 (Statistics Canada, 1992). According to the 1991 Census, 1.5 million children (17% of all Canadian children) live with only one parent; of this number, 17% live with their father (Statistics Canada, 1992).

Like research conducted in other western countries such as France (Le Gall & Martin, 1987) or Great Britain (Hardy & Crow, 1991), the studies undertaken in Canada have indicated the generally more favourable situation of single fathers compared to single mothers (Oderkirk & Lochhead, 1992). Single fathers tend to be more mature and more educated than single mothers; and, being more likely to be employed, they also earn higher revenues (Oderkirk & Lochhead, 1992). Single-parent families headed by a male generally involve school-aged children; very young children living in the exclusive custody of their father are relatively few (Cloutier, 1990a, 1990b).

Previous Canadian research on the dynamics of single-parent families has focused exclusively on women (Moore, 1989; Desrosiers et al., 1993a, 1994) and on children (Marcil-Gratton, 1989, 1993). These studies show that single-parenthood is clearly more widespread than cross-sectional studies would appear to indicate, and that this phenomenon is becoming increasingly important in the lives of women and children, at least as a transitional situation. According to the data collected by the General Social Survey on Family and Friends, conducted by Statistics Canada in 1990, one female out of three is likely to experience single-parenthood at some point in her life, if the trends observed in 1990 continue (Desrosiers et al., 1994). Eighteen percent of all Canadian children born at the beginning of the 1980s have lived in a single-parent family before reaching their sixth birthday. It is estimated that nearly one out of two children will witness the separation of their parents before reaching twenty years of age, if recent trends continue (Marcil-Gratton, 1989, 1993; see also Furstenberg et al., 1983). About a third of these children will live with their father, and the remaining two-thirds with their mother, regardless of their age at the moment of separation; however, the former group of children will live in a single-parent family for a much shorter period than the latter group (Marcil-Gratton, 1993). Other recent studies conducted in various western countries indicate that a significant proportion of children experiencing the separation of their parents (approximately one-half) will, in fact, lose contact with their father or will only have occasional contact with him (Bawin-Legros, 1991; Bertaux and Delcroix, 1991; Cloutier, 1990a; Jacobsen & Edmondson, 1993). In Quebec, only one-third of divorced men see their children at least once each month, compared to two-thirds of divorced women. Further, after a divorce, only 40% of single-parent families headed by women benefit from the regular contact between their ex-spouse and the children, and receive financial support from the ex-spouse (Renaud et al., 1987).

Step-families have been the object of very little research in Canada. This lacuna results from the fact that, excluding censuses, few data sources exist for studying contemporary family forms. Like the majority of censuses carried out around the world, the Canadian census rarely collects retrospective data on the life history of individuals — information that makes possible the reconstitution of family episodes. In addition, census data do not distinguish between natural and step-children and thus do not enable one to identify step-families within two-parent families (Le Bourdais & Desrosiers, 1993). Step-families are not by any means new, however. In the past, remarriage and family recomposition were much more closely associated with the death of a spouse than they are presently, when a new type of step-family formed around one or two separated parents is emerging (Moxnes, 1991; Théry, 1993).

Data on remarriage lead one to suppose that step-families are more frequent among men than among women. Men clearly have a higher propensity than women to remarry quickly after a divorce: according to data from the mid-1980s, it is estimated that three-fourths of divorced men will remarry, compared to two-thirds of divorced women (Adams, 1990). To these figures, one must also add common-law marriages which are increasingly popular among couples in which one or both partners have already been divorced. Census data reveal that cohabitation rates for persons likely to engage in such an activity (i.e., those single, separated, divorced or widowed) were higher among 30-44 year-old men, and thus suggest a high propensity of the latter to form a common-law union after a separation or divorce (Dumas & Péron, 1992).

A recent longitudinal study shows that one Canadian female out of six will experience at least one episode of life in a step-family, if trends observed in 1990 continue (Desrosiers et al., 1994). Another study reveals that more than 60% of children born at the beginning of the 1970s and who experienced the separation of their parents have lived in a step-family before reaching their sixteenth birthday; the likelihood of belonging to a step-family is, however, proportionally higher among children living with their father rather than among those living with their mother (Marcil-Gratton, 1993). What place, then, do family recompositions occupy in men's lives? Part of the following analysis attempts to answer this question.

Data and methodology

Data
Our study is based upon retrospective data from Statistics Canada's General Social Survey on Family and Friends, conducted in 1990. This survey collected the matrimonial (marriage and common-law unions) and parental histories for a sample of 13,500 respondents who were at least 15 years old

in 1990; 6,600 of the respondents were male. The data provide the age[3] of the respondents at the moment of the formation and the dissolution of each union in which they were involved, including the age at marriage when it was subsequent to a common-law union; the circumstances surrounding the end of a union (separation, divorce, death) are also indicated. In addition, the data file includes the age of respondents at the birth or the arrival in their household[4] of each child (biological, adopted, step-child[5]) that they raised, as well as respondents' age when a child left home in a definitive manner. These data enable one to reconstruct the family history of respondents, including the periods they spent in a single-parent or step-family; for each of these periods, the mode of entry into the episode, its duration and the manner in which it ended are known[6]. In order to ensure the comparability of results with previous studies that we have conducted on women (Desrosiers et al., 1994), only respondents aged between 18 and 65 years at the moment of the survey were included in the analysis; this approach also has the advantage of minimising the chances of bias related to memory difficulties among older persons. For purposes of analysis, our data base includes information on 5,537 Canadian males.

An episode of single-parenthood is defined here as any period, regardless of its length, during which a man lives without a spouse, while having the custody of at least one child[7]. A family ceases to be considered as 'single parent' when the father begins living with a partner or when the youngest child earns his living. In the absence of data that enable us to identify the latter moment in the life of a young person, we have chosen 21 years of age as a threshold. Our definition is thus slightly different than that employed by Statistics Canada, which considers as single parent any family unit containing an adult living without a spouse and with at least one unmarried child, irrespective of the age of the latter.

A step-family refers to any household containing at least one child living with a parent and a step-parent. A step-family can thus include children

---

3   At the time of the survey, Statistics Canada collected the dates of the events (e.g., marriages, births) experienced by the respondents; these dates were subsequently converted into ages (expressed in decimal form) in the files used to conduct the present research.

4   In fact, we have information on the age of the respondents at the *birth* of adopted children and of step-children, rather than the age of the respondents when these children arrived in the household; an allocation strategy was developed in order to convert age at birth to age at arrival in the household (see Desrosiers et al., 1994).

5   A spouse's children, born during a previous union.

6   For more information on the nature of the survey and the method of reconstructing family episodes, see Desrosiers et al. (1994).

7   Note that our retrospective data do not indicate whether persons other than a spouse or children were living with the respondent during these periods.

born outside of the current union of one or both of the spouses, to which children born into the current relationship, if any, must also be added. This definition is thus broader than that used in studies of post-divorce situations, since it includes families reconstituted around parents who had never been involved in a previous union as well as those who experienced the death of a spouse. According to our definition, a step-family ceases to exist when there is a union dissolution or when the last child, who is not born to the current couple, leaves home. In the latter case, the step-family becomes a childless couple or, by analogy, an 'intact' two-parent household, in the sense that all children living there are born (or adopted) within the existing union. As we wish to take account of the complexity of the relationships that can exist within step-families, all children present in the household are taken into account, regardless of their age.

The Survey on Family and Friends is not without limitations. This survey furnishes no information on the situation of ex-spouses or on the child-care arrangements adopted after a separation or divorce, and it thus forces us to reduce single-parenthood and step-parenthood to the cohabitation between parent (or step-parent) and child, irrespective of the specific manner in which the role of parent is carried out. This constraint is relatively minor in studies on the family situation of women since, most frequently, custody is awarded to the mother after a separation or divorce. It does cause significant problems, however, in the case of male respondents, who rarely obtain the exclusive custody of their children after a rupture of the union. Finally, the survey contains no information on the periods during which the children temporarily left the respondent household; only age at the moment of a final departure of the children is known. Lacking more detailed data, we thus must assume that the children are present within the family until they finally leave home.

Methods of analysis

Our analysis proceeds in two steps. We first estimate the magnitude of the single-parent and step-family phenomena observed in Canada in 1990, and present certain demographic characteristics of these family types. Secondly, for males, we examine the processes of formation and dissolution of the first episodes of single-parent and step-families. This part of our analysis is based upon the life table method. The principle underlying this method is relatively simple. It consists of calculating, at each time interval considered, the probability that males will undergo a given family transition, by comparing the number of respondents that experience the transition during the period to the number who have not yet experienced the event and who are still under observation. The advantage of the life table method is that it enables one to use the entire set of information gathered and, above all, to use family histories which are underway but have not yet been completed.

The method thus enables one to identify to what extent the intensity and the timing of entering a given family type differ from one generation to another, and to estimate the proportion of males who would experience the phenomenon under consideration if the observed behaviours were to be maintained in the future.

Single-parenthood is first examined, for all males, in function of type of entry into the episode. Three types of entry are considered: 1) the birth of a child outside of a union; 2) separation or divorce; and 3) death of a spouse. Entry into single-parenthood, irrespective of the mode involved, is then analyzed by generation in order to see to what extent male behaviour has changed over time. The same type of analysis is undertaken for the termination of single-parenthood. Four types of exits are identified: 1) the departure (or death) of the last child under custody; 2) marriage; 3) common-law union; and 4) the attainment of 21 years of age by the youngest child.

The same approach is adopted in the context of step-families. Four family situations are considered at the moment of entry into a step-family. On the one hand, the category 'childless' refers to men having no children or who were not living with their children at the moment of the formation of a step-family. On the other hand, among those men living with children when they formed a union, three categories may be distinguished: 1) entries subsequent to an extra-union birth (unattached parent); 2) entries following a separation or divorce; and 3) those subsequent to the death of a spouse. Three types of termination of a step-family are identified: 1) separation or divorce; 2) death; and 3) departure of the last child who was not born to the current couple.

The multiple decrement life table method is employed for the analysis of modes of entry into single-parent and step-families, as well as for the analysis of types of exits. As several modes of entry (or exit) are envisaged simultaneously, these are treated as competing risks and the table provides the net probabilities of each transition[8]. The events in the table are then summed in order to provide cumulative probabilities of entry (and exit) in these two types of families; it is these probabilities, established by age (or duration), that are illustrated in the figures presented below.

A portrait of single-parent and step-families: male — female differences

Single-parent families
Table 1 presents selected characteristics of the single-parent families observed in 1990, according to the sex of the parent. The data indicate that

---

8   For a detailed discussion of this method, see Burch and Madan (1986) and Desrosiers et al. (1993a).

Table 2.1.   Characteristics of single-parent families[a] surveyed, according
                  to sex of parent, Canada, 1990

Characteristics	Sex of parent	
	Male	Female
At the time of the survey		
Percentage of single parents:		
- among all respondents	1	7
- among all respondents with children[b]	4	15
Average age of respondent	45.9	36.2
At entry into the current episode		
Type of entry:		
- extra-union birth	3	16
- rupture of union	82	80
- death of spouse	15	4
Average age of respondent	41.7	31.5
Age of youngest child		
- less than 6 years	22	54
- 6-15 years	52	31
- 16-20 years	26	15
Average age	8.8	5.5
Average number of children	2.0	1.7
Respondents living in a single-parent family N[c]	81	359
%	18	82

Source: *Statistics Canada. General Social Survey (cycle 5): Family and friends, 1990.*

a   A single-parent family household can include other related or unrelated persons,
    excluding a spouse.
b   Children less than 21 years of age.
c   Respondents between 18 and 65 years only. Weighted data scaled to the size of the
    initial sample.

only 1% of males aged between 18 and 65 years were living in single-parent families, as defined in the previous section, when the Survey on Family and Friends was conducted. These single fathers represent only 4% of all respondents living with children younger than 21 years of age; the mean age of these men was 45.9 years. These figures are comparable to results obtained in the US in 1990, which indicate that 4% of all families having children younger than 18 years of age were headed by a single father (Meyer & Garasky, 1993). The proportions are clearly higher for women: 7% of all female respondents and 15% of female respondents living with children were single parents when surveyed in 1990.

The second section of Table 1 presents selected characteristics of single-parent families at the moment of their formation. The dissolution of a union (either a marriage or a common-law relationship) is the underlying cause of the majority of single-parent situations observed; for both men and women, in approximately eight out of ten cases, the episode of single-parenthood current at the time of the survey was the result of a separation or a divorce. Women, however, are more likely than men to undergo single-parenthood as the result of an extra-union birth (16% versus 3%); on the other hand, males are more likely to find themselves as single parents following the death of their spouse (15% versus 4%).

On average, men were 42 years old when they began their current single-parent episode; they had 2.0 children in their custody, and the average age of the youngest child was 8.8 years. Single fathers rarely had the custody of pre-school-aged children: only 22% were living with children less than 6 years old when they became single parents and, in about one case out of four, the youngest child was between 16 and 20 years of age (for the US, see Meyer & Garasky, 1993). For women, entry into single-parenthood occurs earlier; on average, women were 10 years younger than men when they became single parents. Their children were also younger; more than one-half of all women (54%) had the custody of at least one pre-school-aged child at the beginning of their period of single-parenthood.

Although the definition of single-parenthood varies from one country to another, one can see that the results derived from the Canadian Survey on Family and Friends are very similar to those obtained from various studies conducted in the US and in Europe (Hardy & Crow, 1991; Le Gall & Martin, 1987; Meyer & Garasky, 1993). Together, these results illustrate the fact that the situation of single fathers differs in several respects from that of single mothers.

Table 2.2.   Characteristics of step-families[a] surveyed, according to sex of
               responding parent, Canada, 1990

Characteristics	Sex of responding parent	
	Male	Female
Percentage of respondents living in a step-family at the time of survey		
- among all respondents	6	5
- among all respondents with children	13	9
- among respondents living in two-parent family (spouse and children)	14	11
Type of family		
- with step-father	49	79
- with step-mother	39	12
- with step-father and step-mother	11	8
- other[b]	1	1
Average age of respondents at time of survey	39.2	35.9
Average number of children living in the family surveyed	2.1	2.0
Type of union:		
- marriage	35	57
- common-law	65	43
Average age at start of episode		
- respondent	31.8	29.6
- youngest child	5.8	5.8

(Table continues on next page)

Table 2.2.   (continued)

Characteristics	Sex of responding parent	
	Male	Female
Average number of children having lived in family at some time or another	2.4	2.2
- respondent's children	1.5	1.9
- step-children	0.9	0.3
- adopted children	0.01	-
Respondents living in a step-family		
N^c	328	266
%	55	45

Source: *Statistics Canada. General Social Survey (cycle 5): Family and friends, 1990.*

a   The household may include other related or unrelated persons.
b   Step-families of various types that include at least one adopted child.
c   Respondents between 18 and 65 years only. Weighted data scaled to the size of the initial sample.

Step-families
The 1990 Survey on Family and Friends makes possible, for the first time in Canada, the study of step-families among men[9]. Estimates established using this source indicate that 6% of Canadian males aged between 18 and 65 were living in step-families, as defined above; these respondents represented 13% of all males living with children (Table 2). Life in a step-family thus appears to be slightly more frequent among males than among females; 11% of women living with a spouse and child belong to a step-family, compared to 14% of men. This difference is the result of the higher proportion of females living in single-parent families in 1990; it also reflects the higher propensity of men to enter into a new union rapidly after a separation or divorce.

---

9   Data from the 1984 Family Survey did not permit the analysis of family transformations among males. Formulated differently for male and for female respondents, questions on fertility encouraged men to omit the children born in the context of a previous union and who were not living with them at the time of the survey.

The data presented in Table 2 also indicate that single-parenthood is not the sole route through which males enter into a step-family. In approximately one-half of all cases, step-families are formed when males, who are either childless or are living without their children, join a single mother and her child (children). In nearly four out of ten cases, families are organised around the children of male respondents (families with step-mother) and 11% of families consist of children of both the male and female spouses (families with step-father and step-mother). It is interesting to note that complex family forms consisting of three types of children (i.e., children of each spouse born from a previous union, plus those born to the current union) are relatively rare; only 2% of step-families investigated blend the three types of children (data not presented).

As shown in Table 2, male respondents living in a step-family in 1990 were 39.2 years old on average, and nearly two-thirds of them (65%) were cohabiting without being married. Obviously, they were younger (an average of 31.8 years) when they joined the step-family; the youngest child living with them had then an average age of 5.8 years (Table 2). The average number of children living in the families surveyed was 2.1, which is slightly below the average of children having belonged to a step-family at one moment or another. This difference can be attributed to the departures of children (to live with their mother or to assume their own life) that were not compensated for by the births of children to the couple.

There exist important gender-based differences in step-families. For example, it is much more frequent for women than men to raise their own children in this type of family: in nearly 80% of all cases, family recomposition involves only the children of the female, and in 12% of cases it includes children of both spouses. Women living in step-families were slightly younger (35.9 years) than their male counterparts at the time of the survey; they were also less inclined (43%) to live in a common-law relationship.

Male family dynamics

The estimates of the magnitude of single-parenthood and step-parenthood presented above furnish only a static portrait of these phenomena and provide little information on the importance that they take in male life. In order to gain such a perspective, one must consider respondents who had already experienced these phenomena but who were no longer living in such families at the time of the survey, and take into account those who were too young to have experienced the phenomena but who could do so later in their lives.

Male single-parenthood: a transitory situation

Summarising the multiple decrement life table, Figure 1 presents the cumulative probabilities of males who, at each age, have already experienced a first episode of single-parenthood. Figure 1 reveals that, if the behaviours observed in 1990 continue, nearly one-fourth (23%) of men will experience at least one period of single-parenthood at some point before reaching their 66th birthday. Recall that the definition of single-parenthood employed here covers any period during which a man declared to be living with his own children but without a spouse, regardless of the specific custody arrangements adopted (i.e., exclusive custody, shared custody, or partial custody).

Figure 1 shows that the first episode of single-parenthood was most often provoked by a voluntary rupture of the union: 13% of males become single parents as the result of a separation or divorce, while 4% do so following the death of a spouse, and 6% following the birth of a child while not living with a partner. The latter type of entry into single-parenthood tends to occur at relatively young ages; few males experience this event after 30 years of age, as the shape of the curve indicates. On the other hand, entry into single-parenthood due to the death of a spouse occurs later in life, increasing gradually after 40 years of age. Finally, separations and divorces tend to occur at intermediate ages, i.e., between 30 and 50 years.

The relatively high frequency of single-parenthood episodes following an extra-union birth may appear surprising when one considers the low propensity of men to assume the custody of young children. These episodes can include, however, a certain number of males who will form a couple with the child's mother in the months following the birth; unfortunately, our data do not permit us to identify these cases. 'Single' fathers who assume the full custody of their child after birth are no doubt relatively rare. In this latter case, as in the case of a union dissolution involving young children, there is reason to believe that male single-parenthood will be of short duration or that it will initially involve only occasional contact with the child, possibly leading to shared custody.

Figure 2, based upon single-parenthood entry tables by age group, reveals that the likelihood of males to experience at least one episode of single-parenthood varies slightly over time. For any given age, the data show a minor increase in the phenomenon moving from the 55-65 age group toward the 35-44 age group. By age 35, for example, 11% of respondents aged between 35 and 44 years at the time of the survey had already experienced a first episode of single-parenthood, compared to 10% of the 45-54 age group and 9% of the 55-65 age group. There is, however, a rapid increase in single-parenthood between the early 30s and the mid-40s among men aged between 45 and 54 years at the time of the survey. This acceleration of entry into single-parenthood must be seen in the context of the adoption of the

Canadian divorce law in 1968, which exerted a marked influence upon the men of the 35-44 cohort. Men of more recent generations were relatively unaffected by the passage of this law, and the more regular progression of single-parenthood among the 35-44 age group leads one to believe that the proportion of men experiencing this phenomenon could eventually overtake that reached by the 45-54 age group. Finally, one can note the relatively small likelihood of men younger than 35 years to have experienced single-parenthood; the explanation for this may lie in the delay in forming a first union among these age groups.

Do men experiencing single-parenthood remain in this situation for a long period? What type of event most frequently marks the end of this family episode: children leaving home or entry into a step-family? Summarising the multiple decrement life table, Figure 3 reveals that almost all single fathers (97%) will have exited single-parenthood 15 years after the beginning of the episode, if the trends observed in 1990 continue. The rapidity with which men leave the single-parent status is striking: four men out of ten will have ceased to be single parents at the end of one year, and only one out of ten men will remain single parents for at least ten years.

As the data clearly indicate, the formation of a couple constitutes the most frequent manner for males to end a single-parent episode. All together, slightly more than two-thirds of first experiences of single-parenthood ended by union formation before attaining the seventeenth year, by marriage in 40% of cases and by a common-law union in 26% of cases. The rhythm of union formation by single fathers is very rapid: at the end of two years of single-parenthood, nearly 40% of males have already formed a union. The termination of single-parenthood due to the departure of children also occurs relatively early in the episode. Among the 24% of all episodes that end through the departure of children, more than one-half (13%) last less than one year, and almost all last less than 5 years. By comparison, exits from single-parenthood related to the aging of children occur later; in total, 7% of episodes end in this way.

Figure 4, based upon single-parenthood exit tables by age group, clearly illustrates the shortening periods of single-parenthood as one moves from the older to the more recent generations. Three years after the beginning of the first period of single-parenthood, 85% of single fathers aged between 25 and 34 years have already ceased to be so, compared to 66% of men between 45 and 54 years and to only 47% of men in the 55-65 age group. The rapid rates of exit observed among the younger generations are no doubt attributable to the increase in voluntary ruptures of unions as the principal cause of single-parenthood, as well as to the fact that these ruptures occur earlier in the lives of males.

Males in step-families: an increasingly common situation

As a general rule, family recompositions follow a period of single-parenthood, however brief that it may be, experienced by one or another of the spouses. For males, as we saw, some individuals will enter into a step-family without going through a period of single-parenthood. What then is the most common trajectory for males entering into a step-family for the first time?

Figure 5 indicates that one respondent out of six will experience at least one step-family episode if the behaviours observed in 1990 continue. A non-negligible fraction of males (nearly 6%) will enter this situation without bringing children with them (childless men or men not living with their children). A slightly higher proportion (6.4%) will arrive with one or more children, following a separation or divorce; 4% with a child born outside of a union, and barely one percent with children born to a union that was terminated due to the death of a spouse.

The majority of men forming a step-family following an extra-union birth ('unattached fathers') or of those who are without children generally do so at a relatively young age; conversely, step-family episodes linked to the death of a spouse occur later in life. Between these two extremes, family recompositions following a separation or divorce occur at intermediate ages and become more important than the other forms of entry after 47 years of age.

As in the case of single-parenthood, the relatively high proportion of step-family episodes that follow an extra-union birth is surprising, especially since the formation of couples in the six months following the birth of the child were not counted as family recompositions; in the latter case, we supposed that the unattached fathers had formed a union with the mother of the baby[10]. The relationship between the father and his child could have been sporadic, however, during this family episode.

Figure 6 reveals an increase in step-families among the more recent generations. Only the 18-34 age group does not follow this general trend; this is most likely due to the delay in forming a first union among this age group, which, in turn, postpones separations and divorces. With the exception of this group, the more recent generations are more likely than their elders to have experienced a first episode in a step-family. Thus, 12% of males aged between 35 and 44 years at the time of the survey had already, by age 35, belonged to a step-family, compared to 7% of the

---

10 It is, however, impossible for us to be certain that this is the case, given that the Survey on Family and Friends does not contain any information on the spouses or ex-spouses of the respondents.

respondents aged 45-54 years, and only 4% of the respondents aged 55-65 years (see Figure 6).

What is the duration of step-family episodes identified for male respondents? Figure 7 indicates that 85% of males belonging to a step-family will have terminated this episode 25 years after its beginning, if the trends observed in 1990 continue. Nearly two-thirds of these episodes will end with the departure of the step-children, and 21% by a union dissolution. It is interesting to note that, for the shorter durations, there is little difference in timing between these two exit modes: 11% of family episodes will have terminated by one or another of these two modes before having reached their fifth anniversary. In the long term, however, the departure of children is far more important as a way of ending a male's step-family episode.

The cumulative probabilities of exiting step-families vary across generations. Respondents aged between 35 and 44 years and those older than 55 years experience similar rates of exit. Compared to these two generations, men aged 45 to 54 years exit their step-family episode more rapidly and in greater proportion, and the 25-34 age group, on the contrary, seems to experience a higher degree of family stability. Among the latter group, men who experienced family recomposition did so at a relatively early age; it is thus difficult to predict the future behaviour of the whole cohort from this particular sub-group.

Ten years after the beginning of the first episode of step-parenthood, slightly more than one-third of the respondents aged between 35-44 years and between 55-65 years had already exited from this type of family, compared to nearly one-half of men aged between 45-54 years. The examination of detailed data indicates that men in the 45-54 age group, who were at the centre of family transformations provoked by the adoption of Canada's divorce law, simultaneously present certain characteristics of both the preceding and the following generations; like their elders, they are characterised by a high propensity to exit a step-family by the departure of children, and like their younger counterparts, they are characterised by a strong tendency to exit by separation or divorce.

Male and female family trajectories: similarities and differences

Our analysis of the dynamics of single-parenthood indicates that nearly 25% of males will find themselves, at one time or another in their lives, at the head of a single-parent family, if the trends observed by the survey continue. While this percentage may appear high, it is, however, lower than that (35%)[11] observed for women, and the experience of single-parenthood is

---

11 The data on women presented in this section come from Desrosiers et al. (1994).

likely to have different implications for males and for females. On the one hand, very few men obtain the exclusive custody of their children after a union dissolution, particularly when the children are very young. On the other hand, most children that are in the custody of their father maintain very strong ties to their mother; the converse is not necessarily true, however. A large proportion of the episodes of single-parenthood declared by males can thus involve a period in which the father will have joint or occasional custody of his children with his ex-spouse. As Cloutier (1990b:8-9) observes, "in a sense, a single father is less of a single parent than a mother in the same situation".

In addition to variations in the relative magnitude of single-parenthood and in the distinct modes of parenting involved, three major differences distinguish males and females. First, females experience single-parenthood for a longer period than do men: more than twice as many single mothers (22% versus only 9% of single fathers) will remain single parents for a period of at least ten years; conversely, the proportion of single-parenthood episodes of very short duration (i.e., less than a year) is nearly twice as high among males (38% versus 22% for women). Second, even if men do not seem in the long run to be more likely than women to exit single-parenthood by the formation of a union, the former do tend to start living with a partner much more rapidly than the latter: it is only after 8 years of single-parenthood that women catch up to men in terms of the relative percentage that have formed a union. The third difference involves the higher propensity of men to terminate their single-parent episode as the result of the departure of their children; 24% of males, as compared to 15% of females, exit single-parenthood in this manner, and 18% (versus 2% of women) will do so during the first three years of single-parenthood. Conversely, women are much more likely (13% compared to 7% of men) to live with their children until the latter reach 21 years of age. These results reveal marked differences in the experience of single-parenthood between the two sexes. In effect, if the formation of a new union does not necessarily signal the end of parental responsibilities, the departure of the children from the household can radically change the nature of parenthood. These departures are not inconsequential, since several studies indicate that a number of 'part-time' fathers prefer to sever the ties with their children rather than to maintain sporadic contacts that may be rather superficial (Lund, 1987).

Our analysis of the dynamics of step-families has demonstrated that nearly one male out of six will, at some point in his life, be a member of this type of family, if the trends observed in 1990 continue. This proportion is almost identical to that characterising women. In the case of both men and women, we are witnessing a progression of the phenomenon over time, the more recent generations being more likely than their elders to experience at least one episode in a step-family.

Finally, two points deserve to be emphasised concerning male/female differences in step-family life. First, males with children from a previous union that has been terminated due to separation or divorce are less likely to become members of a step-family than are females in a similar situation (approximately 6% versus 9%). Conversely, men more frequently enter into a step-family without children (6% versus 2%), and they are more likely to play the role of step-parent (Le Gall, 1992). Second, unlike single-parent families, step-families identified from male respondents appear to be more stable than those observed for women. Not only are males less likely to have exited from this family status 20 years after the family recomposition occurred (75% versus 87% of women), but they are also clearly less inclined to see their family status altered because of a union dissolution; ten years after entry into a step-family only 17% of males had experienced a separation or a divorce, while more than one woman out of four had experienced such an event. Among the various factors that can be cited to explain these sex-related differences, the type of family organisation in which males and females live doubtlessly plays a major role. Given that women assume the custody of their children in a higher proportion after a separation or a divorce, they are clearly more likely than males to live in a family including a step-father (i.e., composed of their own children plus a partner without children). Several studies have indicated the greater instability of this type of step-family, compared to those involving a step-mother (Desrosiers et al., 1993b; Ferri, 1993). Several hypotheses have been advanced to explain this difference, among which are the particular profile of families in which males have custody of their children and the involvement of women in such families (Ambert, 1986; Ferri, 1993).

Conclusion

Our examination of new forms of male family life, based upon an analysis of the matrimonial and parental histories of respondents of Statistics Canada's 1990 Survey on Family and Friends, can only furnish a first approximation of the extent of transformations that have occurred in the lives of males. By combining the series of dates provided by the respondents for each event (union formation and dissolution; birth or arrival of children; final departure of the latter from the household) that they have experienced during their lives, we have reconstructed their past episodes in single-parent or step-families. This type of exercise is not without difficulties, however.

First of all, the information collected from male respondents is not always of high quality. Previous studies have shown that male retrospective fertility histories tend to be less reliable than those of females, since men tend to 'forget' to declare those children that are not living with them at the time of a survey (Furstenberg, 1988). Second, our data are imprecise in several ways, with the interpretation of specific questions possibly varying from one respondent to another.

One of the major limitations of our study lies in the fact that it is impossible for us to verify if the children of the respondents (including adopted children and step-children) were really present in the household during the family episodes considered and, if so, to identify the frequency and the duration of their presence. In fact, since we only have the dates of birth (or of the arrival in the household) and of final departure of the children, it is necessary to assume that the children live continuously with the respondent as long as they have not finally left the household, irrespective of the fraction of time spent with the respondent. The periods of single-parenthood (or of step-parenthood) studied could thus include a wide range of situations, going from the father who assumes the total custody of his children to the 'Sunday father' who only sees his children one weekend out of two. This latter situation would not have been identified as a single-parent episode if the respondent considered that his children were no longer living with him, having definitely left his household at the moment of the rupture of the union.

This constraint could affect the study of male family transformations more seriously than those of females, since the latter are much more likely to have the custody of their children on a daily basis. It could also lead to an over-estimation of the frequency and the duration of male episodes in both single-parent and step-families. One can assume that as long as a minimal form of contact is at least maintained with a child (e.g., monthly visits or during holiday periods), the respondent will not have considered the child to have definitively departed from his household. However, the specific conditions of parenthood can vary widely over time, as various studies have indicated (e.g., Seltzer, 1991).

In spite of these important limitations inherent in the source of the data employed, our analysis nevertheless remains highly instructive. It furnishes an estimate of the percentage of males that are likely to experience single-parenthood or to belong to a step-family during the course of their lives. It also reinforces several results from studies conducted in the US and in Europe. For example, our results confirm that single-parenthood is a situation that is much more temporary in the lives of males than in those of females. They also reveal the greater stability of step-families identified for males, compared to those observed for females.

The family transformations noted over the past 25 years have significantly modified the form of families and the place of the latter in the lives of individuals. The majority of studies conducted up to now have examined the impact of these transformations upon the lives of women, and they have emphasised the growing feminisation of child custody (see Björnberg, 1991 for a review). Conversely, men appear to have progressively removed themselves from their parental responsibilities (Bertaux & Delcroix, 1990). Unable or unwilling to maintain a meaningful contact with their children from a distance after separation or divorce, men tend to abandon their former parental functions for a new role as step-parents within a step-family; this practice has been referred to as 'serial parenting' (Jacobsen & Edmondson, 1993) or child swapping (Furstenberg, 1988). Is this form of parenting really wide-spread among males? Does it represent a major trend that is likely to endure, or is it rather a temporary situation that is a response to recent conjugal changes? In what way do step-fathers involve themselves on a daily basis in the care of children, and how does their behaviour differ from that of fathers living in an intact two-parent family? At the present time in Canada, little data exist with which to answer such questions. Clearly, further research needs to be undertaken in order to more carefully document the conditions of fatherhood in the various types of families.

References

Adams, O. (1990). Divorces in Canada, 1988. *Health Reports* (Statistics Canada) 2 (1): 57-66 (cat. 82-003).

Ambert, A-M. (1986). Being a stepparent: Live-in and visiting stepchildren. *Journal of Marriage and the Family 48*, 4, 795-804.

Bawin-legros, B. (1991). From Marriage to Remarriage: Ruptures and Continuities in Parenting. In U. Björnberg (Ed.), *European Parents in the 1990s. Contradictions and Comparisons* (pp. 229-242). New Brunswick/ London: Transaction Publishers.

Bertaux, D. & Delcroix, C. (1991). La fragilisation du rapport père/enfant: Une enquête auprès des pères divorcés. In B. Bawin-legros & J. Kellerhals (Eds.), *Relations intergénérationnelles, parenté-transmission-mémoire* (pp. 103-113). Actes du colloque de Liège (May 1990). Liège: Université de Liège and Genève: Université de Genève.

Björnberg, U. (1991). Parenting in Transition: An Introduction and Summary. In U. Björnberg (Ed.), *European Parents in the 1990s. Contradictions and Comparisons* (pp. 1-44). New Brunswick/London: Transaction Publishers.

Burch, T.K. & Madan, A.K. (1986). *Union Formation and Dissolution. Results from the 1984 Family History Survey.* Ottawa, Statistics Canada (cat. 99-963).

Cloutier, R. (1990a). *La garde de l'enfant après la séparation des parents.* Report submitted to the Conseil québécois de recherche sociale, Québec, Université Laval.

Cloutier, R. (1990b). Seuls pour élever leurs enfants. *Revue Notre-Dame 5*, 8-9.

Dandurand, R.B. & Saint-Jean, L. (1988). *Des mères sans alliance.* Québec: Institut Québécois De Recherche Sur La Culture.

Desrosiers, H., Le Bourdais, C. & Lehrhaupt, K. (1994). *Vivre en famille monoparentale et en famille recomposée: Portrait des Canadiennes d'hier et d'aujourd'hui.* Montréal: INRS-Urbanisation, Collection Études et Documents no 67.

Desrosiers, H., Le Bourdais, C. & Péron, Y. (1993a). La dynamique de la monoparentalité féminine au Canada. *Revue Européenne De Démographie 9*, 2, 197-224.

Desrosiers, H., Le Bourdais, C., Laplante, B. & Lehrhaupt, K. (1993b). *Les dissolutions d'union dans les familles recomposées: L'expérience des femmes canadiennes* (19 pp.). Paper presented at the XXllnd Congress of the International Union for the Scientific Study of Population (IUSSP). Montreal, 26 August.

Dulac, G. (1992). L'intimité masculine en éveil: Le désir d'enfant suite à la rupture d'union. *Revue Internationale d'Action Communautaire, 27/67*, 81-88.

Dumas, J. & Péron, Y. (1992). *Marriage and conjugal life in Canada.* Ottawa: Statistics Canada (cat. 91-534).

Ferri, E. (1993). *Research on the stepfamily in Great Britain* (9 pp.). Paper presented at the international conference *Les recompositions familiales aujourd'hui.* Paris, 3 December.

Furstenberg, F.R. (1988). Good Dads-Bad Dads: Two Faces of Fatherhood. In A. Cherlin (Ed.), *The changing American family and public policy* (pp. 193-218). Washington: Urban Institute Press.

Furstenberg, F.R., Winquist-Nord, C., Peterson, J.L. & Zill, N. (1983). The life course of children of divorce: Marital description and parental contacts. *American Sociological Review, 48*, 656-668.

Gauthier, P. (1987). Les 'nouveaux' pères. La paternité en émergence. In R.B. Dandurand (ed.), *Couples et parents des années quatre-vingt* (p. 69-80). Québec: Institut Québécois de Recherche sur la Culture.

Hardy, M. & Crow, G. (Eds.) (1991). *Lone Parenthood. Coping with constraints and making opportunities in single-parent families.* Toronto: University of Toronto Press.

Jacobsen, L. & Edmondson, B. (1993). Father figures. *American Demographics,* August, 22-62.

Le Bourdais, C. & Desrosiers, H. (1993). *Perspectives internationales: Évolution de la recherche sur les familles recomposées au Canada* (21 pp.). Paper presented at the international conference les recompositions familiales aujourd'hui. Paris, 3 December.

Le Gall, D. (1992). *Parâtres d'aujourd'hui. Formes du rôle beau-parental dans les familles héritières d'une union antérieure avec enfant(s)* (16 pp.). Paper presented at the conference La construction de la parenté. Genève, 11-12 December.

Le Gall, D. & Martin, C. (1987). *Les familles monoparentales*. Paris: Les Éditions ESF.

Lund, M. (1987). The non-custodial father: Common challenges in parenting after divorce. In C. Lewis & M. O'Brien (Eds.), *Reassessing fatherhood: new observations on fathers and the modern family* (pp. 212-224). Beverly Hills: SAGE.

Marcil-Gratton, N. (1993). Growing up with a single parent, a transitional experience? In J. Hudson & B. Galaway (Eds.), *Single parent families. Perspectives on research and policy* (pp. 73-90). Toronto: Thompson Educational Publishing Co.

Marcil-Gratton, N. (1989). Les enfants d'aujourd'hui et les comportements nouveaux de leurs parents. In J. Légaré, T.R. Balakrishnan & R.P. Beaujot (Eds.), *Crise de la famille: Crise démographique?* (pp. 343-358). Ottawa: Fédération Canadienne de Démographie et Société Royale du Canada.

Meyer, D.R. & Garasky, S. (1993). Custodial fathers: Myths, realities, and child support policy. *Journal of Marriage and the Family, 55*, 1, 73-89.

Moore, M. (1989). How long alone? The duration of female lone parenthood in Canada. *Transition, 19*, 1, 4-6.

Moxnes, K. (1991). Changes in family patterns-changes in parenting? A change toward a more or less equal sharing between parents. In U. Björnberg (Ed.), *European parents in the 1990s. Contradictions and comparisons* (pp. 211-228). New Brunswick/London: Transaction Publishers.

O'Brien, M. (1991). Changing Conception of Fatherhood. In U. Björnberg (Ed.), *European parents in the 1990s. Contradictions and comparisons* (pp. 171-180). New Brunswick/London: Transaction Publishers.

Oderkirk, J. & Lochhead, C. (1992). Lone parenthood: Gender differences. *Canadian social trends* (Statistics Canada) 27, 16-19 (cat. 11-008).

Renaud, M., Jutras, S. & Bouchard, P. (1987). *Les solutions qu'apportent les Québécois à leurs problèmes sociaux et sanitaires. Trois types: s'occuper d'un parent âgé, soulager son mal de dos, être chef de famille monoparentale.* Report submitted to the Commission d'enquête sur les services de santé et les services sociaux. Québec: Les Publications du Québec.

Seltzer, J.A. (1991). Relationships between fathers and children who live apart: The father's role after separation. *Journal of Marriage and the Family, 53*, 1, 79-101.

Statistics Canada (1993). *A portrait of families in Canada*. Ottawa: Statistics Canada (cat. 89-523).

Statistics Canada 1992. *Lone-parent families in Canada*. Ottawa: Statistics Canada (cat. 89-522).

Théry, I. (1993). Introduction générale: Le temps des recompositions familiales. In M-T. Meulders-Klein & I. Théry (Eds.), *Les recompositions familiales aujourd'hui* (pp. 5-21). Paris: Nathan.

Figure 1.
   Cumulative probabilities of experiencing an episode of single-
   parenthood, by type of entry. Males 18-65 years

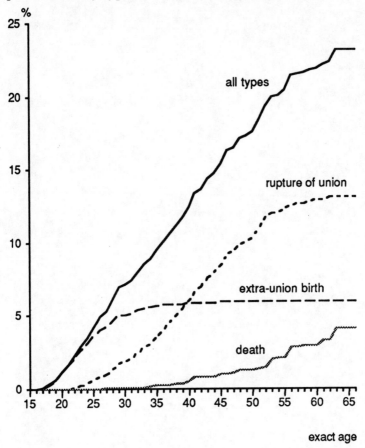

Figures 1 to 8 are derived from *Statistics Canada, General Social Survey
(cycle 5): Family and friends, 1990.*

Figure 2
Cumulative probabilities of experiencing an episode of single-parenthood, for age groups at time of survey. Males 18-65 years.

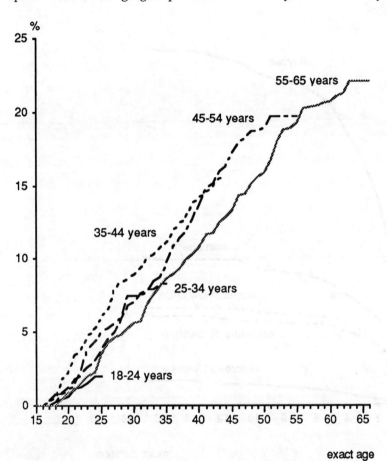

Figure 3
Among males having experienced single-parenthood, cumulative
probabilities for existing from this family status, by type of exit. Males
18-65 years[*]

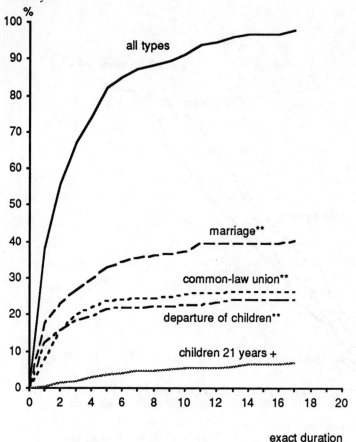

exact duration

*   Curves are terminated when the number of respondents exposed to
     the risk of experiencing the transition considered is less than 10.
** Among men whose youngest child is less than 21 years.

Figure 4
　　Among males having experienced single-parenthood, cumulative
　　probabilities for existing from this family status, for age groups at time
　　of survey. Males 18-65 years[*]

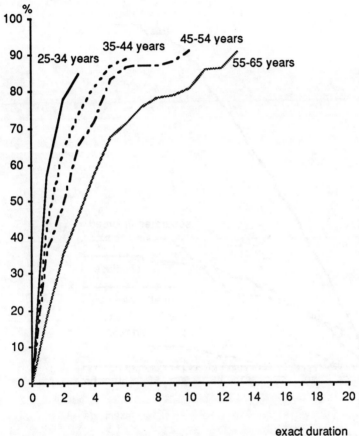

exact duration

* 　Curves are terminated when the number of respondents exposed to
　　the risk of experiencing the transition considered is less than 10.
** Among men whose youngest child is less than 21 years.

Figure 5

Cumulative probabilities of experiencing an episode in a step-family, by family status at entry into episode. Males 18-65 years[*]

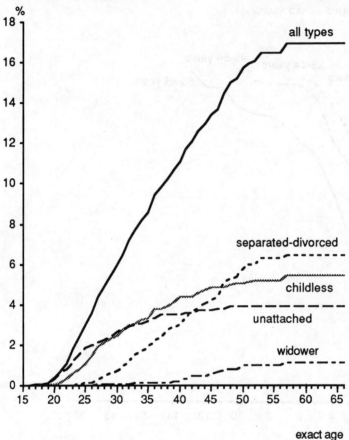

exact age

[*] The categories unattached, separated-divorced and widower refer to men residing with their children at the time of entry into a step-family; the category unattached is composed of men who have never cohabited with a woman, i.e. men who have children outside of a union. The category childless refers to men without children or those children were not living with them at the time of entry into step-family.

Figure 6
Cumulative probabilities of experiencing an episode in a step-family, for age groups at time of survey. Males 18-65 years[*]

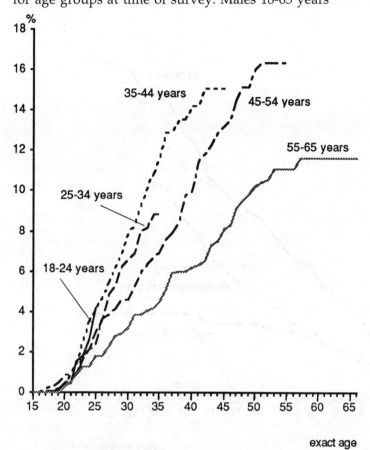

exact age

* The categories unattached, separated-divorced and widower refer to men residing with their children at the time of entry into a step-family; the category unattached is composed of men who have never cohabited with a woman, i.e. men who have children outside of a union. The category childless refers to men without children or those children were not living with them at the time of entry into step-family.

Figure 7

Among males having lived in a step-family, cumulative probabilities of
exiting from this family status, by type of exit. Males 18-65 years

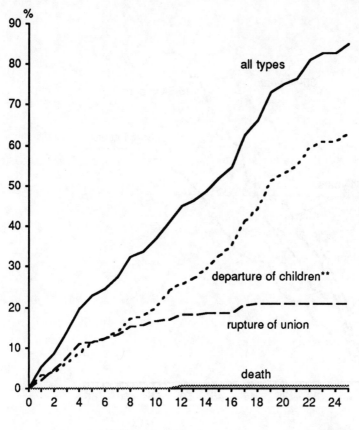

* Curves are terminated when the number of respondents exposed to
  the risk of experiencing the transition considered is less then 10.
** Refers to the departure of the last child that is not born to the recent
  couple.

Figure 8
Among males having lived in a step-family, cumulative probabilities of exiting from this family status, for age groups at time of survey. Males 18-65 years[*]

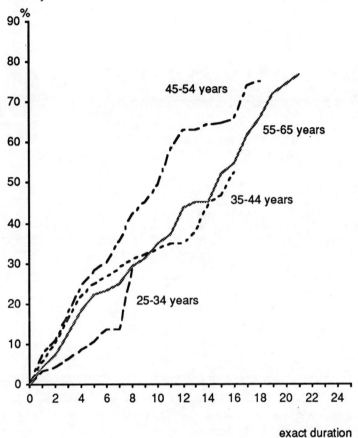

exact duration

[*]   Curves are terminated when the number of respondents exposed to the risk of experiencing the transition considered is less then 10.

Anton Kuijsten

I would like to start by stating clearly that the paper by Desrosiers and Le Bourdais is a welcome and good contribution to the too long neglected field of the 'demography of fatherhood'. The study of fertility has long been female-biased. Until recently, this could be explained, if not excused, by the (in)availability of data: almost all data sources provided fertility data by characteristics of mothers only, neglecting those of fathers. Curiously, the reverse was often true for household and family statistics, which often had the household head — by definition male — as their main marker. The predictable result, then, was enormous difficulties for people who were working on dynamic household and family modelling, in which the two have to be dovetailed.

Fortunately, this situation has changed. We have witnessed the emergence of both large-scale surveys, sometimes as substitutes for censuses, and retrospective surveys, and both include men as well as women. We have also witnessed the emergence of event history analysis and other types of life course analysis methods that can assist in exploring the wealth of these retrospective data sets. One would have expected, then, now that this was finally possible, that the entire community of demographic analysts would have rushed into exploring and analyzing these male data on fertility, fatherhood and living arrangements. Surprisingly, nothing of the sort has happened, as is also mentioned by Desrosiers and Le Bourdais: most of the studies remained exclusively focused on women's fertility and partnership careers.

The layman's intuition might lead him to the question: So what? Intuitive logic seems to suggest that, on average, men must have exactly as many children as women have, perhaps at an average age of about three years older, because men marry approximately three years later than women do, but that's it. This intuitive logic, however, is wrong. Dinkel and Milenovic (1993) have shown, on the basis of pooled German survey data sets, that there is indeed an existing and varying difference between male and female age-specific and cumulative fertility. First, the reproductive life spans of both sexes have different lengths. Second, since men enter unions at an older average age than women, there is an age difference in entering fatherhood: at younger ages, female fertility exceeds male fertility, whereas at older ages the opposite is true. Moreover, among males the variation in age around this mean age at entering a union is much greater than among females, so the male age schedule of fertility may be expected to be flatter than that of females. Register-based analysis of male and female fertility in Denmark in the 1980s (Knudsen, 1993) points in the same direction. An interesting finding in the study of Dinkel and Milenovic is that among older German cohorts (born before the 1930s) male completed fertility is consistently somewhat higher than that of women three years younger. Among more recent cohorts they find the opposite: lower male than female fertility. Their explanation is as simple as it is convincing: it is the effect of the so-called marriage squeeze. In the older cohorts, men were relatively 'scarce', so they had a higher nuptiality level than women; at the aggregate level of the entire cohort they ended up with a higher average fertility. After the war this situation was reversed. The post-1965 fertility decline will probably further deepen this post-war trend of a growing gap between male and female fertility since this fertility decline has further improved the chances of younger female partners on the marriage and cohabitation market.

I read the paper by Desrosiers and Le Bourdais as a welcome extension of the aforementioned argument. Gender differences in terms of fertility and parenthood might in fact be much greater than this marriage squeeze argument alone suggests. First, now that cohabitation has really matured, we must take this living arrangement into account as well and think in terms of 'union squeeze' instead of marriage squeeze. Next, union dissolution has quite different repercussions for fathers than for mothers. Moreover, second unions are much more frequently sought after by once-married males than by once-married females. Finally, men enter second unions that are reconstituted, so-called 'blended' unions, more than women do, bringing together children of different biological backgrounds. All these phenomena are reasons to expect growing disparities between male and female fertility and parenthood experiences with longer duration of the fertility and partnership careers, especially in the social sense of everyday childrearing. In that sense, fatherhood seems to be more fluid, more fuzzy, but also more dynamic than motherhood.

I think it is a major asset of the paper that it is this basic but under-researched fact of life that is demonstrated quite aptly by the authors, and I wish that all who read it will read it as a call for more of this kind of research. Notwithstanding this positive overall view, I would like to make a few comments.

First, I think that the paper would have gained very much by making the overview of male life-course partnership and fatherhood experiences even more complete than it is now by adding what is lacking: the very first beginning, in the sense of *entering* fatherhood for the first time. The focus of the paper is on lone parenthood and on reconstituted unions; i.e. on *later phases of fatherhood*. The series of graphs at the end give an idea of sequences of events that can happen to fathers once they have entered lone parenthood, but the sequence really starts with entering fatherhood as such, in a first union. So one can wonder, for example, to what extent the between-cohort differences in cumulated proportions by age who have already experienced lone parenthood (Figure 2, page 53) can be explained by between-cohort differences in cumulated proportions by age who have experienced fatherhood as such.

Second, focusing on lone parenthood and family reconstitution as "new forms of family life" is the authors' good right, of course, but I wondered whether they are not overdoing this a little. This has to do with their definition of lone parenthood in particular, or rather, with what seems to me to be a lack of consistency in that definition throughout the paper. On page 32, a spell of lone parenthood is defined as each period — whatever its duration — in which a man lives without a partner and with at least one child to care for. This looks like a very clear definition, and it is what I expected after having read that the authors knew the age of respondents at the moment of formation and dissolution of each of the unions they experienced, the reasons of each union disruption, and the age of respondents at the moment of entry or exit of every child of whatever type (natural, adopted, stepchild) that had ever lived in their household. So, I would assume that it was possible to determine, for any moment in the respondent's life, his or her exact household composition. But later on, in their analyses, the authors use a kind of lone parenthood definition that seems to hold for everybody who has experienced the disruption of a union-with-children. All kinds of legal and everyday custody, care and visiting arrangements are lumped together and called lone parenthood. No wonder then, that it is found that 23% of men and 35% of women have experienced lone parenthood at least once during their adult life. But isn't there the danger of exaggeration? What relevance does such a figure have in real life, or for social policy? Because of the description of what is in the data set that I just quoted, I was quite surprised to find later on in the paper that Desrosiers and Le Bourdais did not make any distinction between all these types of custody-and-care arrangements of divorced fathers, and thus more or less included every arrangement in this lone parenthood category. In this way, and that is what I meant by 'danger of exaggeration', Desrosiers and Le Bourdais used a kind of maximum definition. Was it not possible to do some second runs of the survival table models, now using a minimum definition by incorporating those cases only in which — from the data — it was absolutely clear that the children were in the household of the lone parent almost full-time? I think such an analysis would come much closer to the concept of lone parenthood as used in current household and family statistics, although I would never deny the usefulness of trying out other conceptual approaches.

Third, Desrosiers and Le Bourdais' paper is almost completely descriptive, making no mention of theory that might have guided them when making their models and doing their analyses. I am sure there was theory in the research project as a whole, but it is not in this paper. Theory could, or must, have guided their decisions when arranging the data and constructing the models, because theory has repercussions for modelling. I will give two examples. The first one has to do with the decision to treat the various ways to exit from a given status as 'competing risks'. Within the framework of the survival table as such — from a purely technical point of view the authors are right of course — you can only leave the status through a single door; after that, leaving through other doors is no longer possible. But from a more substantial point of view things may be somewhat different. Look, for example, at the exits from the state of lone parenthood, depicted in Figure 3 on page 54. As one of my Ph.D. students pointed out (Manting, 1994), one can look at the risk to enter a marriage and the risk to enter a 'free union' as two competing risks. But one can also look at them as being two variant outcomes of the same process of union formation, triggered by a first decision to enter a union, and in a second stage only determined by a preference for direct marriage or a preference for starting (at least) as a cohabitor. These different ways of looking at the phenomenon can have quite different consequences for modelling. My second example has to do with this status of cohabitor, or, more precisely, with the operationalisation of the duration of leaving, for example, the lone parent status through the door of 'free union' as the authors call it. How did Desrosiers and Le Bourdais determine that duration? Did they have proof of when exactly people started to cohabit (something comparable with a marriage certificate, for example)? Or did respondents subjectively indicate at what time they had the feeling that they were really cohabiting? We all know that cohabitation often starts by 'gradually moving in' (Manting, 1994), in post-marital situations perhaps even more so than in first-union situations. Especially in that early phase, cohabitation can be a very fuzzy concept, as fuzzy as the lone parenthood definition used sometimes seems to be. How did Desrosiers and Le Bourdais deal with these potentially ambiguous situations?

My final comment (I leave out matters of detail) has to do with the life course approach. Although Desrosiers and Le Bourdais mention the expression only a few times in their text, their analysis has been done from a life course perspective. I clearly see their attempt to summarise and compare the results for men with those for women (page 43). But at the same time they do a kind of life course analysis in which people's lives are chopped into small slices, and then one slice after the other is placed under the microscope and analyzed and discussed separately. Much research that is sold as life course analysis is conducted in this way. Too much I would say, because it is hardly more than the old multivariate analysis of event determinants, with the help of the modern tool of event history or lograte analysis. But where is the integration of these parts? In my view, the message of the life course approach is not that each individual past experience has some influence on that individual's future behaviour. No, it is the *combination* of all past experiences that, at each moment when a new event may announce itself, may exert its influence on whether or not that new event will occur. And once it has occurred, that new event immediately shifts, so to speak, from the right side of the equation to the left side, and becomes part of the battery of past experiences that from then on together will influence the occurrence of new events. Real life course analysis, in my view, should be dynamic, and recursive in its modelling. I think it is a pity that the authors have treated the events they studied as isolated occurrences, because I believe that with more than five-and-a-half thousand cases they could have proceeded in the direction I just stipulated, looking at the influence of sequences-of-past-events much more than at that of individual past events in describing and explaining next steps in people's partner and parental careers.

References

Dinkel, R.H. & Milenovic, I. (1993). Male and female fertility: A comparison of age-specific and cohort fertility of both sexes in Germany. *Genus, IL*, 1-2, 147-158.

Knudsen, L.B. (1993). *Fertility trends in Denmark in the 1980s: A register based socio-demographic analysis of fertility trends.* Copenhagen, Danmarks Statistik (Statistiske Undersøgelser nr. 44).

Manting, D. (1994). *Dynamics in marriage and cohabitation: An intertemporal, life course analysis of first union formation and dissolution.* Amsterdam, Thesis Publishers, 1994 (PDOD-Publications Series A: doctoral dissertation).

3

The wish to become a father
How do men decide in favour of parenthood?

Menno Jacobs

In this article I will describe some of the most important, past and present, social scientific investigations into the wish to become a father. I will start with a brief overview of the theories that concern choice processes on fertility. Then I will present a conceptual model of possible determinants with regard to the fertility decision by men, illustrated with and partly validated by a small survey I conducted recently.

Theoretical perspective

One important issue in demography is the procreative behaviour of societies. Demography has traditionally been the scientific discipline concerned with measuring, explaining and forecasting fertility rates. Although the first task (measuring) was always done quite accurately, the other two have been widely criticised. Once it was recognised that demographic theories were poor predictors of the future procreative behaviour of a social system, it was time to look for other possibilities to improve the predictive power of demographic theories. One suggestion often heard was to improve the 'conceptual base' of demography. Another suggestion stressed a switch from macro-level theories to micro-level theories, or an integration of both types of theory. These suggestions came together when demographers embraced other disciplines such as neoclassical economics and (social) psychology (Burch, 1980; De Bruijn, 1993; Vermunt, 1993). Since then an important issue in demography became the procreative behaviour of a couple.

Even before the shift in focus in demography took place there was considerable interest in fertility from a psychological point of view. We might say that the *expectancy-value model* designed by Fishbein (Fishbein, 1972; Fishbein & Ajzen, 1975) triggered a new way of looking at fertility. It became popular to speak of fertility not only in terms of graphs and rates, but also in terms of beliefs, attitudes and intentions. Up until then attempts had been made to make an inventory of the motives for having children. Consider for example Rabin (Rabin, 1965; Rabin & Greene, 1968) who classified 'motivation for parenthood' into four categories, or Hoffman and Hoffman (1973) who made a nearly exhaustive list of possible motives to have children.

Due to a number of social, ideational and medical shifts, having children has increasingly become *a choice*. After the introduction of *the pill* in 1960 this contraceptive method became very popular. It can not simply be a coincidence that the US total fertility rate curve shows a sharp decrease after 1960 (in Western Europe 5 years later). This means that fewer (Western) women get fewer children, and if they do, they get them at a later age (Westoff & Ryder, 1977; De Beer, 1992; Vermunt, 1993). Having children has become a very difficult choice for many people since many women have a job, aspire to a career and no longer automatically take responsibility for the nurturing and raising of their children. 'Taking' children is not something that goes without saying, but a topic of much negotiation between married or cohabiting couples (Avort, 1987).

Since having children seems to have become such a difficult and deliberate choice for many people, scientific programmes reacted by looking at the 'fertility decision' in a similar way, namely in terms of weighing *costs and benefits*.

Clear examples of theories whose axiom is the (rational) weighing of costs and benefits are the theories of neoclassical economics (e.g. New Home Economics), designed by Becker (1960; 1981). "The demand for children would depend on the relative price of children and full income. An increase in the relative price of children reduces the demand for children and increases the demand for other commodities (if real income is held constant)" (Becker, 1981 96). Considering having children as a pure financial matter has often been criticised. The theory of New Home Economics would be applicable to predicting the outcome of a choice between refrigerator A and B, but not to the choice between having children or remaining voluntarily childless (Hull, 1983; Simon, 1987). However, New Home Economics has contributed to the fruitful idea of considering difficult choices or decisions, such as the fertility decision, as a weighing of costs and benefits, whether entirely rational or not.

Another example of a cost/benefit theory is the Exchange Theory. Exchange Theory assumes a maximisation of utility in the exchange between people of costs and rewards; for example, of paid and unpaid labour. It focuses mainly on three human resources, namely education, profession and income. Applied to the fertility decision the theory 'predicts' that socio-economic status and gender role orientation influence perceptions of the costs and benefits of having children (Seccombe, 1991). Seccombe found that the higher the male's occupational prestige, the less likely he is to rate either opportunity or financial costs as very important. For women no such relationship was found. She also noted that traditional men see more benefits in having children than do non-traditional men. It is here that we find that the couple as a unit of analysis is split into the two individuals, man and woman.

Men only

Most studies on procreative behaviour conducted so far have focused on women, some have focused on both sexes, and only very few on men. Some of these studies suggest that there are only small differences between men and women regarding the motivation for parenthood (Rabin & Greene, 1968; Hoffman, 1972). Recent sociological developments, (individualism, increasing labour force participation of women and the changing gender-identity of men and women) make it necessary for decision-making on parenthood by men and women to be regarded separately (Gerson, 1986; Lesthaeghe & Surkeyn, 1988; Seccombe, 1991; Marsiglio, 1991). It was because men were scientifically underexposed in fertility research, that a project was started at Tilburg University to investigate the role of men in the decision either to have children or to remain childless.

The aim of this project is to describe, and to some extent analyse, the determinants that contribute to the decision to become a father. The first task was, of course, to indicate these determinants. The *expectancy-value model* provides us with the concept of the wish for children in terms of, thanks to micro-economics, costs and benefits. Exchange theory supplies other determinants such as socio-economic status and the division of paid and unpaid labour between men and women. The second task was to bring these determinants together in a conceptual model. The third task was (and is) to validate the model empirically. Before detailing the model and the empirical findings, I will elaborate upon the determinants.

The wish for children

A wish has two components: change and timing. If you want to have something or become someone, then you feel a need to change the present situation. A mental incongruity is felt between the present situation and a desired situation. Feeling a need for change does not necessarily mean that you want it instantly. There is a timing aspect. You might want it now, or within a year, or not within the next five years. In fact, an incongruity can exist for a long time without the subject doing anything to diminish this incongruity (Tazelaar, 1980). In this case I call the wish latent. If the incongruity leads to some kind of action, I call the wish manifest. Action is interpreted rather broadly in this respect. Besides behaviour to fulfil the wish, deliberating or doubting, *making* a choice is also considered to be action. A latent wish does not have any strings attached, it is free of obligations. This means that a latent wish has no timing aspect other than 'sometimes' or 'maybe after some five or ten years'. As soon as one begins to contemplate the fulfilment of a wish, a more specified timing will be attached. If we assume that people's behaviour always has *some* goal or function, we might say that it is unlikely that someone would spend much time on making a difficult choice which will never, or only in the very distant future, become reality. Thus, the distinction between a latent and a manifest wish can be made by looking at action and timing.

An interesting aspect of wishes is their origin. Some wishes seem to have always existed or to have emerged spontaneously, others are clearly induced by some external source (people, advertising agencies). Some people feel they have a disposition, or intrinsic motivation for desiring something ('always wanted to drive a Ferrari'), whereas others admit that they were influenced ('neighbour drives Ferrari, I want it too'). It is a bit precarious to look for the origin of a wish as being *either* internally or externally induced. Genetic factors, childhood and adolescent experiences and present circumstances all play a role. To unravel at least a bit of the complex interplay of these factors a distinction is made between childhood and adolescent experiences (including past influences by others) on the one hand, and present, felt and admitted influence on the other. Miller (1992) found convincing empirical support for the childhood and adolescent experiences as predictors of a childbearing motivation later in life.

We can now connect this distinction to the former one of the latent and manifest wish. A latent wish is by definition a long-term, 'hidden' incongruity, which therefore eliminates the possibility of being induced by present influences. This leaves us with a rather simple statement: A latent wish is induced by genetic factors and past experiences, and a manifest wish is induced by a latent wish or present influence. Since a latent wish is defined as being shaped by genetic factors and past experiences, we may view it as a set of personal values and norms regarding having children. If and when a latent wish becomes manifest depends on the timing aspect. Therefore age and duration of the relationship are important determinants for this change. Moreover, situational factors (e.g. more financial scope) may shorten the postponement.

A manifest wish is considered to be a three-phase construct. As noted before, a manifest wish is characterised by action, meaning conscious mental activity (thinking about it) as well as goal-directed behaviour. I call the first phase of the manifest wish a *desire*. This corresponds with the doubting phase. One begins to think about realising the desired new situation, which means that advantages and disadvantages are juxtaposed. It is hypothesised that, speaking of a desire, advantages *and* disadvantages of the desired situation are valued both as high.

The next phase is called an *intention*. In this phase the advantages are still highly valued, but the importance of the disadvantages has diminished. This means that a positive decision is at hand.

The last phase of the manifest wish is characterised by instrumental behaviour. In this phase the wish has transformed itself into goal-directed behaviour in order to actually fulfil the wish (see also Miller, 1994).

Socio-economic status and gender role orientation

As mentioned before there are other indicators of the fertility decision than only the wish for children. I refer to socio-economic status and gender role orientations. It has been argued that socio-economic status plays a role in fertility (Lewis et al., 1982; Beckman, 1983; Hollerbach, 1983; Seccombe, 1991). Unfortunately it is not clear in which direction this influence works. Seccombe argued that men with a higher socio-economic status see more benefits in having children. This is only true if these men do not have to give up their role of breadwinner. They expect their wives to be at home, cherishing their so-called traditional gender role orientations. The link between socio-economic status and fertility is thus mediated by gender role orientation. Socio-economic status is considered to be partly responsible for having modern or traditional gender role orientations: people with a lower socio-economic status are more traditional.

One of the hypotheses in this study is that either modern or traditional gender role orientations may facilitate the fertility decision. If a couple agrees on a traditional division of tasks (i.e. the man takes care of the income, the woman takes care of the child) there are less barriers to wanting a child. But it can also be the other way around. If a couple agrees on a modern division of tasks (i.e. the man and the woman want to share the responsibilities of earning an income and caring for the child) there are also less barriers to wanting a child. The facilitating factor is therefore the agreement between man and woman. This does not alter the fact that there can be other barriers (financial barriers, for example) that overrule the barrier of disagreement on the division of paid and unpaid labour.

Conceptions on fatherhood

Modern or traditional gender role orientation is part of a construct called 'conceptions on fatherhood'. The most important conceptions on fatherhood are economic and social responsibility, ideas and plans about taking care of the child, and gender identity. These are considered to be the determinants of the wanted and expected division of paid and unpaid labour after the baby is born. There may be a difference between wanted and expected, since the gap between 'in principle' and 'in practice' among today's fathers is quite big (Knijn, 1990). Many men have to compromise between the demands of their employer, the demands of their partner and their own demands.

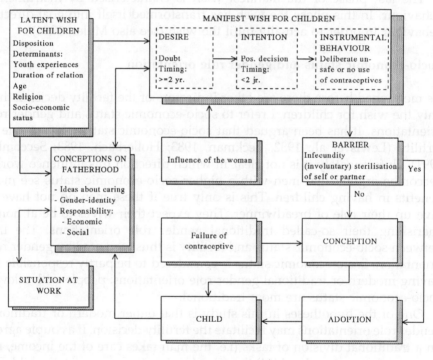

Figure 1

Conceptual model

The aforementioned constructs can be brought together into a conceptual model. In figure 1 we see that a latent wish for children of the man as well as a manifest wish for children of the woman[1] may induce a manifest wish. The manifest wish may influence the conceptions on fatherhood, which initially were shaped by the latent wish, the values and norms regarding having children. Furthermore the model allows for a complex interplay between the situation at work, the conceptions on fatherhood and the manifest wish.

In the following I will examine in more depth the proposed determinants of the fertility decision and their connections. Some empirical support will be presented, based on a small survey I conducted recently.

Empirical validation

The concepts of the conceptual model werge operationalised into attitudinal and concrete questions, and incorporated in a questionnaire. The aim was to test the operationalisations and to validate the questionnaire, compared to and in relation with the model. Students of sociology were asked to select three men from their circle of friends and family who met each of the following three criteria: They had been married or cohabiting with a woman, for longer than one year; their partner was younger than 40; if they had a child, it was younger than 2 years of age. Each student interviewed three men, unknown to them, using a structured questionnaire. Couples not capable of having children were filtered out of the sample. 177 usable cases were collected; in 62 there already was a baby.

The group of respondents is slightly higher educated than the average Dutch population; a well-known problem when gathering information in the way just described.

There are four groups:

1. Those who have decided not to have a child, at least not within the next 5 years.
2. Those who have not yet decided. They are still in doubt, and cannot give a term within which they want their first child.
3. Those who have decided that a child would be welcome, preferably within one or two years. Those who do not use any contraceptive also fall into this category.
4. Those who already have a child.

---

1   The manifest wish of the woman is only one of the external factors that may influence the manifest wish of the man. It is considered to be the most important external factor. For the sake of simplicity other possible influences have been left out of the model.

These groups are equivalent to the phases of the manifest wish. Those who have decided not to have a child (1) obviously do not have a manifest wish for children. Those who are in doubt (2) are in the desire phase. Those who have made a positive decision (3) are in the intentional or instrumental phase[2]. The last group, the fathers, is a control group.

It was more difficult to establish those who had a latent wish for children. In fact, the questionnaire showed to be not sufficiently adequate to that. However, some indicators proved to be useful. The question 'Do you want children during your lifetime?' was connected to a question about when at what age this was decided. This led to the conclusion that 28% of the men who expressed a wish for children had always known they wanted to become a father sometime, 13% knew it at the time of cohabitation, 17% at the time of marriage or cohabitation contract, and 42% knew it only at the time of the interview. Religiosity and size of the parental family proved to be good predictors of 'the always present wish for children'. It should be noted, however, that more research has to be done to empirically support the latent wish for children hypothesis (see also Miller, 1992).

To measure the manifest wish for children 13 advantages and 13 disadvantages of having children were mentioned in the questionnaire. The items were collected from several studies, some of which have already been mentioned (Hoffman & Hoffman, 1973; Out & Zegveld, 1977; Niphuis-Nell, 1981; May, 1982; Bell, Bancroft & Philip, 1985; Morahan-Martin, 1991; Seccombe, 1991; Van Balen, 1991). The overall question, concerning the advantage items, was: 'Do you consider the following statement as a reason to want a child?'. If a respondent already had one child, the question was if they considered it a reason to want *another* child[3]. The question with respect to the disadvantages was analogous. A separate factor analysis of both the advantages and disadvantages clearly pointed to three factors each. The advantage items were divided into 4 items concerning affective aspects, 4 items concerning instrumental aspects and 5 items concerning situational aspects. The affective aspects refer to the emotional side of becoming a father, such as giving love and affection to the child and taking care of it. The instrumental aspects refer to achieving a goal, such as enrichment of the relationship with the partner, continuing the family name, and giving meaning to life. Finally, the situational aspects allude to external factors

---

2   A distinction between intentional and instrumental can be made, but it is not considered particularly relevant to the purpose of this article.

3   Strictly speaking the question to want *another* child is different from the question to want the first child. The group 'men with one child' is therefore considered as a control variable in the model, and is always regarded separately from the group 'men without children'.

contributing to the wish for a child, such as the opinions of family and friends in this respect, and to what Rabin (1965) calls *fatalistic* motives, such as 'it's part of life', or a logical consequence of getting married.

The disadvantage items were divided into 4 items concerning freedom-constricting aspects, 4 items concerning responsibility aspects, and 4 items concerning practical impediments. One item constituted a factor on its own, namely the fear of having a child with a serious handicap. Freedom constriction has two aspects. First, the loss of freedom in general, and second, difficulties in combining paid labour or education with having children. The second category responsibility refers exactly to what the word suggests: The responsibility of having children is too big to handle. The third category refers to what Hoffman and Hoffman call *barriers*. Well-known barriers are a shortage of money, a home that is not suitable etc. Other 'practical impediments' are disagreement on housekeeping tasks and the situation in the world.

Results

To get a good overview of the scores on these items I set out the four groups against a weighed percentage of agreement on the various advantage and disadvantage items. A score of 100% on one item indicates that everybody agrees on this item and finds it very important. The results are shown in two graphs. I will first examine the advantages.

Advantages
The general pattern is that the advantages are seen as being more important when the decision to get a child is more likely. Most important are the affective aspects of having children. Some advantages, especially the instrumental ones, are only seen when the woman is pregnant, or when the baby has been born. We see a significant difference between those who do not want a child and those who have one on the item 'seeing children growing up is an experience I do not want to miss'. The same goes for 'children provide meaning to life' and 'it enriches my relationship'. That does not alter the fact that affective and instrumental advantages of having children are considered to be quite important by every group. Situational aspects are not seen as clear advantages, except for the item 'my own childhood and upbringing play a role', which, after all, is not the prototype of a 'situational aspect'.

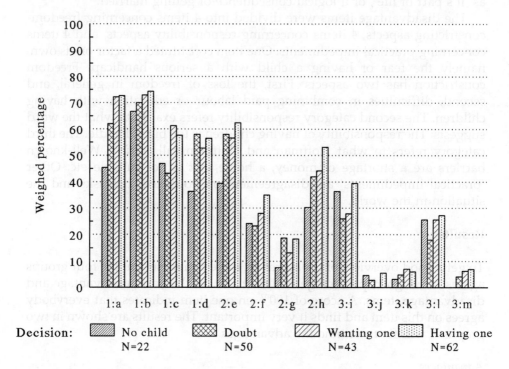

Figure 2. Advantages of having children

Category 1: Affective aspects
a: Seeing children growing up is an experience I do not want to miss
b: I can give love and affection to children
c: I would like to take care of children
d: Raising children seems a challenge to me
Category 2: Instrumental aspects
e: Children provide meaning to life
f: Having children is convenient when I am old
g: I want to continue my family name
h: Having children enriches my relationship
Category 3: Situational aspects
i: My own childhood and upbringing play a role
j: The opinions of family and friends are important to me
k: Having children is a consequence of being married or cohabiting
l: Having children is part of life
m: My religion plays an important role

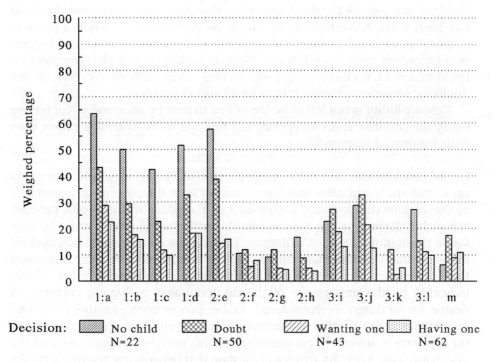

Figure 3. Disadvantages of having children

Category 1: Freedom constricting aspects
a: Having children curtails my freedom
b: I want to do things which are difficult to do if you have a child
c: Having children is difficult to combine with my work
d: Having children is difficult to combine with my partner's work
Category 2: Responsibility aspects
e: I do not feel ready for having children
f: I am not sure whether I can cope with it
g: I can not handle the responsibility
h: The upbringing is too difficult for me
Category 3: Practical impediments
i: My dwelling is not suitable
j: I can not afford it financially
k: We do not agree on the division of household tasks
l: The situation in the world
m: Fear of having a child with a serious handicap

Disadvantages

Looking at the disadvantages, we see a roughly similar pattern, but in the opposite direction. Freedom-constricting aspects and 'not feeling ready for children' are seen as the most important disadvantages, even once the child has been born. Nevertheless, the decrease in importance when a positive decision is at hand is spectacular. Practical impediments are the biggest problem when there is still doubt. What is striking is that disagreement on the division of housekeeping tasks is rare. Only 12% of the men in the doubting phase considered this to be a (major) problem.

Responsibility is not felt to be too heavy to bear by most men. Not feeling ready for children is an exception, but this has to do with age rather than with feelings of responsibility.

Let us consider the influence of age more closely. Although the sample is small this study indicates that age interferes with the perceived importance of the various disadvantages, *regardless* of the phase in the choice process. No such influence of age is found on the advantages[4], which are relatively stable throughout a person's lifetime. There is one cohort effect, however, in the sense that younger men consider affective motives to be more important than older men do. The phase in the decision process is most clearly indicated by the importance of the disadvantages of having children. A desire for children is considered to be proportional to the perceived importance of the affective advantages of having children; the manifest wish for children is inversely proportional to the perceived importance of the disadvantages. Also McCormick et al. state that benefits are relatively stable, costs being both more likely to change and sensitive to the environment (McCormick et al., 1977). Seeing the advantages of having children is similar to a disposition for wanting them, and overcoming the disadvantages paves the way for a positive decision.

Earlier, I indicated that socio-economic status and gender-role orientations influenced the fertility decision as well. I suggested that there should be agreement between man and woman on the division of housekeeping and child care tasks. As we saw before, there is only a small group of men who consider this to be an impediment to having children in the short term. Those who, for the time being, do not want children do not consider it a problem at all. Only those who are in the doubting phase mention it. This supports the supposition, but it cannot be considered an important factor.

---

4   One clear exception to this is the statement 'Having children enriches my relationship'. A lot of childless men answered this question with 'I don't know', which was interpreted as 'I don't agree'.

When we use socio-economic status and gender-role orientations as sociological variables, a positive effect on the fertility decision should be found, several studies say (Lewis et al., 1982; Beckman, 1983; Hollerbach, 1983; Seccombe, 1991). However, socio-economic status is partly determined by age. The finding, also in this study, that men with a high socio-economic status are more likely to come to a positive decision is therefore useless. Older people have a higher socio-economic status, fewer financial barriers and therefore they are more likely to make a positive decision. This study was too small to control for age and cohort effects.

Gender-role orientations are very difficult to measure. That is to say, the link between attitudes and behaviour on this topic is very weak. On the 'Attitude towards Women Scale' (Spence & Helmreich, 1972; Nelson, 1988), for example, a score of 80 (with 100 as a maximum) is considered 'low'. Modern gender-role attitudes are common, and social desirability plays a major role. This means that people do not act according to their uttered ideas (Willemsen, 1992). Earlier I mentioned the gap between 'in principle' and 'in practice'. One example from the data might illustrate the fact that men seem to be quite flexible in their gender identity. In the survey under study here, men were interrogated by male and female students. On the proposition 'Men and women should divide household tasks equally' 66% of the men agreed when they had a male interviewer. When they had a female interviewer this percentage was 79%. This example illustrates that before being able to estimate the influence of gender-role orientation, a good instrument has to be developed, specialised on aspects of the fertility decision.

At this stage it is difficult to estimate the influence of the latent and the manifest wish for children on the conceptions on fatherhood, partly due to the difficulty of measuring gender identity. However, men in the intentional phase do have more explicit ideas about their role as a father (70%) than men in the doubting phase (61%), or those who only have a latent wish for children (45%). Furthermore it turned out that men with more traditional ideas about fatherhood see more instrumental and situational benefits in having children than do non-traditional men who stressed the emotional benefits.

Conclusion

The data support the conceptual model in many ways. It proved to be useful to connect a timing aspect to the wish for children in order to operationalise the three-phased manifest wish. Also, the three phases correlated with the perceived costs and benefits (or advantages and disadvantages) of having children, as predicted. A desire for children means that costs and benefits are perceived as being high, whereas an intention points to a decrease in the perceived costs, the perceived benefits remaining the same or even rising.

However, the link between a manifest wish for children and conceptions on fatherhood is diffuse. It could be that this is a result, or an indicator, of the relative confusion of (expectant) fathers of today's Western world.

References

Avort, A.J.P.M. van der (1987). *De gulzige vrij-blijvendheid van expliciete relaties.* Tilburg: Tilburg University Press.

Balen, F. van (1991). *Een leven zonder kinderen. Ongewilde kinderloosheid: beleving, stress en aanpassing.* [The Life-Situation of Childless Couples. Involuntarily Childlessness: Experience, Stress and Adaption] Amsterdam: UvA.

Becker, G.S. (1960). An Economic Analysis of Fertility. In National Bureau of Economic Research. *Demographic and economic change in developed countries* (pp. 209-231). Princeton: NBER.

Becker, G.S. (1981). *A Treatise on the Family.* Cambridge, MA: Harvard University Press.

Beckman, L.J. (1983). Communication, power, and the influence of social networks in couple decisions on fertility. In R.A. Bulatao & R.D. Lee *Determinants of fertility in developing countries.* New York: Academic Press.

Beer, J. de (1992). General time-series models for forecasting fertility. In N. Keilman & H. Cruijsen (Eds.), *National population forecasting in industrialized countries* (pp. 147-175). Amsterdam/Lisse: Swets & Zeitlinger.

Bell, S., Bancroft, J. & Philip, A. (1985). Motivation for parenthood: A factor analytic study of attitudes towards having children. *Journal of Comparative Family Studies, 16,* 1, 111-119.

Bruijn, B. de (1993). *Interdisciplinary backgrounds of fertility theory.* PDOD Working Paper, No. 16. Amsterdam: Graduate School of Research in Demography.

Burch, T.K. (Ed.) (1980). *Demographic behaviour. Interdisciplinary perspectives on decision-making.* Colarado: Westview Press.

Corijn, M., Liefbroer, A.C. & Jong-Gierveld, J. de (1994). *It takes two to tango, doesn't it? The influence of characteristics of both partners on the timing of the birth of the first child.* Paper presented at the Zesde Sociaal-Wetenschappelijke Studiedagen, Amsterdam 7-8 april, 1994.

Crawford, T. (1973). Beliefs about birth control: A consistency theory analysis. *Representative Research in Social Psychology, 4,* 53-65.

Fishbein, M. (1972). Toward an understanding of family planning behaviour. *Journal of Applied Social Psychology, 2,* 214-227.

Fishbein, M. & Ajzen, I. (1975). *Belief, attitude, intention and behaviour: An introduction to theory and research.* London: Addison-Wesley.

Gerson, M-J. (1986). The prospect of parenthood for women and men. *Psychology of Women Quarterly, 10,* 49-62.

Heath, A. (1976). *Rational choice and social exchange.* London: Cambridge University Press.

Hoffman, L.W. (1972). A psychological perspective on the value of children to parents. In J.T. Fawcett (Ed.) *The satisfactions and costs of children: Theories, concepts, methods* (pp. 27-56). Honolulu: East-West Population Institute.

Hoffman, L.W. & Hoffman, M.L. (1973). The value of children to parents. In J.T. Fawcett (Ed.), *Psychological perspectives on population* (pp. 19-76). New York: Basic Books.

Hollerbach, P.E. (1983). Fertility decision-making processes: A critical essay. In R.A. Bulatao & R.D. Lee (Eds.) *Determinants of fertility in developing countries.* New York: Academic Press.

Hull, T.H. (1983). Cultural influences on fertility decision styles. In R.A. Bulatao & R.D. Lee (Eds.), *determinants of fertility in developing countries.* New York: Academic Press.

Knijn, T. (1990). Hij wil wel, maar hij kan niet: over zorgend vaderschap en mannelijke gender-identiteit. *Psychologie en Maatschappij, 51,* 99-111.

Lesthaeghe, R. & Surkeyn, J. (1988). Cultural dynamics of fertility change. *Population and Development Review, 14,* pp.1-45.

Lewis, C., Newson, J. & Newson, E. (1982). Father participation through childhood and its relation to career aspirations and delinquency. In N. Beail & J. McGuire (Eds.) *Fathers: Psychological perspectives.* London: Junction.

Lindenberg, S. (1991). Social approval, fertility and female labour market behaviour. In J. Siegers, J. de Jong-Gierveld & E. van Imhoff (Eds.), *Female labour market behaviour and fertility: a rational choice approach* (pp. 32-58). Berlin/New York: Springer Verlag.

Marsiglio, W. (1991). Male procreative consciousness and responsibility: A conceptual analysis and research agenda. *Journal of Family Issues, 12,* 3, 268-290.

May, K.A. (1982). Factors contributing to first time father's readiness for fatherhood. *Family Relations, 31,* 353-362.

McCormick, E.P., Johnson, R.L., Friedman, H.L. & David, H.P. (1977). Psychosocial aspects of fertility regulation. In J. Money & H. Musaph (Eds.), *Handbook of sexology, section vii: Regulation of procreation* (pp. 621-653). Amsterdam/London/New York: Elsevier.

Miller, W.B. (1992). Personality Traits and Developmental Experiences as Antecedents of Childbearing Motivation. *Demography, 29*(2), 265-285.

Miller W.B. (1994). Childbearing Motivations, Desires and Intentions: A Theoretical Framework. *Genetic, Social and General Psychology Monographs, 120*(2), 223-258.

Morahan-Martin, J. (1991). Consider the children: Is parenthood being devalued? *The Psychological Record, 41*, 303-314.

Mott, F.L. (1983). *Fertility-related data in the 1982 national longitudinal surveys of work experience of youth: An evaluation of data quality and some preliminary analytical results.* Columbus: Ohio State University, Center for Human Resource Research.

Nelson, M.C. (1988). Reliability, validity and cross-cultural comparisons for the simplified attitudes towards women scale. *Sex Roles, 18*, 289-296.

Niphuis-Nell, M. (1981). *Motivatie voor ouderschap. Een onderzoek naar de invloed van attitudes op het proces van gezinsvorming.* [Motivation for parenthood] Deventer: Van Loghum Slaterus.

Out, J.J. & Zegveld, P. (1977). Motivatie voor ouderschap: Een onderzoek [Motivation for parenthood: An inquiry]. In R. Veenhoven & E. van der Wolk (Red.), *Kiezen voor kinderen?* [Choosing in favour of children?]. Assen/Amsterdam: Van Gorcum.

Rabin, A.I. (1965). Motivation for parenthood. *Journal of Projective Techniques and Personality Assessment, 29*, 405-411.

Rabin, A.I. & Greene R.J. (1968). Assessing motivation for parenthood. *Journal of Psychology, 69*, 39-46.

Seccombe, K. (1991). Assessing the costs and benefits of children: Gender comparisons among childfree husbands and wives. *Journal of Marriage and the Family, 53*, 191-202.

Simon, H.A. (1987). Rationality in psychology and economics. In R.M. Hogarth & M.W. Reder (Eds.), *Rational Choice.* Chicago: University of Chicago Press.

Spence, J.T. & Helmreich, R. (1972). The attitudes towards women scale: An objective instrument to measure attitudes towards rights and roles of women in contemporary society. *Catalog of Selected Documents in Psychology, 2*, 66-67.

Tazelaar, F. (1980). *Mentale incongruenties-sociale restricties-gedrag: Een onderzoek naar beroepsparticipatie van gehuwde vrouwelijke academici.* [Mental incongruities-social restrictions-behaviour: A study of labour force participation of married women with an academic degree]. Utrecht.

Vermunt, J.K. (1993). De geboorte van het eerste kind: Uitstel of afstel? [The first birth: Are delays dangerous?]. *Gezin, 4*, 1, 31-52.

Voets, S. (1994). *The concept of choice and relocation behaviour.* PDOD Working Paper, No. 25. Amsterdam: Graduate School of Research in Demography.

Westoff, C.F. & Ryder, N.B. (1977). *The contraceptive revolution*. Princeton, NJ: Princeton University Press.

Willemsen, T. (1992). Sekse als cognitieve categorie: Een sociaal-psychologische benadering van sekse. [Gender as a cognitive category: A social-psychological approach of gender]. In T. Top & J. Heesink (Red.), *Psychologie en sekse*. Houten/Zaventem: Bohn Stafleu Van Loghum.

Frank van Balen

The decision to become a father

The role of the husband concerning the decision to have a child is often underexposed in scientific research and discussion. Most attention is paid to the motives, drives or incentives of the wives.

In Western societies the decision to have a child is often carefully planned. The existence of highly reliable contraceptives enables couples to prevent unwanted pregnancies and to choose the most convenient moment for having children. The couples often think that desired procreation can be completely planned. Husband and wife may discuss the best time for birth with respect to their careers, and they sometimes even reserve a place in kindergarten before conception has taken place. Also, there is a tendency to share the burden and the joy of parenthood more equally between the partners. These developments may have altered the process of opting for fatherhood.

The motives behind human procreation have been the subject of much speculation. Within the psychoanalytical tradition great value has been attached to biological drives. Deutsch describes an inborn need of women to procreate (Deutsch, 1944). Benedek discernes an instinctive motive for motherhood and an instinctive drive for survival as the root of fatherhood (Benedek, 1970a; 1970b). Also the sociologist Rossi is inclined to attach great importance to biological drives (Rossi 1977; 1985). In contrast to these views, radical feminists state that wanting to have a child is a consequence of social enforcement. Rowland sees procreation as dictated by the dominant norms and values of society (made by men) (Rowland, 1984). Hamner accentuates the need for women to be free from enforced motherhood (Hamner, 1984) and Corea describes motherhood as a consequence of masculine politics and patriarchal rule (Corea, 1985). These two different viewpoints ('instinct' versus 'social pressure') are difficult to test empirically. However, we can ask what people themselves see as reasons for wanting children. This area is accessible to empirical research.

Within the empirical tradition research into the motives for wanting children has been centred on the cost and benefit model. Since Hoffmann and Fawcett proposed this model, it has been the dominant way of analysing people's reasons for wanting a child (Fawcett, 1972; Fawcett, Albores & Arnold, 1972; Hoffman, 1972; Hoffman & Hoffman, 1973; Fawcett, 1978). There are two versions of this model: a macro-model and a micro-model. The macro-model starts from sociodemographic and economic data. Based on these data, forecasts are made, about fertility decisions. In this version the researcher evaluates the advantages and disadvantages of having children. In the micro-model the judgements of the individuals themselves are the subject of study. Advantages and disadvantages may be sociopsychological (feelings of happiness versus loss of freedom) and economic (old-age care versus costs of upbringing). In both versions research is centred on the positive and negative sides of having children, not on the reasons for wanting them in the first place. Within this model children are seen more or less as commodities. People are expected to make rational choices based on pros and cons. This model has been frequently used in studies about the determinants of fertility in developing countries, especially with respect to the upper limit of the number of children. However, as Hoffman and Manis noted cost-benefit analyses are not useful for analysing the transition to parenthood, i.e. the choice for the first child (Hoffman & Manis 1979). They are only useful when analysing decisions regarding the number of children. Also, Dutch studies have shown that (at a particular moment in their lives) around 95% of the couples decide that they want to have a child (Niphuis-Nell, 1976; Beets & Van Hoorn, 1988). Surveys in several Western countries indicate a voluntary childlessness of approximately 5%. In the USA only 2% of the women who wed, want to be childless (Schroeder, 1989). Just a few couples are kept from opting for parenthood because of a rational evaluation of costs and benefits.

Like the cost-benefit model, Jacobs' model is based on an evaluation of the advantages and disadvantages of having children. An important improvement in his conceptual framework, however, is the distinction between a latent desire (I would like to have a child, but not now and not in the present circumstances) and a manifest desire (I would like to have a child, now and in the present circumstances). Jacobs focuses on the transition process from a latent desire to a manifest desire. He describes a three-phased transition. In the first phase one begins to think about realising the desire to have a child. This first phase has been coined — somewhat confusingly — the 'desire phase'. I think 'doubting phase' would be a more appropriate description. In the second phase the intention to have a child has taken shape. In the third phase (instrumental phase) the intention is transformed into goal-directed behaviour: actively striving to have a child.

Jacobs assumes that the three phases are accompanied by the diminishing importance of the perception of the disadvantages of having a child. However, perceived advantages are said to remain high during all phases.

In his pilot study Jacobs found confirmation of the assumed diminishing perception of disadvantages during the phases of transformation. However, contrary to his expectation, the advantages of having a child become more important when the decision to have a child is more likely to be made. Furthermore, age appeared to be of great influence on the perception of advantages and disadvantages, regardless of the phase of transformation. I suspect that the duration of the relationship with the female partner could be important in this respect.

Two studies, one by Mozes and the other by Van Luijn and Parent focused on the decision-making process about having a child among women and men, and the relative power of the partners with regard to this issue (Mozes 1989; Van Luijn & Parent 1991). Both studies concerned couples who thought seriously about the choice to have a child. The studies reported that the opinion of the wife was more important than that of the husband. Van Luijn and Parent reported in two-thirds of the cases it was a shared decision, in which, however, the opinion of the woman was decisive. In most other cases the wife decided. Mozes also, describes the wife as being the decisive partner. Usually she is the one who chooses to have a child, while the husband only consents to this choice.

Conclusion

The three phases discerned (doubt, intention and instrumental behaviour) are helpful in analysing the transformation of a latent desire to have a child into a manifest desire. However, the model is only partly supported by the results of the pilot study and may need some revision. Jacobs' study is important in that it focuses on the often neglected role of the husband in the process of decision-making about having a child. However, I think the influence of the female partner is very important in the development of a latent desire to have a child and in the transformation of this latent desire into a manifest desire for fatherhood. An integrated model that incorporates both partners would be better equiped to explain the process of decision-making about parenthood.

References

Beets, G.C.N. & Van Hoorn (1988). Vrijwillig kinderloze vrouwen geportretteerd. *Maandstatistiek der bevolking, CBS, 6,* 11-16.

Benedek Th. (1970). The Family as psychological field. In E.J. Anthony & Th. Benedek (Eds.), *Parenthood, its psychology and psychopathology* (pp. 109-136.). Boston: Little, Brown & Co.

Benedek Th. (1970). Fatherhood and providing. In E.J. Anthony E.J. & Th. Benedek (Eds.), *Parenthood, its psychology and psychopathology* (pp. 195-200). Boston: Little, Brown & Co.

Corea G. (1985). *The mother machine, reproductive technology from artificial insemination to artificial wombs.* New York: Harper & Row.

Deutsch H. (1944). *The psychology of women. Vol. II.* London: Research Books.

Fawcett J.T. (1972) Introduction and Summary of workshop discussions and conclusions. In J.T. Fawcett (Ed.), *The satisfactions and costs of children: Theories concepts, methods* (1-10). Honolulu: East-West Centre Population Inst.

Fawcett J.T., Albores, S. & Arnold, F.S. (1972). The value of children among ethnic groups in Hawaii: exploratory measurement. In J.T. (Ed.), *The satisfactions and costs of children: Theories concepts, methods* (pp. 234-259). Honolulu: East-West Centre Population Inst.

Fawcett J.T. (1978). The value and cost of the first child. In W.B. Miller & L.F. Newman (Eds.), *The first child and family formation* (pp. 244-265). Chapel Hill, NC: University of North Carolina.

Hamner J. (1984). A womb of one's own. In R. Arditti, R. Duelli Klein & S. Minden (Eds.), *Test tube women* (pp. 438-448). London: Pandora.

Hoffman L.W. (1972). A psychological perspective on the value of children to parents: concepts and measures. In J.T. Fawcett (Ed.), *The satisfactions and costs of children: Theories concepts, methods* (pp. 27-56). Honolulu: East-West Centre Population Inst.

Hoffman L.W. & Hoffman M.L. (1973). The value of children to parents. In J.T. Fawcett (Ed.), *Psychological perspectives on population.* New York: Basic Books.

Hoffman L.W. Manis D.B. (1979). The value of children in the United States: a new approach to the study of fertility. *Journal of Marriage and the Family, 41,* 583-596.

Luijn H. van & Parent A. (1991). *Laatste kans-moeders.* Delft: Eburon.

Mozes M. (1989). *Uitstel of afstel, kiezen voor kinderen in een veranderende samenleving.* Culemborg: Lemma.

Niphuis-Nell M. (1979). Hoeveel huwelijken blijven kinderloos? In R. Veenhoven R. (Ed.), *Vrijwillige kinderloosheid* (pp. 33-50). Rotterdam: Kooyker.

Rossi A. (1977). A Biological perspective on parenting. *Daedalus, 106,* 1-32.

Rossi A. (1985). Gender and parenthood. In A. Rossi (Ed.), *Gender and the life course* (pp. 161-191). New York: Aldine.

Rowland R. (1984). Reproductive technologies: The final solution to the woman question. In R. Arditti, R. Duelli Klein & S. Minden (Eds.), *Test tube women* (pp. 356-369). London: Pandora.

Schroeder P. (1989). Infertility and the world outside. *Fertility and Sterility, 49,* 595-601.

4
Men's aspirations concerning child care
The extent to which they are realised

Mirjam van Dongen

Introduction

My prime focus in this article is the gulf between men's aspirations with regard to child care and their parental behaviour. I will start by giving a brief overview of the three most common hypotheses that concern men's involvement in child care and household chores. Then I will present an introduction of a concept of care and its implications, based on the definition of care given by Fisher and Tronto (1990). I will use this concept as a guideline for analysing men's aspirations and the extent to which these are realised.

Three most common hypotheses

Men's changing role in the family, their aspirations with regard to having and caring for children and the manner and degree to which they put these aspirations into practice, have received increasing psychological and sociological attention. Men's role as fathers and precisely what they do in the home have been widely discussed (e.g. McKee & O'Brien, 1982; Jackson, 1983; Russell, 1983; Lewis, 1986; Lewis & O'Brien, 1987; Lamb, 1987; Sandqvist, 1987; Wheelock, 1990; Bozett & Hanson, 1991; Hood, 1993; van der Lippe, 1993; Mozes-Philips & Wester, 1994; de Jong & van Olde, 1994). Results indicate that most men today desire and seem to have a closer relationship with their children than did their fathers. But although they seem to be prepared to participate to a greater extent in certain child care activities, particularly where mothers are employed, this usually involves the more pleasurable and non-committal aspects of child care with routine care being left to women.

Sociological research on how and why housework and child care are divided between men and women is often based on three hypotheses derived from role, exchange and rational action theory. The key concepts of these hypotheses are (a) *relative resources*, including the power relationship between partners; (b) *ideology*, often operationalised as gender role attitudes; and (c) *time availability*, or demand/response capability (Coverman, 1985; Spitze, 1986; Ross, 1987; Kamo, 1988; Coltrane & Ishii-Kuntz, 1992; Duindam, 1991; Van der Lippe, 1993).

Relative resources
Explanations based on men's and women's relative resources derive from the notion of 'fair' exchange. The assumption is that the division of child care and household chores depends on a rational and maximally efficient allocation of household members' time to paid labour, domestic labour and leisure. It is assumed that couples try to maximise their earning potential by allocating tasks in a rational manner. The pattern of domestic task sharing is typically determined by negotiations between spouses, which are based on their power relationship. The underlying assumption is that the spouse with greatest power and authority can minimise his or her participation in undesirable activities, including (many) household and child care tasks. Power within a marriage derives, at least in part, from resources that reflect socio-economic status in society in general, for example education, earnings, and occupational position. The hypothesis, therefore, is that the more resources men have compared to women the less time they will spend on domestic labour; and the more resources women have vis-à-vis men the more time men will spend on domestic labour.

In my view at least three fundamental objections against this neo-classical explanation of the allocation of time can be made. The first objection deals with the view that men and women as free individuals make rational choices. Men and women can not be considered to be free individuals, because they act within a cultural context. Powerful images of masculinity and femininity as well as societal norms concerning fatherhood and motherhood influence the choices men and women make. Although normative influences are sometimes discounted, most explanations based on relative resources do not discount them. Rational choice is another difficulty in this perspective. The choice whether or not to care for children can not be entirely rational. People are not able to determine every possible advantage or disadvantage and they may act contrary to their own interests. Furthermore, emotions, distorted perceptions of own and shared interests, psychological needs for confirmation, habits, etcetera, may also play an important role in choices men and women make.

The second objection is the inequality between men and women. Socially valued resources, such as education, knowledge, income, status and occupational position, are unequally divided between men and women. When an average man and an average woman get married, this inequality is carried over into marriage. As a result, the inequality of power becomes an inherent part of the relationship. In the perspective based on relative resources it is presupposed that the spouse with more power (which in most cases will be the male partner) is able to delegate child care and household chores as undesirable activities to his or her partner. This means that child care and household chores are valued less than paid (market) labour and are implicitly viewed as onerous and menial. Care in our society is indeed valued less than paid labour, but personal preferences can run counter to this: paid labour may be experienced as an undesirable activity and care as a desirable one. How should we understand men who do participate in domestic labour to a great extent? The relative resource perspective is not able to answer this question.

My third objection is that this perspective does not take (sufficient) account of the fact that women might have emotional or domestic power. Women often are the gatekeepers when it comes to men's involvement in child care and household chores. Due to part-time work, many women stand little chance of getting an interesting job (which may also lead to promotion). The option to accept the responsibility for care with the matching power position may be rather attractive to many women. When it comes to child care and household chores women often set the rules, while men have to gain their position in the 'caring arena'.

Ideology
The ideology perspective is based on the argument that the division of labour reflects ideological views on gender equality. The assumption is that the sex role ideology into which people have been socialised influences their sex role behaviour. It means that partners who endorse the principle of gender equality are expected to share domestic labour fairly. Therefore, the more egalitarian one or both spouses are, the higher the husband's relative share is. This ideology factor is often measured by means of gender role attitudes. Education is often assumed to be an indicator for these attitudes. Modern gender role attitudes are supposedly associated with high levels of education; traditional gender role attitudes with low levels of education.

An interesting fact is that the ideology hypothesis counters the relative resources hypothesis in its predictions concerning men's contribution to domestic labour. The ideology hypothesis argues that education and occupational status will increase the time men spend on child care and household chores, while the relative resources hypothesis predicts that education and occupational status will decrease the time men spend on such activities.

I think that the ideology hypothesis can be challenged on at least three grounds. First of all, gender roles nowadays are hardly ever so specific that people know exactly how to behave in every situation. Fathers and mothers of the late 1980's and early 1990's have been taught a pattern of parenting and division of labour between men and women on the basis of the role models by which their own parents lived. But these transmissions of values and practices contradict with many of the ideals of parenthood which are prevalent in the present generation of parents. Given the fading boundaries between masculinity and femininity and the lack of role models for caring fathers, there is scope for people to act on the basis of their own beliefs. As a result, fatherhood practices vary.

My second point refers to the supposed relation between behaviour and attitudes. A change in paternal participation in caretaking does not necessarily result in changed values or gender role attitudes; nor do gender role attitudes necessarily lead to changed paternal behaviour. Internal and external impediments may give rise to a less clear relationship between paternal behaviour and gender role attitudes. Factors such as internalised values, education, age, income, work schedules, social networks and household composition are all capable of influencing the degree to which the practice reflects men's attitudes.

The third comment refers to the fact that maternal attitudes, which are in part influenced by the mothers' perceptions of their own fathers, may have an important effect on the likelihood of paternal involvement. Lamb and Oppenheim (1989: 17) mention that somewhere between 60% and 80% of women do *not* want their husbands to be more involved in child care than they currently are. Backett (1982: 79) describes that women construct an involvement on the side of the father based on a belief that he would be able to do things 'if the necessity arose'. It seems that although many mothers would like their husbands to do more, a substantial majority are satisfied with 'the way things are'.

Time availability
The time availability (or demand/response capability) hypothesis emphasises the relative amounts of time available for performing domestic labour. The amount of time husbands spend on child care and household chores depends on the time they have available for such activities. The mere fact that most men work full time outside the home decreases the time available to them for domestic labour. The fact that an increasing number of women work outside the home decreases the amount of time available to them as well. The theory is that factors such as female occupational status, number of children and number of hours spent on paid labour influence male participation in child care.

Again, some fundamental comments should be made. First of all, factors like female occupational status and number of children present do not tap the time available to husbands. The wife's occupational status may indicate the time available to *her*, but not the time available to *him* to perform domestic labour. So, time availability can only provide a meaningful explanation of men's domestic participation, if the demands placed on men to perform household and child care tasks are taken into consideration. Therefore, the hours men devote to domestic tasks are a function of (a) the demands placed on them to fulfil domestic responsibilities and (b) their ability to respond to these demands.

Secondly, the time availability hypothesis suggests that work and care are complementary, but they are not. Fatherhood may have a diversity of meanings for men and they may enact being a father in different ways, regardless of whether they themselves or their partners have no job or a part-time or full-time job. Men who work long hours may, for example, involve themselves heavily in the educational aspects of childrearing such as reading (bedtime) stories, watching children's programmes on television, talking to the child, and playing with it. These caretaking tasks may not interfere with daily routines. So, the question should be asked whether or not a low level of participation in caretaking signifies a low level of interest, commitment or motivation.

Thirdly, the time availability hypothesis disregards the insight that men and women have different gender-identities. They do not simply exchange time. Wheelock (1990) for example found no relation between (unemployed) men's use of time in child care and household chores and the division of labour outdoors between men and women. The way in which different activities are socially valued is at stake once more.

The aforementioned perspectives based on role, exchange and rational action theory can all be challenged on several grounds. For this article it is important that the comments are based on the gulf between men's thoughts and deeds. The three most common hypotheses fail to sufficiently explain this inconsistency. Why is it that some men who voice egalitarian aspirations share care to a great extent while others do not? It seems that the normative context plays a major role. The definition of care (and responsibility for care) could be an intervening factor. It is the dependent variable in much research, and yet it is hardly questioned. What is (child) care? How is involvement in (child) care measured?

Reflections on care

The way in which fathers' involvement in child care is measured can be criticised on several counts. Involvement in child care is often measured as performance: the degree to which fathers care is seen as a function of the regularity and frequency with which different caretaking tasks are performed. These tasks are seldom weighted and the choice of these different caretaking tasks seems arbitrary and is rarely justified (see for example Coverman, 1985; Vollebergh, 1986; Ross, 1987; Antill & Cotton, 1988). The question is whether such a range of caretaking tasks can adequately measure fathers' involvement in child care. For instance, the meaning and importance of tasks may differ from one household to another. In some households the contact between father and child is experienced as being very important, whilst in other households the income earned is given greater importance. When measuring fathers' involvement in child care we should not simply include the performance of representative caretaking tasks, but also how these tasks are contemplated, arranged and organised. In other words, to what extent do fathers take responsibility for initiating and maintaining caretaking activities? Even when the list of activities show that the fathers' share is more or less equal to that of the mothers, this does not mean that fathers genuinely share the responsibility. It is possible that mothers tell fathers what to do, that fathers 'help out'.

What's more, the use of such a list of caretaking tasks assumes that the researcher takes the view that all fathers make the list in the same manner. But when it is not specified what precisely the researcher wants to know, each father may make a list from his own point of view concerning his involvement and performance. That is to say, the researcher will not know whether the answers given represent the factual or perceived situation. Even when it is clear whether the researcher is interested in the factual or perceived situation, the way in which fathers answer the question remains unclear. Every man can have his own definition of 'relatively shared'. Their own perceptions colour the way they view and experience their involvement and performance. Resemblance as well as variation between fathers may be greater than random, because of conflicting poles of affectionate concern and successful breadwinning.

Hence from the aforementioned remarks on the manner in which involvement in child care is measured, it follows that the definition of involvement is too limited. Involvement in child care is often seen as direct participation. The underlying assumption is that the more a father does, the more involved he is. But is this really so? Depending on the situation, possibilities and ideas, parents choose the best possible arrangement. In some families this arrangement means that the father is the sole (or main) breadwinner, whilst the mother carries (prime) responsibility for child care. But does this mean that this father is less involved in child care than the father who shares both responsibilities with his wife more equally? There is a tension between what can be done and what is realised. Part of this tension seems to result from a low valuation of certain caretaking tasks by men. Perhaps we will be able to clarify this tension more successfully if we look at the concept of care more precisely.

Caring has been defined as a 'labour of love' (Finch & Groves 1983). It has been described as a part of maternal thinking, as a difficult and demanding practice (Ruddick, 1980). The moral dimensions of caring have been considered as an ethic of care. Some authors appeal to women's morality (for example Gilligan, 1982), while others place such an ethic of care in its moral and political context (for example Tronto, 1993).

Care is not something which can be neatly defined. It is a strange mixture of labour and love (Finch & Groves, 1983). We care for others practically *and* emotionally. In broad terms, caring is a concept which encompasses that range of human experiences associated with feeling concern for, and taking charge of the well-being of others. Care implies a reaching out to someone other than oneself and carries the implicit suggestion that this will lead to some kind of action. The needs of others are seen as providing a starting point for what must be done.

In the light of an ethic of care, Fisher and Tronto (1990) have recognised the complexities of care as a practice. Their thoughts on care could be applied to the issue of paternal behaviour. As far as I know, this has rarely been done until now.

Fisher and Tronto (1990: 40) define care as an activity that includes everything we do to maintain, continue, and repair the world surrounding us so that we can live in it as well as possible. This caring process contains different components that may clash with each other, namely caring about, taking care of, caregiving and care-receiving.

Caring about
'Caring about' is based on feelings of concern. In ordinary usage, the expression 'caring about' is often used to suggest love and affection. Caring about does not necessarily entail skills, but skills relating to perception and trained attention may influence what we care about. Caring about, therefore, entails noticing the existence of a caring need and making an assessment that — but not how — this need should be met. So, caring about involves a certain degree of attentiveness to the needs of others: how can one care about something one does not even notice? For caring depends on having knowledge which is peculiar to the particular person being cared for. To provide such knowledge, the caring person must devote a great deal of attention to learning what the other person might need. This attentiveness is not instinctive, but rather something which can be learned. Because inattentiveness is not the same as ignorance, the question is: when is ignorance of caring needs truly ignorance, and when is it inattentiveness?

Taking care of

Taking care of involves assuming some responsibility for the identified need of others and determining how to respond to it. It involves the recognition that it is possible to act to address these unmet needs. It suggests responsibility for initiating and maintaining caring activities. It presupposes the idea that it is possible to take the action required. Therefore the combination of contemplating, decision-making, arranging and organising caring activities forms a major part of taking care of others. Sufficient knowledge and skills are necessary to be able to assess which caring activities are needed and to predict the outcome of these actions, since responsibility implies accountability. This means that in many cases participation without engagement is insufficient.

Caregiving

Caregiving involves the direct meeting of the needs for care. It involves concrete caretaking tasks. It entails responding to the particular, concrete, physical and emotional needs of others. Caregiving requires continuous and intensive time commitments. The knowledge involved in caregiving requires a detailed, everyday understanding, since it may be necessary for people to revise their caregiving strategy to respond to circumstances which change from one minute or day to the next. Making revisions of this kind requires experience, skill and judgement. Competence in child-rearing is dependent on both practical experience in caregiving and on personal knowledge of the individual person in question (see attentiveness). Intending to provide care and even accepting responsibility for it, but then failing to provide good care, means that the need for care is insufficiently met.

Care-receiving

The person who is being cared for responds to the care he or she receives. After feeding the hungry person, he or she will no longer be hungry. Care-receiving provides the knowledge that caring needs have actually been met.

Following Fisher and Tronto's thoughts, child care consists of four components. Caring about children involves paying attention to them in such a way that we focus on their physical and mental well-being. Taking care of children involves responding to these aspects: taking responsibility for activities that ensure children's well-being. Caregiving involves the concrete caring tasks, such as feeding and comforting. Care-receiving involves children's responses to the care they receive.

Fisher and Tronto see these components as phases in a caring process. Each component operates as the general precondition for the next. In order to take care of children, one or both parents must care about them; in order to give care, one or both parents must take care of them. The caring components or phases may be carried out by one parent or may be divided between both parents. Mothers are usually engaged in these caring phases.

These phases are not always orderly stages of caring. Phases may be intertwined in a chaotic or even contradictory way. A mother who *gives care* to her child, often finds herself also having to *take care* of the child because of a vacuum of responsibility: fathers give care to their children more often, but seldom really share the responsibility. The relationship between taking care of and caregiving is more complex than might be supposed at first glance. It is likely that the parent who is entrusted with responsibility for care will be more frequently involved in caregiving, but it is equally probable that the parent who is more frequently involved in caregiving is entrusted with responsibility for child care.

Furthermore, ability factors such as skills, knowledge, time and resources are necessary. Nowadays both parents are assumed to have the skills and knowledge required, but fathers are still seen to be the ones who provide the financial resources, while mothers are thought to have the requisite time to give care. Social arrangements create these fragmentations.

Measuring care according to the four caring phases may have major implications for understanding the practice of fatherhood. We can gain deeper insight into the father's role by identifying the part men play in caregiving and in the contemplating, decision-making and arranging of caretaking activities as well as child care arrangements; by examining men's attentiveness and sensitivity to children's cues; by identifying how men experience and define the care they provide; and by evaluating the way in which men experience the broader context of care.

Men's aspirations and the extent to which they are realised: some findings

Perhaps we can gain a better understanding of fathers' involvement in child care if the aforementioned reflections on care are taken as a starting point. I will test men's aspirations with regard to child care and the degree to which these are put into practice against the concept of care. The data used were collected by means of a small survey which I conducted recently. The survey consisted of structured interviews with 215 randomly selected, although not representative, married or cohabiting men with children until the age of five. Questions were asked about men's aspirations with regard to paid labour, having children and child care, and the manner and degree to which men put these aspirations into practice.

The inspiration for this project was based on the fact that there has been a shift towards a more nurturing father who participates in active child care. This shift, however, entails that fathers are more sensitive to the areas where mothers are in need of assistance rather than signifying a move towards a genuine sharing of responsibility for child care. Why is this so? Are men's aspirations aimed at specific aspects of care? What exactly is the part that caregiving plays in the aspirations voiced by men? And what about taking care of children, the responsibility for initiating and maintaining caretaking activities?

Caring about

We have seen that caring about children entails noticing the caring needs of these children. In order to notice their caring needs, recognising those needs is indispensable. So, if a father is not attentive to the caring needs of his children, he can not possibly address those needs; how can someone care about something he or she does not notice? Attentiveness goes hand in hand with specific knowledge about the child cared for. A possible way to measure men's attentiveness is to ask them to compare their own paternal behaviour with the way in which their fathers enacted fatherhood.

Almost every father reports that he perceives a great shift in attitudes toward children when comparing the way in which he experiences fatherhood with the parenting by his own father. Today's fathers seem to be more interested in, and aware of many of the details of their children's behaviour and they give more attention to their children than their own fathers did. One might conclude that children have become more central to fathers' lives. Fathers describe themselves as being inclined to spend more time with their children and to play with the children more than their fathers did. During the interviews, fathers position themselves as competitors to women in terms of having the skills required to raise and care for children. Fathers mention no differences in the physical and psychological attention they and their partners give their children. They believe they are just as sensitive to children's cues as their wives are. At moments when they are less attentive to these cues, it is not because of ignorance but because they were absent during the day — due to work — and therefore lacked information about their children's activities, feelings and experiences during that day.

Taking care of

To measure the aspect of taking care of children, the fathers were asked questions about their perceptions of their share in taking responsibility for breadwinning and caregiving. For much of the 20th century working and the responsibility for breadwinning was associated with men, whilst caring and the responsibility for caregiving was associated with women. Nowadays the picture is less clearly defined.

Although a large number of men (36,5%) felt that the responsibility for breadwinning was more or less shared, most fathers (63,5%) felt they had prime responsibility for providing financial security for their families. These fathers appeared to be strongly committed to their work. Financial considerations and possible negative consequences for their careers were given as arguments for not working fewer hours after their (first) child was born.

The division of responsibility for care is less clear (51.4% consider the responsibility for care to be shared, 48.6% believe the prime responsibility is carried by their wives). An interesting finding is that fathers view their share in the responsibility for child care as more or less equal to their partners' share, regardless of whether they see themselves as the (main) breadwinner or not. For men, being the main breadwinner and being less involved in direct caregiving does not automatically lead to female responsibility for child care. The reason seems to be the fact that work is not looked upon as being in opposition to family life; rather, it is considered to be complementary. Although paternal strategies are mainly directed towards diminishing the negative influence of work on family life, reducing fathers' working hours is hardly seen as a solution whereas a reduction in the working hours of mothers occurs very often. How can it be that fathers feel just as responsible while they spend far less time on caretaking tasks?

It seems that men use a diffuse definition of taking care of children, in the sense of some sort of on-going responsibility and commitment, not directly connected to the practical responsibility for initiating and maintaining caring activities. So, even though fathers spend many hours away from home, they still feel very responsible for the well-being of their children and the care their children receive. This emerged from the judgement men gave of fathers who are not 'fully there' for their children when they do not work. These fathers are said to leave the well-being of their children to the mother only, while they should receive the love and care of both mother and father. Although these beliefs are firmly expressed in the interviews with fathers, they apply them to others — not to themselves. They say the difference between themselves and most other fathers is the mere fact that they spend much time on the children, they are completely there to meet their children's needs (physically and mentally), while in the case of many other fathers it is the other way round: children are there to meet their fathers' needs and desires.

Perhaps the feelings of responsibility men express are indicative of a general agreement with regard to shared parenting, namely that being a parent entails taking responsibility for caring for children. And of course, each man may have his own definition of sharing. It may also be an indication of the fact that in practice most fathers cannot see any alternative to assuming the chief breadwinning role. Indeed, the men interviewed felt that their jobs interfered with their opportunities for having contact with their children. They wished they could spend more time with them. For fathers, involvement is both activity and disposition.

Caregiving
Caregiving entails the direct meeting of caring needs. The extent to which fathers were involved in caregiving was measured in two ways. First, a list of caretaking tasks which had to be performed regularly was compiled. Secondly, men were asked to assess their own share compared with that of their partners and other people (for example day-care providers).

All fathers are involved in child care tasks, but what is the minimum for one may be the maximum for another. The involvement emerged from the differences between the way the fathers fulfilled their parenthood role and the way this was done by their own fathers. The fathers cited differences in contact with children: that they intervened more in issues concerning child-rearing and spent more time with their children than their fathers had.

In practice most men are the (main) breadwinners. Single-earner households have been a firmly established family model in the Netherlands. Dual-earner households are rather exceptional. In the Netherlands only 24% of women with children under the age of five have a (small, part-time) job (Hooghiemstra & Niphuis-Nell, 1993). Due to work schedules most men spend far more time away from home than their wives. As a consequence their *absolute* share in routine caretaking tasks such as feeding and nappy-changing, does not equal that of their wives. At the same time they all feel, and their wives seem to agree with this, that their *relative* share equals their wives' share. What's more, because their available time is limited they find it more important and in the children's best interest to spend time on affective aspects of child care such as cuddling and romping, and educational activities such as playing games, reading (bedtime) stories and watching children's programmes on television.

Most fathers believe they are more involved in child care than their own fathers were. This emerged from the differences between the way they fulfilled their parenthood role and the way this was done by their own fathers. The fathers cited differences in contact with children: that they intervene more in issues concerning child-rearing and spend more time with their children than their own fathers did.

Although all men said they are involved in caregiving, women are still in charge: many of them make preparations. If father is to spend time with his children without mother being present, she often makes sure that he lacks nothing: she prepares food in advance and writes a note with things to remember. As we saw earlier, men's participation in certain child care activities usually involves the more pleasurable and non-committal aspects. Fathers seem to involve themselves particularly in affective activities, such as cuddling and romping with children, and in educational activities, such as playing games, reading (bedtime) stories and watching children's programmes on television.

Conclusions

An inconsistency exists between paternal thoughts and deeds, between men's aspirations and the extent to which they are realised. Fathers want to be more involved in child care, yet actual practice is different. The three most common hypotheses — relative resources, ideology and time availability — fail to provide an adequate means of gaining insight into men's aspirations and the extent to which they are realised. According to the relative resources hypothesis many fathers minimise their share in child care tasks. And yet most fathers do not view child care as an undesirable activity. On the contrary, they all want to be *more* involved. The ideology hypothesis presumes a relationship between attitudes and behaviour. But this relationship seems rather diffuse. Men who believe they share the responsibility for child care with their partners may still be the main breadwinner and, as a result, spend less time on child care. The time availability hypothesis suggests that work and care are complementary. As the data show, such complementarity does not always exist, even though many men experience their available time as a bottleneck.

The concept of care proved to be useful in gaining deeper insight into the inconsistency between men's reported behaviour and values. By developing a concept of men's participation in child care in this manner, it may be possible to narrow the gap between thoughts and deeds and to make a better evaluation of fathers' participation in child care. We can extend the range of tasks to take account of indirect and non-physical caretaking, particularly with regard to decision-making. We can discover what fathers feel about the division of labour, how their share was established, and how it is maintained.

Fathers should not automatically be regarded as workers first and parents second; the entire spectrum of men's experiences and ideas about child care, placed in a moral and political context of care, should be taken into account.

References

Antill, J.K. & Cotton, S. (1993). Factors affecting the division of labour in households. *Sex Roles, 18*, 9/10, 531-553.

Bozett F.W. & Hanson, S.M.H. (Eds). (1991). *Fatherhood and families in cultural context*. New York: Springer Publishing Company.

Coletrane S. & Ishii-Kuntz, M. (1992). Men's housework: A life course perspective. *Journal of Marriage and the Family, 54*, 43-57.

Coverman, S. (1985). Explaining husbands' participation in domestic labour. *The Sociological Quarterly, 26*, 1, 81-97.

Duindam, V. (1991). *Ouderschapsarrangement en geslachtsidentiteit. Geslachtsspecifieke socialisatie, geen onverdeeld succes bij een verdeeld subject?* Utrecht: Lemma.

Finch, J. & Groves, D. (1983). *A labour of love. Women, work and caring.* London: Routledge & Kegan Paul.

Fisher, B. & Tronto, J. (1990). Towards a feminist theory of caring. In K. Abel & M.K. Nelson (Eds.), *Circles of care: Work and identity in women's lives.* Albany: State University of New York.

Gilligan, C. (1982). *In a different voice.* Cambridge: Harvard University Press.

Hochschild, A. (1989). *The second shift. Working parents and the revolution at home.* New York: Viking Press.

Hood, J.C. (1993). *Men, work, and family.* London: SAGE.

Hooghiemstra, B.T.J. & Niphuis-Nell, M. (1993). *Sociale atlas van de vrouw. Deel 2. Arbeid, inkomen en faciliteiten om werken en de zorg voor kinderen the combineren.* Rijswijk: Sociaal-Cultureel Planbureau.

Jackson, B. (1983). *Fatherhood.* London: George Allen & Unwin.

Jong, A. de & Olde, C. van (1994). *Hoe ouders het werk delen. Onderzoek naar de totstandkoming van de verdeling van het betaalde werk en het werk thuis tussen partners met jonge kinderen.* Den Haag: VUGA.

Kamo, Y. (1988). Determinants of Household Division of Labor. Resources, Power and Ideology. *Journal of Family Issues, 9*, 2, 177-200.

Knijn, T., Nunen, A. van & Avort, A. van der (1994). Zorgend vaderschap. *Amsterdams Sociologisch Tijdschrift, 3*, 70-97.

Lamb, M. (Ed.) (1987). *The father's role: Cross-cultural perspectives.* Hillsdale: Erlbaum.

Lamb, M. & Oppenheim (1989). Fatherhood and father-child relationships. Five years of research. In S. Cath, A. Gurwitt & L. Gunsberg (Eds.) *Fathers and their families* (pp. 11-26). Hillsdale: The Analytic Press.

Lewis, C. (1986). *Becoming a father.* Milton Keyes: Open University Press.

Lewis, C. & O'Brien, M. (Eds.) (1987) *Reassessing fatherhood. New Observations on fathers and the modern family.* London: SAGE.

Lippe, T. van der (1993). *Arbeidsverdeling tussen mannen en vrouwen. Een interdisciplinaire studie naar betaald en huishoudelijk werk binnen huishoudens.* Amsterdam: Thesis Publishers.

McKee, L. & M. O'brien (1982). *The father figure.* Londen: Tavistock Publications.

McKee, L. (1987). Fathers' participation in infant care: A critique. In M. Lamb (Ed.), *The father's role: Cross-cultural perspectives* (pp. 120-138). Hillsdale: Erlbaum.

Mozes-Philips, M. & Ester, F. (1993). *Zorgen voor de toekomst. Een onderzoek naar carrièreperspectieven van verzorgende vaders.* 's-Gravenhage: VUGA.

Ross, C.E. (1987). The division of labor at home. *Social Forces, 65*, 3, 816-833.

Ruddick, S. (1980). Maternal thinking. *Feminist Studies, 6*, 342-367.

Russell, G. (1983). *The Changing role of fathers.* Milton Keynes: Open University Press.

Sandqvist, K. (1987). *Fathers and family work in tow cultures. Antecedents and concomitants of fathers' participation in child care and house work.* Stockholm: Almqvist & Wiksell International.

Spitze, G. (1986). The division of task responsibility in U.S. Households: Longitudinal adjustments to change. *Social Forces, 64*, 3, 689-701.

Tronto, B. (1993). *Moral boundaries: A political argument for an ethic of care.* New York: Routledge.

Vollebergh, W. (1986). De a-symmetrie in het symmetrisch gezin. *Sociale Wetenschappen 29*, 4, 295-315.

Wheelock, J. (1990). *Husbands at home. The domestic economy in a post-industrial society.* London: Routledge.

Charlie Lewis

What are men's aspirations as parents?

About ten years ago, as part of a study of fathers' involvement with their one-year-old children, I interviewed a lorry driver. When describing his daily life he told me that he woke at around five am. and worked a long day loading up his lorry and delivering goods up to 150 km away from his home town. It was clear that he did very little towards caring for his young child, while his wife had given up her full time job in order to care for their baby and home. He clearly felt guilty that her 'job' took up more time than his, for she took the major responsibility for the child at evenings and weekends particularly as he worked on Saturdays. Yet he did not especially enjoy his job and he explained an incident which had raised a lengthy discussion among the two spouses over the fortnight before the interview.

One afternoon the lorry driver found himself on his way back to the yard and with a bit of time to spare he decided to call in on his family. He found his wife and child asleep on the living room sofa. While he realised that everyday routines often exerted great demands on his wife, the incident alerted him also to the realisation that some aspects of her lifestyle did have advantages over his. While their spousal discussions that followed concerned the possibility of reversing roles, he reported that these were conducted in a light-hearted manner because with the best joint will in the world the couple could not afford to transfer from what he earned to what she could earn.

This example demonstrates the validity of Mirjam van Dongen's and Fisher and Tronto's analyses. 'Care' is a highly loaded term, which cannot be divorced from its moral and political context. The distinctions between the four levels of caring which are highlighted in this paper alert us to the problems illustrated by the case of this lorry driver and his family. It is clear that his wife was involved in a large proportion of the 'taking care of' and particularly the family's necessary 'care giving'. On the domestic front she prepared an evening meal for him and performed most of the domestic tasks (i.e. housework) and in many respects he was a 'care-receiver' while he was at home. So, on one level this father's main contribution to domestic care was in terms of 'caring about' his wife and child — his reason for calling in that afternoon was because he wanted to check that they were both fine. As with so many men, an understanding of their role in care must surely come to terms with the discrepancy between thought and deed. Most fathers care about rather than take care of their dependants, unless a more broad definition of the latter term is made to include economic provision.

Van Dongen's paper is correct in pinpointing the theoretical problems with over-simple theoretical analyses, based on resources, ideology and time. She also neatly points out that men define their involvement in child care in diffuse ways, contrasting their relatively small contributions at home with their high levels of commitment to family life in general and their young children in particular. Yet there are some fundamental assumptions and claims made in the paper that I would like to take issue with.

The final paragraph of the chapter starts: "The concept of care proved to be useful in gaining deeper insight into the inconsistency between men's reported behaviour and values. By developing a concept of men's participation in child care in this manner, it may be possible to narrow the gap between thoughts and deeds and to make better evaluation of fathers' participation in child care". These comments give rise to my three major concerns with Van Dongen's analysis: a presupposition that we are witnessing shifts in paternal roles, a claim that the four levels of 'care' represent a process model of parental involvement and finally a dismissal of the influences represented by the three 'perspectives' discussed at the start of her paper. I will deal with these in turn, paying most attention to the last.

At three points in the chapter it is claimed that paternal roles are becoming more involved. The only evidence that is offered in support of this assertion is that contemporary men report that they are more involved with their children than their own fathers were with them. I have grave worries about the validity of such assumptions. Like the fathers studied by Van Dongen, those whom I have studied over the past sixteen years have also continued to contrast their own high commitment to their children with their own fathers' relative detachment. Yet I have been fortunate to have a database on paternal roles collected (largely in interviews with mothers, but some fathers were involved) in the late 1950's. As I have reported elsewhere (Lewis, 1986), there is a striking similarity between parental accounts of fatherhood in the 1950's with those of the 1980's (like the accounts of the fathers in van Dongen's study from the 1990's). The repeated story is that fathers with young children feel more involved than their fathers were and that by implication paternal involvement is increasing, albeit in limited terms. My concern is that we should be focusing upon which, if any, aspects of child care may be witnessing shifts in paternal involvement. The analysis presented in the chapter fails to address the complexities of assessing real or possible change, and this has strong implications for my second and third points, which I will turn to now.

It is clear that we need a more sophisticated understanding of what caring is about, but my second concern is with the assumption that the four types of care represent 'phases'. Even though Van Dongen admits that the phases are not orderly, the implication seems to be that men's aspirations about parenting are now being realised in 'caring about', but may progress to greater 'taking care of' or 'care giving'. Fathers are showing some commitment but not in terms of meeting children's direct needs. Yet just to say that the relationship between the various types of care is complex seems to duck the questions of why contradictions exist and how we may understand them. An equally plausible alternative view is that fathering is more about caring about, because for some generations it has been about parenting at a distance. In 1943 Pearl Gardner published a study conducted in the 1930's in which a dominant theme was fathers' confusion about wanting to be involved but not being able to. Whenever they have been studied in the twentieth century, it seems necessary to explain why there is so much variation between fathers, particularly as a few men men care for their children more than any other carers. In the last analysis Van Dongen's typology does not explain these important dimensions of fatherhood.

My third critical point encapsulates the first two and concerns Van Dongen's analysis of three theoretical perspectives which are criticised at the start of the chapter. I agree with her that resources, ideology and availability cannot by themselves account for paternal involvement in care of children and other dependants. Yet this does not mean to say that these aspects of care may not be important. If we return to the lorry driver, his time at home was severely limited. Like most fathers with preschoolers he worked long hours and seized every opportunity to work overtime. In Britain today approximately 50% of mothers with preschoolers work outside the home, but their earnings and hours indicate that they 'help' the family in paid employment in the same way as their husbands or partners 'help' by conducting a limited set of domestic or child care tasks. The same seems to hold in other advanced economies. Men's time is thus usually restricted to caring about their family rather than caring for it. In most families knowledge about children's material and psychological needs is more likely to be vested in those who spend time with those children. Thus to some extent relative differences in parental resources and time can explain why men so often take a subservient part in care.

But most importantly ideological conflicts explain why sex differences in parenting are so hard to shift — if indeed the bulk of men and women fully want a change in the parental balance of power. So many fathers I have interviewed clearly exploit their partners in terms of the care expressed at home. They will not change nappies because they are offended by the smell, they do not clean the house because either they feel that it doesn't need to be cleaned or because they say their partners do the job better. Some studies of unemployed men show that even when they are around for considerable periods of time they still leave managerial decisions about and many jobs in the home to their partners. Van Dongen claims that ideology cannot account for patterns of child care because, firstly, male and female roles are somewhat confused, secondly there are discrepancies between behaviour and attitudes and, thirdly, maternal resistance may play a part in reducing paternal involvement. While I agree with her 'critique', I feel that she uses too narrow a definition of the term ideology. Other sociological (Backett, 1982; La Rossa, 1977) and psychological (Lewis, 1986) analyses have drawn upon Marxist and other recent accounts of ideology which involve contradictions and 'false consciousnesses'. These authors have assumed that role confusions are the very stuff of ideological issues between mothers and fathers. Men and women have different interests in parenthood — mothers tend to invest more in motherhood, partly because their interests are limited in the sphere of paid work. It is as important to them to take care of others directly in the home as it is for fathers to fulfil the provider role. Yet at the same time men and women also have obligations in other spheres. The ideology of spousal equality or symmetry makes most men committed to doing their bit in the home and with their children, even though 'their bit' involves a mixture of 'caring about' and token commitments to 'taking care of' their children.

Only occasionally do the ideological issues in most parental relationships surface or become explicit. For example, they become paramount in many cases of parental separation. On a more mundane level the lorry driver's realisation that his wife has obvious perks in her role of caring for the child is a typical example of how spouses only rarely address the other's perspective on parenthood. Feminist analyses have pinpointed the stress points which emerge from those issues of male exploitation of women in the family (e.g. Oakley, 1979). Perhaps the image of surprise, even jealousy, experienced by this man reveal how much we need to know about issues over which men have relatively less power. In response to Van Dongen I would suggest that her distinction between the different phases of parental involvement will come to life if more analysis is made of why so few men move beyond 'caring about' their children.

5

Fatherhood and the law in a modern society
The legal role of the father in the Netherlands

Paul Vlaardingerbroek

Introduction

> Men are nothing more than mobile sperm banks, it has been said, their role is over as soon as conception has been achieved. They fulfil only decorative purposes... It could even be said that in England and in a number of other scientifically advanced countries the unmarried father has come to be seen as sexually and socially unnecessary, merely a man who pays, or should pay: nicknamed in Germany a 'Zahlvater', expressing the idea that the duties of paternity are a form of perpetual payment for sinful and stolen pleasures, the act of insemination as the occasion for a lifetime of financial obligation. Of the positive and familial aspect of fatherhood, we hear little in law.

This quotation has been taken out of a chapter in the book *Parenthood in modern society*, written by Ruth Deech. Of course, its intention was critical, but it is true that the definition of fatherhood has changed dramatically in recent years.

In this contribution I will deal with the question whether the father has a more important role to play than merely being a 'mobile sperm bank'.

In modern family life many factors play a role in the relationship between family members. In most countries the social and legal position of the father has changed dramatically in the past two decades. Thanks to artificial insemination the same can be said of the biological/genetical role of the father. In a leading article in the Sunday Times of 3 July 1994 attention was given to the question: "Do fathers still have a leading role to play?" and the following quotation is interesting for this contribution: "The day has already dawned when he [the father, PV] has to categorise himself as the genetic father (the sperm donor), the biological father (the father who implanted the fertilising sperm), the legal father (who in some countries is the sperm donor) or the social father (whom the child regards as a father figure). Such groups may already be meeting for a post-natal cup of tea." Although this article has a bit of a negative background, the same developments can be found in other modern countries.

In the following I will try to show that the legal position of the father has changed in several respects, such as in the law on affiliation, parenthood, custody and access rights. I will deal with the Dutch legal aspects of the role of the father, but these items can be compared with developments in other countries in Europe. To make it easier to compare these developments in family law in different European countries, I will give a rather detailed overview of the (changes in the) legal position of the father in Dutch law. I will conclude that in the Netherlands the legal position of the father has been strengthened in some ways while in other respects the father's legal status has been weakened. The growing international dimension of family law demands that we find international answers to the changing (legal) position of the father and the social role he has to play. However, I will first give a short description of the Dutch concept of the family.

The concept of the family

In 1991 more than half the respondents of a representative survey considered divorce a better solution than staying in a bad marriage, even when the children were still living with their parents. In 1965 only 12% of the respondents were of this opinion. Also in 1965, almost three out of four respondents found voluntary childlessness unacceptable, as against only 5% in 1991. The majority of respondents in 1991 had no difficulty in accepting artificial insemination. Repudiation of a child born to a cohabiting couple was indefensible for a majority of the respondents. According to 85% of the respondents cohabitation is a good preparation for marriage; 71% find that cohabitation is absolutely not a topic for concern and discussion any longer. An even greater tolerance is expressed towards living alone (91%), and towards living in a homosexual (male or female) relationship (86%).

In the Netherlands, 'family' and 'family life' are not limited to traditional concepts of the family. Apart from the traditional family of a man and a woman who are married and have children, the notion of family is also used to describe other *primary living units in which the care and upbringing of children takes place*, such as single-parent families or persons who live together without being married, be it of two opposite sexes or of the same sex. Regardless of the composition of the couple living together, as soon as there are children, the living unit is called a family. So the definition of the family is more than merely the description of the (broken) nuclear family. The Netherlands government considers family life to be an absolutely private affair. The state may not interfere with the way in which people shape their way of life or their family life, unless there is a very good reason, for example if the interests of the children are in danger. So children — not the adults who live together — have the focus of attention of the Netherlands government. Preventative policies dealing with dropping out of the family is one of the priorities of Dutch Youth Policy.

Nowadays there are more than 1 million single-parent families[1] in the Netherlands and there is a widespread tolerance in our society for unmarried couples. As for people of the same sex who prefer to live together, more than 20,000 homosexual and lesbian couples are living together on a permanent basis, including couples who raise children.

Nuclear families represented only 35% of all household forms in the beginning of the eighties. In the near future, one third of all households will be of the nuclear-family type, one third will be of the single-person variant and the remaining third will be made up of other living arrangements. If social policy remains unchanged, it is expected that at the beginning of the 21st century half of all households in the Netherlands will be of the single-person type. These changes and forecasts are not different from those found in other West European countries.

The present size and composition of households reflect the aforementioned demographic trends. Since 1971 population censuses have been discontinued because many people made objections for reasons of privacy. Until 1971 information on households was obtained through these population censuses every ten years.

During the last three decades the composition of private households has changed very much. The number of single-person households increased sharply and, concomitantly, the number of nuclear family households decreased. The number of other types of living arrangements, such as lone-parent families, cohabiting partners with children, and non-family households showed a slight increase.

Moreover, the total number of households is increasing at a faster rate than the total population. This decline in the number of members per household has been called 'the thinning' of the family.

Changing fatherhood and the affiliation law

During the past 25 years more or less substantial reforms of the affiliation laws have been carried through in almost all continental West European countries. Three common elements can be noted:

---

1   Out of a total of almost 16 million inhabitants.

1. *equalisation*: the primary object and result of the reforms has undoubtedly been the elimination of discrimination between various categories of affiliation;
2. *liberalisation*: the reforms have suppressed numerous restrictions on the establishment and contestation of affiliation;
3. *modernisation*: the final objective of all these reforms has been to modernise affiliation law, although this modernisation cannot compete with the new medico-genetic techniques which permit a child to be conceived without sexual intercourse.

Dutch law is partially based on the Napoleonic Code (which was in force from 1811 to 1838). In 1970 the affiliation code was reformed in the framework of the law introducing Book 1 of the new Civil Code. Following the decision by the European Court in the Marckx-case the first draft for the revision of affiliation law was published in 1981. Small changes took place in the affiliation law because of the Marckx-case, but in 1988 the government submitted a Bill for revision of the affiliation. In 1993 this Bill was repealed. A new Bill has been sent to the Council of State for comments.

In all Western industrialised countries the sixties marked a turning point, especially in matters of demography: a decline of the birth rate, fewer legal marriages and more de facto marriages, a growing number of separations and divorces, and therefore an increasing number of children born out of wedlock or living with only one parent or a parent and a step-parent. At that time, it was a straightforward task to describe the rules of affiliation. Dutch affiliation law is based on the presumption that a husband is the father of his wife's children.

When a child is born within marriage, the man who was married to its mother at the time of conception or at the time of birth, is presumed to be the father of the child. When the child is born within marriage only the husband is entitled to take legal action (within 6 months from the time when he acquired knowledge of the birth) to contest his paternity. This action will not succeed if the husband has given his consent to an act liable to lead to conception (e.g. artificial insemination, approved adultery). In the Napoleonic Code, the restrictions on the scope of contesting the presumption of fatherhood were expressed in three ways:

i.   only the husband was allowed to contest his paternity;
ii.   he could do so only within a very short time-limit;
iii. the law strictly and narrowly defined the circumstances under which he could deny paternity.

Now, the protection of family harmony and the importance of safeguarding the long-established status of the individual are considered to be valid reasons for restricting paternity contests. Nevertheless, in the Netherlands these rules of contestation still form the basis of the law and of the jurisprudence, although these obstacles to the possibility to contest paternity are increasingly seen as an unjustified obstruction in the search for conformity between legal affiliation and the biological truth.

Children born more than 307 days after the marriage has been dissolved will only have a mother at the time of their birth. The paternity of a child born in the 306 days after the dissolution of the marriage can be contested by the mother, but only if she declares to the civil registrar that she contests the paternity of her ex-spouse, and only if the mother marries the man who has recognised the child. The man who recognises the child has to marry the mother of the child and they are to marry in the year following birth. The retention of this presumption of legal fatherhood (the *Pater est* rule[2]) is usually defended by the following empirical rule. When a married woman bears a child, an identified man exists of whom it can be presumed that he is the biological father of her child. As a matter of fact, the husband of the married mother is usually the biological father of the child, not so much because married women are generally faithful to their husbands, but simply because couples who commit adultery generally do not wish to beget a child, and the availability of contraception and abortion allows them to avoid an adulterine birth[3].

A child born out of wedlock only has a mother (Art. 1:221 BW[4]). However, paternity can be established outside marriage when the child is acknowledged by another man (not necessarily the natural father). A voluntary acknowledgement by the man is required. The mother has to give her consent. If the child is aged twelve years or more, the child itself must consent to the acknowledgement (Art. 1:221-225 BW).

The child cannot be acknowledged by a married man[5] (whose wife is not the mother of the child) or — in the case of a child born as a result of incest — where the sexual intercourse resulting in the conception of the child occurred between the mother and her (grand)father or brother. The father can acknowledge his child after the dissolution of his own marriage or if he got married less than 306 days before the birth of the child. The mother of the child has to give her consent to voluntary acknowledgement.

---

2   Pater est quem nuptiae demonstrant.
3   Senaeve, P., 1993: 95.
4   BW = Dutch Civil Code.
5   However, the Hoge Raad (i.e. the Supreme Courd of the Netherlands) allowed the prohibition for a married man to acknowledge the child of un anmarried woman to be suspended, but only in certain situations: he has to be the begetter of the child and his wife may not object to this acknowledgement. Her objections can be put aside when she has no serious grounds for this objection; Hoge Raad 10 November 1989, NJ 1990, 450.

Legitimation is possible when the child is acknowledged before or at the time of the marriage, or even after the marriage is dissolved in the event of the mother's death.

If a child has not been acknowledged (because his or her identity is not known, because the child does not wish to be acknowledged, or because the mother does not consent to acknowledgement) there are special proceedings to determine paternity, but only for the purpose of ensuring support of the child by that man (Art. 1: 394 BW).

The above summarises briefly the Dutch statutory rules on affiliation. Since the *Marckx*-case, the Dutch provisions on affiliation have been overruled on a number of occasions. I shall give some examples.

The Dutch legislator revised the provisions contained in the Civil Code on affiliation and inheritance law because the legitimate child had a better legal position than the illegitimate child (Act of 27 October 1982, Stb. 608). The illegitimate child had no kinship with the relatives of his mother and — following acknowledgement — of his father. This legislation came into force with retrospective effect, backdated to 13 June 1979 (the date of the decision of the European Court in *Marckx*).

The legal right of the mother to give consent to a man to acknowledge her child was considered to be a right of absolute veto. However, in a case-law development, a change has been introduced if the mother refuses without valid reason. In that case the man has to state that there has been 'family life' between him and the child[6]. The so-called 'absolute veto' of the mother of the illegitimate child has become a 'suspensive veto'. At the request of the man who wants to acknowledge her child and who can prove that he has enjoyed 'family life' with the child, the judge may decide that the mother's consent can be superseded by a decision on the part of the court.

A draft bill was submitted to Parliament in 1991; this would introduce many changes into the present Articles in the Civil Code with regard to affiliation/parentage. In this draft more weight has been given to the wishes of the natural father of the child who wants to become its legal father. Unjust differences in the field of affiliation law between the father and the mother of the child will disappear. Thus in a case where paternity is at issue, both the man and the woman will have the same legal rights. In the new statute the legislator has also taken into account the problems that may arise with artificial insemination.

To conclude: in the Netherlands the legal status of the unmarried father has improved dramatically, although this has led to a weaker position of the unmarried mother. However, the position of the married (or just divorced) mother has improved, while in the new bill she will have the same position

---

6   Hoge Raad, 8 April 1988, NJ 1988, 170; Hoge Raad 18 May 1990, NJ 1991, 374 & 375.

as her (former) husband with regard to the denial of the fatherhood of the child.

From paternal to parental authority

Section 245 of Book 1 of the Dutch Civil Code contains the following rule concerning the relationship between a child and its parents: "A child, of whatever age, has to honour and respect his parents". Of course, this is a rule of law with a strong moral flavour, and it is hard to enforce it in practice. On the other hand, parents are free to fulfil their basic duties as they think fit. Although the legislator (more exactly: the government) does not prescribe how parents should fulfil these duties, child protection regulations have existed in Dutch law since 1905. When parents abuse or neglect their child, intervention in parental authority is possible.

Since a child has no capacity to perform legal acts[7], someone has to be his legal representative, control his financial affairs, care for him and secure his education. In the natural course of things, these duties fall to the parents. They have parental responsibility which consists of power over the child on the one hand and control over their financial affairs on the other.

Since 1838 the legal regulations relating to parental authority have been drastically revised from time to time. The Civil Code of 1838 contained the concept of *'paternal authority'*. The father exercised this power and had the right to ask the court to take his child into custody when, in his opinion, the child misbehaved. This 'parental disciplinary law' was abolished in 1922. Almost 20 years earlier, in 1905, 'paternal authority' was replaced by *'parental authority'*, but only the father could exercise this right. Also in 1905 some child protection regulations were introduced allowing intervention in parental authority, which until then had been inviolable. Parents or guardians who ill-treated or neglected their child could lose parental responsibility or guardianship. This would also happen if they were unable or unfit to raise their child. In urgent matters it was possible to suspend parental authority, as a temporary measure, by committing the child to the 'Child care and protection board'[8]. In 1922 the so-called supervision order

---

7 These legal acts may include making a contract, but also taking decisions about medical treatment, abortion, religion, what parent to live with, visiting rights, etc.

8 A special Council for the Protection of Children. This Council is a state organisation. It has the obligation to investigate the well-being of the child when there is a suspicion of child abuse or child neglect, for instance after a report or request has been submitted by the Confidential Doctor, the school, family or neighbours. This council also has the legal task to advise the judge in many family disputes (where children are involved), as to requests for access orders or child support.

(or in Dutch: 'ondertoezichtstelling') was added. This new regulation was a compromise between the extremes of either taking the child away from its parents or doing absolutely nothing. In 1948 the law was changed again.[9] Both parents have to exercise parental control, but where the parents differed the *father's opinion prevailed*. If his decision seemed to be contrary to the moral and material interests of the child or detrimental to its health, the children's court magistrate, at the mother's request, could nullify the decision. In 1984 the statute *Gelijke behandeling* (Equal Opportunities for Men and Women) changed this. So now, if the parents differ over the child's education and upbringing, either of them may request the children's court magistrate to decide on the issue. This is also the case when the father is not interested in his child's education and leaves this to his wife. When there is a dispute between the parents with regard to the upbringing of the child the judge will attempt to find a compromise between the parents' conflicting opinions and take a decision which is in the child's interest (section 1:246 Civil Code). Some minor changes to the Civil Code are not discussed here.

In literature, court decisions and legislation, the notion of parental control has being developed. Specialists in family and child law have long been pleading both for more rights and for more duties for young people. When children get older, they acquire more rights and duties for themselves, at the expense of those of their parents. Some specialists propose a step-by-step approach: when the children reach a certain age (e.g. 10, 12, 14 or 16) they obtain certain rights. Others prefer a sort of 'sliding scale' giving parents the right to decide when their child is capable of doing certain things, because children do not mature at the same rate. Dutch judges tend to regard parental control after or outside marriage as important. As far as legislation is concerned, a governmental committee published a report in 1971 with a number of recommendations concerning control over minors and related problems. A bill was drafted in 1986 but it received such sharp criticism that it had to be revised. In early 1993 (3 February) a bill concerning parental authority was submitted to the Dutch Parliament. This bill is in closer harmony with developments in the law (court decisions) and literature (Tweede Kamer, 1992-1993, 23 012, Nos. 1-3) regarding the issue of legal custody and parental authority. It proposes the legal continuation of parental authority after divorce and in out-of-wedlock situations by means of a simple declaration to the clerk of the subdistrict court. Parental authority can be exercised by both parents or by a single parent.

The requirement of a family relationship remains, as a result of the advice of the Council of Europe concerning parental responsibility, which was accepted by the Council of Ministers on 28 February 1984 (Recommendation

---

9   Law of 10th July 1947, Staatsblad H 232, enforced on 1st September 1948.

No. R(84)4 concerning 'parental responsibility', Strasbourg, 1984). In the near future, legal guardianship will only be possible if a third party, not being a parent, is appointed (Tweede Kamer, 1992-1993, 23 012, No. 3, p. 22).

Until now, parental control in the Netherlands has been related to marriage. According to the law, legitimate children are subject to parental control; illegitimate children are under guardianship. However, when the father has acknowledged the child, he and the mother[10] of the illegitimate child may ask the subdistrict court judge to grant them parental authority. If there is no authority over a child[11], for example, when the marriage of the parents has ended or the parents lose their parental authority by a decision of the district court, guardianship can be given to the parent (usually the mother) or to a third person. The third person could be a natural or a legal person (usually specialised in guardianship). Guardianship and co-guardianship may not be given to the same person. If the parent's marriage ends (by death or divorce), parental authority will be transformed into guardianship and co-guardianship. In the case of divorce this can lead to severe disputes between the parents as to who should have full authority (guardianship) over the child(ren). There are a number of distinctions between parental authority and 'guardianship'. Only two parents can have parental authority; they both have the same right to educating and bringing up the child. A guardian has the absolute right in this matter. The principal task of the co-guardian is merely to supervise the responsibility of the guardian with regard to the child. Apart from these differences, there are hardly any differences between parents with parental authority or guardianship. However, the guardianship of a third person differs from parental authority or the guardianship of one parent. So, the third person does not have to support the child with his own money.

In the 1970s and early 1980s there was an increasing movement towards retaining parental authority after divorce instead of (co-)guardianship. Fathers in particular wanted their parental authority to continue[12]. They felt that the co-guardianship they were usually granted (because they did not have day-to-day care of the child), was no right at all. Although their partnership had come to an end, it was argued that this should not terminate their joint parental authority. This was eventually achieved as a

---

10 She will be the guardian if she is unmarried, adult and not insane at the time of birth of her child.
11 When, for example, the mother is a minor, or when the child is a foundling.
12 Thanks to the 'fathers' rights' movement for instance.

result of the influence of the European Convention on Human Rights (ECHR), especially after the famous Marckx-case[13].

So, the Convention could not only protect a citizen against the administration, but could also be used as an incentive for governments to bring their national legislation in line with the European Convention. The Dutch legislator was forced to act after a number of important rulings by the Hoge Raad.[14] On 4 May 1984 the Hoge Raad granted the request of two parents to retain joint parental authority over their legitimate child after their divorce, despite the fact that Dutch statute law provided otherwise. The Hoge Raad ruled that parents could retain their parental authority jointly, provided that: (i) they *both* explicitly requested this; (ii) they were able to act in co-operation and (iii) this solution did not conflict with the child's best interests. As parental authority was now detached from marriage, judges in the subdistrict courts were confronted with requests by *unmarried* couples seeking for parental authority over their children instead of (co-) guardianship. After some contradictory rulings by regional courts, the Hoge Raad decided on 21 March 1986[15] that unmarried couples could also have parental authority, if:

i.   both parents have a legal relationship with their child (so the illegitimate child of an unmarried mother has to be acknowledged by its father[16]) and are capable of exercising parental authority;

ii.   evidence is given that *both* parents wish to have this parental authority;

iii.   there appears to be co-operation between the parents; and

iv.   this does not conflict with the child's best interests.

With regard to point iii., the Hoge Raad added that if the parents of the child were living together at the time of their request, it could be assumed that this condition was fulfilled. If the parents were not living together, they had to provide evidence that this condition of co-operation had been fulfilled[17].

This was the first time the Hoge Raad ruled that it was not incompatible with the Dutch legal system nor with the rationale of Articles 8 and 14 of the European Convention that unmarried parents who have a legal relationship with their child should have parental authority. Furthermore, Art. 14 requires that the law be interpreted such that no distinction is made between

---

13 European Court on Human Rights 13-6-1979, Publ. ECHR A, vol. 31.

14 NJ 1985, 510.

15 NJ 1986, 585.

16 The acknowledgement of a child has the consequence that the child will have his father's nationality and name and will inherit from him. The father has to support his child and may apply for (co-)guardianship. The ackowlegdement as such does not give (parental) authority.

17 NJ 1986, 585.

divorced and unmarried parents who have legal ties with their child. So since 1986, parental authority and marriage have been detached.

It is remarkable that this interpretation of the Hoge Raad was not in accordance with that of the European Commission which, two years earlier, had stated in the case of a complaint by two unmarried parents who could not receive joint custody, that (EC 9519/81, March 15 1984, X versus FRG, not published):

"Article 8 protects the illegitimate family. Nevertheless, by virtue of Article 12 of the Convention, the family based on marriage enjoys greater protection. Therefore, special legislation concerning children born out of wedlock can be justified, particulary in the interests of these children. In respect of an unmarried couple living together, the award of care and custody exclusively to the mother, in practice, entails few inconveniences."

and, somewhat further:

"The measure here in question only concerns the formal right of care and custody. According to section 1705 BGB [Bürgerliches GesetzBuch, PV] this right is vested in the mother only and exclusively. In practice, however, the mother voluntarily shares its exercise with the applicant or at least she has the possibility to do so. Therefore the regulation in question does not in itself prevent the applicant from enjoying his family life or maintaining a normal father-child relationship with the child born out of wedlock, as he is living with the child and the child's mother."

With regard to Article 14 in conjunction with Article 8 ECHR, the Commission stated that:

"It is not discriminatory to pass special legislation concerning care and custody of children born out of wedlock, such legislation is justified by the greater difficulties met by these children if the relationship of their unmarried parents ends" (ECRM 15 March 1984, No. 9639/82, D and R 36, p130; ECRM 15 March 1984, No. 9519/81, not published, see de Langen, 1990).

Of course the interests of the child remain the criterion by which the joint request of the parents must be reviewed[18].

In spite of the extension of the national legislation mentioned above, the wishes of some citizens went further. The nature of the family relationship between parents and child became the focal point of discussion. The decisions of the Hoge Raad prompted much debate. Judges in the subdistrict courts were confronted with petitions filed by two women or two men, seeking parental authority. The Hoge Raad, however, reiterated that one of

---

18 Hoge Raad, 21 March 1986, NJ 1986, 585.

the conditions for joint parental authority[19] was that both parents must have a legal family tie with their child. So in a de facto marriage the parents can acquire parental authority if the man acknowledges his child, but a couple of the same sex can not do so. In spite of this, emancipation groups have been putting pressure on the Dutch legislator to reform the laws[20] even to the extent of giving joint 'parental' authority to homosexual couples.

In a number of rulings, the Hoge Raad has explicitly upheld this claim. In the first case, the request came from two women who considered themselves to be the social parents of the child, as it was they who were providing everyday care[21]. One of the carers was the mother of the child. In their opinion it was possible that, in spite of the absence of a family tie between the mother's girlfriend and the child, there was in fact family life (as defined by Article 8 ECHR) between the adult and the child. However, the Hoge Raad was of the opinion that the requirement that there be a family relationship between the adult and the child was not incompatible with Article 8 and 14 ECHR, "NB now that it here considers an infringement which as is the consequence of which is herefore [in previous considerations in this ruling it was said that this infringement is allowed by Art. 8 section 2, PV] considered, follows from the Dutch legal system concerning the parental authority and remains within the limits of which is allowed by Art. 8 section 2 regarding legal provisions. NB"

Another case concerned a man who could acknowledge a child but did not wish to do so since this would mean that the child's family name would have to change.[22] Again the Hoge Raad used the same reasoning as in the earlier case, in the so called 'Spring judgements'.

The number of divorced fathers with custody of the child is growing, but usually these children are older than twelve years. A new Bill will make it possible, once it has been enacted, for the partner of the father or the mother (who must have parental authority) to ask for joint custody. This joint custody is a weaker right than the parental authority of the parent. There is no difference in this bill between a heterosexual or homosexual partner of the parent (TK 23 714).

To conclude: With regard to parental authority we see a decrease in paternal authority in favour of joint custody and joint parental authority after and

---

19 It is not possible for one parent alone to have parental authority. However, the district court judge may decide that parental authority can be *exercised* by one parent (e.g. if the father has lost parental authority because he abused the child).

20 To make it possible to give joint parental authority to the couple when the man did not or can not acknowledge the child (e.g. because he is married to an other woman).

21 Hoge Raad 24 February 1989, NJ 1989, 741.

22 Hoge Raad, February 24 1989, NJ 1989, 742.

outside marriage. Nowadays, married parents have equal legal rights and duties with regard to the education and upbringing of their children. In practice, this may be different.

The changing rights of the father to child access

Before 1 October 1971 (Article 161, clause 5 BW, Act of 6 May 1971, Stb. 290), the parent had no legal right to maintain contact with their children who were under custody of another. Access rights existed neither in statute nor in case law.

The initial statutory amendment merely gave judges discretionary powers to make arrangements between the child and the *divorced* parent who did not have custody. The judge was free to determine the grounds on which a request was to be granted or denied. No grounds of legal reviewed were enacted. Nor was there a right for parents and children to have access. Furthermore, the act was only applicable in cases of divorce.

It is not surprising, therefore, that case law interpretations have led to a further interpretation and extension of the right to access. Back in 1957 and 1961 the European Commission accepted that the parental right to access after divorce follows from the right to family life. Breaking off the relationship between the parents does not end the tie between the child and its parents[23].

In 1980, the European Commission concluded that "according to its established case-law, the right to family life also contains the right of a parent to have access to or contact with the child on the understanding that the State may not interfere with the exercise of that right otherwise than in accordance with the strict conditions set out in para. 2 of the Article, that says "protection of health and morals" and "protection of the rights and freedoms of others"[24].

As a consequence, Article 161, paragraph 5 (old version) of the Civil Code was held not to be in accordance with the rights protected by Article 8 ECHR.

Subsequently, the Hoge Raad concluded that the right of the parent who does not have legal custody as stipulated in Article 8 ECHR, exists in principle, but that in specific situations this right can be restricted by the judge's assessment of what is in the best interest of both the other parent

---

23 ECRM, Application No. 172/56, *X* v *Sweden*, Yearbook I, p. 211; ECRM, Application No. 911/60, *X* v *Sweden*, Yearbook IV, p. 198.
24 EComHR 13 March 1980, NJ 1981, 121.

and the child. Only after an evaluation of the actual situation can the content of the right be determined.[25]
This development in actual cases led to an amendment to the legislation on this matter.

Article 1:161a BW superseded Article 161 paragraph 5 BW and came into force on 1 December 1990 (Act of 13 September 1990, Stb. 482). The access rights between the child and the parent who does not have guardianship, are now explicitly guaranteed.

The issue to be assessed is the admissibility of the request; after this has been determined, the possibility of an arrangement concerning parental access is investigated. The central issue here is the best interest of the child.

In February 1985 the Hoge Raad abandoned the requirement that an application is only admissible if the child is a descendent of the adult, or if there have been previous family relations[26]. The only requirement was that the applicant "is or has been in such a relation to the child that he is having family life with his child within the meaning of Article 8 ECHR. It is irrelevant, having regard to Article 14 ECHR, whether the relationship with the child is based on legal parenthood, acknowledgement, biological parenthood or any other relation, which can be considered equal to the previous relation for the purpose of applying Article 8 ECHR." This formula has been repeated several times[27]. By virtue of this ruling by the Hoge Raad, the circle of persons who are able to apply for a right of access has increased substantially. However, this ruling also opened (undesirable) possibilities for semen donors, incestuous (grand)fathers, rapists and other persons to begin legal proceedings for access rights, because the mere fact of being a biological parent would be sufficient to speak of family life. Therefore, the view of the Hoge Raad could not stand. This interpretation was not shared by the European Court of Human Rights. In 1988 the Court considered the issue in the *Berrahab-case*.[28] In this case against the Netherlands, the issue concerned the father and daughter Berrehab, who could not have contact with each other because the father had not received permission to remain in the Netherlands and had been deported. The father

---

25 Hoge Raad 24 August 1974, NJ 1975, 277; Hoge Raad 15 February 1980, NJ 1980, 329; Hoge Raad 2 May 1980, NJ 1980, 537; Hoge Raad 25 September 1981, NJ 1982, 557; Hoge Raad 13 November 1981, NJ 1982, 558; Hoge Raad 19 March 182, NJ 1982, 599; Hoge Raad 16 April 1982, NJ 1982, 560; Hoge Raad 7 May 1982, NJ 1982, 561; Hoge Raad 25 June 1982, NJ 1982, 562.
26 Hoge Raad, 22 February 1985, NJ 1986, 3.
27 Hoge Raad, 10 May 1985, NJ 1986, 5; Hoge Raad, 16 May 1986, NJ 1986, 627; Hoge Raad, 5 December 1986, NJ 1987, 957.
28 ECtHR 21 June 1988, NJ 1989, 746, NJCM Bulletin 1988, p. 579.

and daughter enjoyed family life according to the European Court. The Court held:

"The Court likewise does not see cohabitation as a sine qua non of family life between parents and minor children. It has held that the relationship created between the spouses by a lawful and genuine marriage... has to be regarded as 'family life'. It follows from the concept of family life on which Article 8 is based that a child born of such union is ipso jure part of that relationship; hence, from the moment of the child's birth and by the very fact of it, there exists between him and his parents a bond amounting to 'family life', even if the parents are not then living together. Subsequent events, of course, may br'eak that tie..." (para. 21).

As a result of this judgment, the Hoge Raad *re*considered its position in 1989[29]. It held that:

"For the admissibility of the request it is demanded that the applicant not only states that he is the biological father, but also states additional circumstances as mentioned above, from which follows that between him and the child there are ties which can be considered vie familiale/family life in the sense of Article 8 ECHR, so that there is room for investigation of the possible justification for a right for access."

The consequence of this judgement is that being merely the biological father of the child is insufficient reason to be granted the right to parental access. The father (begetter) also has to allege certain incidental circumstances from which his relationship with the child can be considered to be a close, personal connection and therefore classified under the protected right of family life. Then his request will be sustained. The Hoge Raad does not give a restrictive enumeration of the circumstances necessary for having 'family life'. The general interpretation in judicial literature is "the necessary existence of a concrete family relation of a certain period, continued contact with the child after breaking off the relation with the parent and a demonstrated interest in, and care for, the child"[30].

The next question that must be answered concerns whether the arrangements for parental access in the particular case are appropriate. The rights and interests of other persons also involved in the relationship between the child and the parent, who want to have visiting rights, will be balanced, because the right to access will also influence the child's other relationships.

In accordance with Article 1:161a BW, the judge has the opportunity to honour or to reject a request for access. Paragraph 2 and 3 provide the basis for rejecting the request. The most important criterion is whether access

---

29 Hoge Raad 10 November 1989, NJ 1990, 628.
30 See also the Hoge Raad, 4 January 1991, NJ 1991, 253.

would be against the child's best interests. The contact with the parent who does not have custody of the child can cause serious damage to the development of the child. A second reason is the unsuitability of the parent.

In the draft bill discussed above, the circle of persons who will be able to request a right to access has been increased. The proposed Article 377f grants this right to anyone who has a close personal relationship with the child and is a relative in the second degree, or its natural parent. The so-called social parent who has educated, raised and taken care of the child, treating him as part of the family for at least one year, can also apply for access to the child. With the words 'close personal relationship', the legislator is linking Dutch law to the case law of the European Commission which gives an interpretation of family life as "a relationship...sufficiently close to constitute family life"[31].

The grandparents or separated brothers and sisters are possible candidates for the right to have access, and we believe that even a mother who babysits other people's children will be able, under certain circumstances, to appeal to her close personal relationship with the child in order to obtain certain visiting rights.

A remaining problem is the enforcement of the judgement. Some possible methods of enforcement in the Netherlands are:

i.   financial penalty: however, in most cases the mother has to co-operate, but she is also the financially weakest party;
ii.   imprisonment: a consequence is that the child's educator/caregiver will not be able to look after it;
iii. setting aside of the obligation to pay maintenance: this is unlikely to lead to an alteration in the financial position of the mother as she obtains her money from social welfare;
iv.   placing the child under supervision: such a measure would seem excessive in these circumstances.

Only in very exceptional cases will one of these decisions be taken. The main reason is that it will cause distress to the child and will be against its best interests.

It is very difficult to devise legal provisions for these types of practical problems because we are dealing with people, and the visiting/information problems arise from the non-harmonious dissolution of marriages or other relationships between the parents of the child.

In almost 10% of marriages involving minor children which end in divorce, the dissolution of the marriage does not bring an end to the quarrels between the former spouses.

---

31 EComHR, 8823/78, 12 March 1980, unpublished.

Recently, a new arrangement was introduced for those who do not have access to their children because their former spouse does not allow him or her to have contact with the child. In some cases, the court ruled that the child's father be allowed to receive information about the child regularly (school reports, a photograph of the child, details of illnesses, and so[32].

The legislator goes even further. A new bill with regard to parental authority and access rights, states that in the case of divorce, the parent without parental authority and with no access to the child has the right to be *informed and consulted* in important matters with regard to his or her child (choice of school, school results, sickness of the child, etc.). Many Dutch lawyers and judges are afraid that this new right, once enacted, shall lead to a new battlefield between the parents and others who have information on the child[33].

To conclude: We see that the position of the divorced father with regard to access to his child has been strengthened. However, the unmarried father (begetter) must have had family life (a close personal relationship) with his child before he is allowed to initiate legal proceedings for access. This development has undermined the legal status of the mother, but in my opinion this is justified because of the protection under Art. 8 ECRM.

Child support by the father in the Netherlands

The social significance of marriage, the nuclear family, and the extended family originally found expression in the support duties involving not only spouses, parents, and children, but also more distant relations like cousins, uncles, aunts, grandparents, grandchildren, and so on. It was expected of them that they would support each other, especially financially. State care was secondary. Although it has not quite disappeared, the social importance of family support has been reduced to social care by society. This reduction of support between family relations is reflected in both our family law and public law; for instance, only the ex-spouses and parents of minors can be obliged to compensate for benefits granted by local social services.

The general duty to support has the following elements:

---

32 Hoge Raad 8 February 1991, NJ 1992, 21.

33 The proposed Art. 377c gives an obligation to professionals (e.g. teachers, social workers) to give information about the child to the parent who does not raise the child. Only in a limited number of cases is the professional allowed to withhold this information (see the grounds to reject a request for access to the child).

1. It is strictly personal, which means that it ends at the death of the person who is entitled to this support or at the death of the person who has to give financial support; the right to support can not be alienated or seized.
2. It can always be changed, unless spouses have made an agreement at the time of their divorce that whatever circumstances may arise, their alimony agreement can not be changed.
3. Renunciation by agreement from a right to support is not possible.
4. The possibility to get legal redress of a claim to financial support has been strengthened in many ways (e.g Art. 479b ev. en 598 ev. Rv[34]).

Blood relationship and other kinship ties entail four specific obligations and duties:

First, there is a *reciprocal obligation between parents on the one hand, and their children on the other hand*, when there are legal family ties between them. A natural child (which means a child born out of wedlock) has a duty to support his father if the child, while still a minor, was acknowledged by his father. If the child is an adult, aged 18 years or older but younger than 21, and in need of support, the parents have the obligation to support their child in the costs of living and studying.

Parents only have to pay for their adult son or daughter if he or she is in real need. A student can be self-supporting if able to work, so parents do not have to pay for him or her over the age of 21. Of course, there can be a moral obligation to support one's children. New legislation for the support of children who are studying (a kind of scholarship) obliges parents to support their children during their studies, insofar as their financial means allow them to do so.

Second, there is a *unilateral support duty of the begetter towards his illegitimate child*, as long as the child has not been acknowledged by his begetter or by any other man (this is one of the few legal ties between the begetter and his child if it was not acknowledged by him). Legal family ties between the father and his child are only created by acknowledgement (eventually followed by a legitimation because of a marriage with the child's mother). So the father does not have to be the biological father of the child. This unilateral support duty only exists until the 21st birthday of the child, unless the child is not able — because of mental or physical problems — to earn his or her own living.

As mentioned in the foregoing, the child's father is presumed to be the man who had sexual intercourse with the child's mother in the period between the 307th and the 179th day before the birth of the child.

---

34 Civil Legal Proceedings Act.

Third, there is a *unilateral support duty of the step-parent towards the legitimate and illegitimate children of his/her spouse*. This duty only exists when the children are not over 21 years of age, when they belong to the family of the step-parent, and as long as the marriage lasts.

Very recently, the Hoge Raad ruled that an unmarried 'stepfather' cannot be obliged to support the child of his girlfriend, because the law is very clear on this point[35].

Fourth, there is *a reciprocal support duty between parents-in-law and their children-in-law*, but only when the marriage of the child-in-law still exists.

But who actually pays? In the Netherlands there is no fixed rule about the ranking of family members in terms of support rights and duties. However, in the first place the (ex)husband is always obliged to give support to the (former) spouse. If he pays, the other relatives are not obliged to pay (art. 1:392 BW[36]). Children-in-law and parents-in-law are hardly ever entitled to support.

If more relatives are obliged to give support to one person, everyone has to pay a share. The judge may make allowance for any relevant circumstance (for instance, the kind of relationship).

The duty to support results in an obligation to pay money to the person who is entitled to support. The judge, however, may order that support in kind will be given (for instance, food, clothes, and so on).

The range of support duties is decided by two factors:

a. the needs of the person(s) who is (are) entitled to support; and

b. the financial means of the person who is obliged to pay support.

The judge may reduce the amount to be paid because of misbehaviour of the person who is entitled to support. This reduction is not possible in cases where children are entitled to support.

Until 1993, the infant welfare centre had to give financial advice to the judge in cases where the parents argued about the amount of child support to be paid. The Dutch government is currently working on a new act with regard to the calculation of the amount due (a fixed amount, based on the average costs of raising children).

Support duties for minor children comprise four special aspects:

i.   Support demands more than merely the cost of living; i.e. just feeding and clothing a person; it also includes the costs of care and education (for instance, cultural/sport activities).

ii. The child need not be in need; support must also be given to a child who has an income/inheritance of his own.

---

35 Hoge Raad 29 April 1994, unpublished.
36 Civil Code.

iii.   It is not permitted to reduce the support to a child under the age of 18
       years, even in the case of misconduct by the child.
iv.   The child has — in a certain way — the right to receive support
       commensurate with the parents' living conditions.

Normally most of the support is given in kind; especially when the child
lives at home with its parents. In the case of divorce, the parent without
parental authority must pay alimony for the child. Financial support is also
given when the child does not live at home because of a legal child- care
order. If the judge has made a decision in the case of child support, the
parent who is obliged to pay support must pay the allowance to the infant
welfare centre. Finally, when the child has lost its parents, or when the
parents have no money, there is a wide range of social benefits available.

Marriages end, new relations start and finish, and the production of children
is increasingly becoming a matter of medical science. Nowadays nothing
seems to be certain in family relationships. In general, the idea that children
should be born in wedlock and should be educated by its parents (especially
by its mother) is no longer held, meaning that the present Family Code is
becoming more and more outdated. Specialists in family law, lawyers,
judges, and professionals are asking for new legislation, especially to
strengthen the rights of parents and children who have (had) family life with
each other, in particular in those cases where there is a difference between
genetic/biological, legal and social parenthood. The law should provide for
a pluriform system with regard to the legal consequences of these different
forms of parenthood.

    In my opinion the first person who should be responsible for child
support is the one who is responsible for the education of the child.
However, if there is a parent (genetic/biological or legal), the educator may
try to get some financial allowance from this parent. Only donors who have
given their sperm (or egg) *anonymously in a special clinic* should be free from
support duties because at the time of donation, he or she did not have the
intention of becoming a parent, but merely of helping out infertile people.

Nowadays children are cared for and socialised in a variety of settings that
are very different from the nuclear family environment. Examples of these
settings are: step-families (either based on a marriage bond or not), children
who live with foster parents, children born and/or brought up in
homosexual/lesbian relationships, children brought up by a (non)-kin single
parent, and children procreated or born through modern insemination
methods.

    The expression 'social parenthood' has been coined in the Dutch language
(sociaal ouderschap) to cover these different ways of bringing up children.

This topic is extremely important but it has not yet been systemised because of the rapid rate of change in this area.

The legal aspects can be subdivided into two parts. These are:

a. Those concerning persons who have decided to procreate by medico-technical means and, moreover, to care for and bring up the child. They have taken "the responsibility to bring the child into the world", and have expressed the determination to become parent(s) in the absence of any reference to a biological bond with the child. In my opinion the wish to have a child should have legal consequences and not merely the fact of having a family life with the child.

b. Those concerning persons who at a later date establish a relationship with the child, whether this relationship is combined with legal or social parenthood or whether it stands alone. They have "taken the responsibility to take a child that has already been born". This category of social parenthood is especially relevant to step-families that are formed by either marriage or cohabitation[37]. I think that the new educator of the child has to respect the rights of the former parent (access and information rights) of the child, unless the parent neglects his or her responsibilities towards the child, or when his custodianship has been taken away by a court ruling because of neglect or abuse of the child.

For these two categories of social parenthood the following questions are relevant:

1. Which legal relationships merit consideration in the case of social parenthood, and what should their underlying principle be? Should a legal connection be made between parental authority and an obligation to provide for the child?
2. Does the child become a party to a legal relationship too, because of the legal relationships binding the social parent(s)?
3. Which (legal) procedures should be followed?
4. Could legal relationships be initiated by the child as well?
5. Do the rules on adoption have to change in such a way that one man or woman can adopt a child or that two unmarried persons (heterosexuals or homosexuals) can adopt a child?

Since these questions are more or less the same in almost all Western countries and since the international dimension of family law has become more and more important, finding the answers to these questions should take place at an international level. Special consideration should be given to the importance of international conventions.

---

37 De Hoog, Presvelou, Cuyvers, 1993, p. 40.

Conclusions

In this contribution I have tried to give a short impression of some changes in Dutch society with regard to new families, and the repercussions which these changing living arrangements have for the father. Because of changing ties between parents and children we have to search for new answers to questions with regard to the role of the father, as well as the role of the mother.

We have seen that until the end of the 19th century the father had a very strong (legal) position. In the Netherlands it even took until 1956 before the legal incapacity of the mother was removed from the Civil Code. Until then she was not allowed to perform legal acts; she always needed her husband's permission. Fortunately, this was the case in the old days. The legal position of (married) women has changed.

On the one hand we can see a strengthening of the legal position of the parent without parental authority (usually the father), but on the other hand we are also confronted with the fact that, usually, the mother still raises the child.

Although a lot of children are still born within the marriage of their parents, many children grow up in single- parent families. Infertility can be reduced by medical advances and surrogate motherhood and adoption. Besides biological/ genetic parents, we now have legal and social parents. Who should be responsible for the child: the mother, the begetter, the legal parent(s), the step-parent, or the foster parents? Should there be a link between parental authority/custodianship and support duties? Does the donor have access rights or information rights? Should these different links between the child and the parents be solved in a pluralistic code?

These problems can be solved in the following way:
The person(s) who is (are) responsible for raising the child is also responsible for supporting the child. In most cases, fortunately, the married parents remain responsible for the support of their child, but if the person who raises the child has no legal ties with his child, he may ask for a financial allowance from the legal parent or begetter. In the case of adoption in the Netherlands new legal ties are created between the educator and the child. This means that only the new parents of the adopted child have support obligations.

In my opinion the most sensitive political and legal questions in relation to the role of the father are:
- To which extent should the social context be brought into line with the legal context?
- Who will defend the rights of the child?

- Should the legal position of the father be strengthened, even if this undermines the legal status of the child's mother?
- What is the legal position of the donor of the child? Does a man, who is merely the begetter of a child (e.g. a donor) have rights to access to his child or a right to be informed (and consulted by the mother) about his child?
- Whose legal position should be stronger: the begetter's or the educator's (e.g. in the case of stepfatherhood)?
- Whose legal position should be stronger: that of the child's legal father or that of the person who raises the child?
- How to support parents and how to encourage parents (especially fathers) to assume their responsibility for the upbringing of their child?
- How to prevent all forms of child abuse and neglect by the parents (especially fathers)?

A discussion about this subject by practitioners, lawyers, administrators and legislators could contribute to finding the answers to these complex problems. This discussion should be held at an international level. Since "families (and fathers) across frontiers"[38] are becoming more common, it is becoming increasingly important that national codes be harmonised.

In my opinion, the father (I do not mean the sperm donor) of a child is not merely a 'mobile sperm bank'. He has *legal rights and duties* with regard to the education and upbringing of the child, the support of the child and the mother of the child. At the same time, he has access and information rights when his marriage or relationship with the mother of his child comes to an end. (Future) fathers should be educated to assume the responsibilities of having a child. Modern laws regarding the legal consequences for the father should take account of his status: is he a genetic or social father?

The public officer should register the affiliation of the child. Legal consequences should only apply for the support duties of the father, unless he is a sperm donor and has given his sperm anonymously in a clinic. Only the name and identity of this father have to be registered so that the child may know its identity (Art. 7 UN Convention on the rights of the child). In other cases the genetic father can be obliged to support his child, but this will have no further consequences. Only in cases where there was family life between the genetic father and the mother of his child (or between him and the child) may he ask for access to his child and for information and consultation about his child.

---

38 The theme of an international conference of the International Society of Family Law that was held in Cardiff from 28 June-2 July 1994.

The man who raises the child (the social father) should be regarded as the legal father. This can have legal consequences for matters such as the name of the child, inheritance law, support, education rights and parental authority or custody.

References

Deech, R. (1993). The rights of fathers: Social and biological concepts of parenthood In J. Getelaar & P. Sarcevic (Eds.), *Parenthood in modern society*. Dordrecht: Martinus Nijhoff Publishers.

De Hoog, Prevelou, Cuypers (1983). *Family arangements and policy in the Netherlands*. NGR, Den Haag, p. 12.

Hoog, C. de (1989). Het gezin: Ontwikkeling en actualiteit. *Tijdschrift Gezin*, 3, 128-148.

Senaeve, P. (1993). The reform of Affiliation law in France and Benelux. In *Parenthood in Modern Society* (p. 96). Martinus Nijhoff.

Carol Smart

Fatherhood and the law: The case of the UK

In this brief comment on Paul Vlaardingerbroek's paper on the legal role of the father in the Netherlands, I shall draw on the English experience to provide a picture of the way in which the 'problem' of fatherhood has been, and is being, addressed in a comparable European country. I shall not comment on the specifics of Dutch law or history (since I am hardly equipped to do so) but instead will move to the more general question of whether, as Vlaardingerbroek suggests, there is a legal solution to some of the problems we both identify.

It is perhaps important to note that I am approaching these questions as a sociologist rather than as a lawyer, and thus my focus and emphasis is necessarily somewhat different. It is therefore important to my perspective to consider the social, historical and political context in which the concern over fatherhood has arisen. It is also part of my approach to theorise the law itself, rather than to see it simply as the application of a remedy to problems which society creates, but which law is seen to transcend. My comment therefore falls into three sections. The first will cover the supposedly modern concern over fatherhood; the second will explore contemporary legal/policy responses to fatherhood in the UK; and the third will raise theoretical issues about law and about diversity which will problematise the idea of legal solutions to social developments.

The 'modern' concern over fatherhood

It is usual to see the so-called crisis (both social and legal) of fatherhood as a fairly recent phenomenon. This crisis is usually identified as inhering in the physical separation of fathers from children, and the consequent emotional problems which follow from this (Dennis & Erdos, 1993). Typically it is presented as a problem which has emerged since the second world war. This periodisation of the problem has meant that it has been linked to other recent social changes. The first of these is the rise in the rate of divorce. Thus divorce itself is seen to be the core of the problem because it is divorce which is seen to separate the father from 'his' children. It is presumed that before the availability of divorce such a separation between father and children was either rare, or that the quality of the presumed contact was good. The second link is made with the rise of unmarried motherhood. Whereas this condition has traditionally been seen as resulting from the irresponsibility of men who have classically been seen as leaving the mother holding the baby, more recently understandings of unmarried motherhood have changed as more women 'appear' willing to enter into this condition. Unmarried motherhood has thus been reinterpreted as women's selfishness rather than men's, and also as a sign that women are trying to separate men from their biological offspring. The third link is made with the rise of the second wave of the Women's Movement. This linkage is seen to work in various ways. Typically it might be argued that women have taken over men's roles as income providers thus emasculating them whilst refusing to allow them to be more involved with their children. Or it is argued that women think that they have little need of men and thus, selfishly, think that families (i.e. children too) can do without them.

In the popular imagination all of these three elements can be laid at the door of women who are seen as upsetting a family structure which once worked perfectly adequately. This structuring of the issues in turn depicts men or fathers as the victims of social processes which they never wanted and of legal systems which have mistakenly assumed that it was women who needed the safeguards and protections. Of course, one cannot deny the historical accuracy of divorce rates, illegitimacy rates and the existence of the women's movement. My argument rather, is with the way that this history of events starts its account at a particular moment and the way that it excludes other crucial developments which provide a different understanding of this history. Thus, I would argue that it is vital to start our history of fatherhood somewhat earlier.

A slightly longer historical perspective allows us to see that the father's position, in law at least, begins to change in the mid nineteenth century. Until this period the father enjoys what has been called absolute father right. That is to say that the married father was the sole legal guardian of his children and the wife had no rights at all as a mother. This situation began to change under pressure for reform which came from philanthropic interventions into the working class family. This concern was part of the bourgeois desire to reform the working class family, or perhaps more accurately, one might say the desire to turn working class households into institutions which were recognisably ideological families (see Barrett &

McIntosh, 1982). Thus we can see interventions which not only attempted to turn biological mothers into an approximation of the middle class ideal of motherhood, but also attempts (through mothers) to transform biological fathers into social fathers. This is part of Donzelot's (1979) thesis in which he depicts the domestication of the working class family and the working class husband. The aim of philanthropists was to decrease the working man's use of alcohol and bring him back from the pub and the streets into the home. In so doing it was surmised that he would bring more of his income home with him to benefit his family. For this strategy to work, the mother had to make the home more appealing to him and thus her housewifely skills were to be improved. But this, in turn, required her to be at home, creating for her a greater economic dependence on her husband.

The working class father/husband of the nineteenth and early twentieth century has been depicted as brutal, violent, uncaring and as inflicting multiple pregnancies upon his wife regardless of the consequences and uncaring as to whether these children could be adequately supported. But most sociologies of the family see him as having changed considerably by the mid twentieth century (Young & Willmott, 1957; 1973). Put simply, the question we need to consider is for whose benefit were these changes seen as desirable? Certainly there was a Women's Movement at this time which strove to improve conditions for women. Frances Power Cobbe, for example, campaigned for a change in the law which would allow poor women to leave their violent husbands and to take their children (under 7 years of age) with them if he was found guilty of assault (Brophy & Smart, 1985). But equally, Anna Martin who was working for benefits for mothers at the turn of the century, made it plain that conditions for women in the family must improve *in order that* women could better raise their children (Clarke et al., 1987). There was therefore a very strong argument which suggested that the working class father was a danger to his children and that, even if he was not directly cruel to his children, his cruelty and neglect towards his wife impacted upon the children and hence the ultimate state of the family and the nation.

This history of the working class father should allow us to understand the changing nature of fatherhood somewhat differently. In particular we should start to become aware of a third force in the developments we can perceive. This third force is social work with its primary concern for children rather than women. It is therefore the rise of the welfare principle which is so crucial to the changes in fatherhood in the last century and a half. Whilst the Women's Movement has been significant, the main justification for changes to the status of men within the family has been the motive of child protection.

Even the bourgeois father was not exempt from this movement. Challenges to his authority which began also in the mid nineteenth century with Caroline Norton's campaign for access to her children on separation from her husband, rested on the claims of mother-love and how this was essential for the child of tender years (Norton, 1982, orig. 1854). Put briefly therefore, it is possible to argue that fatherhood has been a matter of social concern and legislative interference, since at least 1850. Our worry about fatherhood is therefore far from new, even if it now takes a slightly different form. Moreover, the concern over fatherhood has been generated by the changing status of childhood rather than the changing status of women. Although I appreciate that it is to oversimplify history to separate out women and children in quite such a clear cut fashion, I think it is important to do so to correct the modern, political rewriting of history which suggests that historical developments can be accounted for by reference solely to an accumulation of women's rights. Such a history is also important in order to enable us to counter the current political idealisation of family life before the 1960s which seems to construct a perfect and unchanging family which existed continuously until the errors of the Women's Movement and permissiveness undermined a perfectly satisfactory social institution.

Contemporary legal/policy responses to the crisis in fatherhood in the UK

In this section I shall concentrate on two major policy developments in the UK since 1989. These developments are encapsulated in the 1989 Children Act and the 1991 Child Support Act. The former, I would suggest, reflects a continuation of the philanthropic concern that men should be 'good' fathers and that good fathering is in the interests of children. The latter reflects the equally long-standing concern that men should be obliged to support their offspring financially and that mechanisms should be created to induce economic responsibility.

The Children Act 1989

As the title of this Act suggests, its main concern is with the welfare of the child. In itself this is not new, but what is new is the re-formulation of what constitutes welfare. Whilst, for example, the welfare of the child on divorce in the 1970s in the UK was understood to be compatible with a clean break divorce and the rapid remarriage of the custodial parent (inevitably the mother), by the 1990s the welfare of the child on divorce had become associated with continuing contact with a biological father, even to the detriment of the stability of the reconstituted family. The private law provisions of this Act sought to maintain contact between father and child at all costs. To achieve this the legal concept of 'custody' was abolished and it is now almost impossible for one parent to deprive the other of their parental rights/responsibilities. In order that fathers should not be alienated by a legal system which seemed only to want to get them out of the way, the new legislation seeks to minimise the grounds for disputes by removing the legal basis of arguments over custody and by minimising the interference by courts and judges. Parents are encouraged to negotiate between themselves or (although this is not part of the legislation) with mediators.

This legislative move should be seen in the context of the growing fear of what happens to children if they 'lose' a father. The fear is the presumption of a rise in delinquency and the ever deepening cycle of deprivation. Fathers then have come to symbolise stability and order in family life when once they symbolised disruption and danger. However, the ultimate goal of this legislation is not dissimilar to legislation in earlier times which sought to make the biological father into a social father rather than an absentee sperm donor.

The Child Support Act 1991
This legislation constructs the father in a slightly different form. Here he is the absentee father who refuses to acknowledge his financial responsibilities. This legislation is not interested in questions of the quality of care provided by an absent father but only with his ability to pay child support. The Act set up a huge machinery which will eventually be the equivalent in size of the Inland Revenue. This machinery is gradually meant to replace the courts and private financial settlements in preference for a standard tariff of payments for a father (or non residential mother) to pay for the upkeep of his children.

The setting up of the Child Support Agency met with organised resistance from fathers and second families and the Government has been forced to soften some of its provisions and powers (DSS 1995). Much of this resistance came from middle class fathers who found themselves depicted in the way that working class fathers had so often been, namely as irresponsible and disreputable. Moreover they were resistant to the idea that the poverty which often follows family breakdown should be more evenly distributed between lone mothers and absent fathers.

These two pieces of legislation are deploying two rather different methods to continue the long-standing tradition of trying to make men into 'good' fathers. One tries to keep the father involved at an emotional level through encouragement and avoidance of conflict, the other tries to keep him involved financially through strict regulatory controls. But each has a rather different idea of what the 'good' father is. For the Children Act the good father is one who sees his children and participates in their care. For the

Child Support Act the good father is one who pays for his first children even at the expense of his second family. In this second model it is clear that the overall principle of the welfare of the child is not paramount, since the well-being of the first children is placed above the well-being of the second cohort. Moreover, lone mothers' benefits are cut (and thus income to children is cut) if they will not assist the Agency. At the same time, in the UK there are no other social policy developments occurring which would make it more possible for fathers to actively care for children. The courts, the benefit system and the pension system all operate to keep men in full time employment (if they are in employment at all). There have therefore been no structural changes which would substantially alter how fatherhood works. Although mothers are now increasingly to be found in the labour market there is little evidence that men are willingly leaving the labour market to engage in caring behaviour. Amongst those unwillingly unemployed the dominant policy concern is that they might provide a poor role model for sons rather than this being seen as an opportunity to engage in better fathering behaviour.

The outcome of these new strategies is unlikely to produce clear changes in fathering or in the opportunities to father in the social sense. Their impact is perhaps more likely to make the position of mothers worse without substantially improving or changing the institution of fatherhood. The position of the mother is worsened because beyond the point of divorce she must now manage, sustain and organise the ongoing relationship between her children and their father (even under conditions where he has been extremely violent). Moreover, early indications of the impact of the Child Support Act suggest that fathers blame their former partners for the financial demands made by the Child Support Agency and that the requirement for financial support has led to some fathers demanding contact and staying contact with their children to reduce the amount of support they must pay. This brings me to the final section of my comment.

Theorising law's relationship to fathers

Feminist theories of law have, perhaps, tended to see the relationship between law and fathers/men in one of two ways. The first way has presumed that the law has largely served the interests of men. The second way has focused more on legal reasoning and logic and has seen the way the law operates as reflecting masculine values and modes of reasoning. There is value in both of these approaches but we must be cautious of elevating either or both to the level of total explanations of the law (Smart, 1995). In particular such analyses seem inadequate when we study modern family law with its central focus on children rather than either men or women, and where men too are subject to disciplinary strategies. Thus we must take other considerations and/or ways of theorising law into account.

The additional consideration we must include is the concept of diversity. Feminist work has argued for a long time for the recognition of the diversity of women. We have been slower to recognise the diversity of men along lines of class, ethnicity, religion, region and so on. Thus we must realise that working class men have been the subject of disciplinary strategies for a long time. We should also recognise that an intervention like the Child Support Act might have a very different impact on informal arrangements for child support in Afro-Caribbean households than in white middle class households. In the former it may worsen considerably the position of the mother and children, whilst in the latter her financial position might be considerably improved. There is unlikely, therefore, to be a unitary outcome which suits all men or disadvantages all women.

We need also to theorise law differently. I have argued elsewhere (Smart, 1995) that we should see law as a gendering strategy. By this I mean that law does not work inexorably to suit the interests of one gender over another, but that it does operate to retain distinctions between the genders and to 'fix' gender difference into certain kinds of forms. Thus law is not so much about giving to men and taking form women, or vice versa, but about confirming certain gender differences, some of which advantage either men or women. This means we cannot know automatically in advance, so to speak, that everything law does will work in one way, or even that the strategies of law will be uni-directional.

Once we begin to approach law in this more fluid way we can also begin to see that it may not be a very reliable tool in the object of social engineering. Thus it is here that I take issue with Vlaardingerbroek's paper. In his final paragraph he suggests that a discussion about this subject by practitioners, lawyers, administrators and legislators may contribute to finding the right answers for these complex problems. To this I would say that these very people have been engaged in such discussions since at least 1850 and, manifestly, as a group they are not able to find the solution to social problems and developments. But my criticism of this strategy is not so much based on the fact that it has so far failed to be successful, but rather because
1. such moves merely empower experts and technocrats and contributes to the legalisation of everyday life, and
2. law is not a *solution* to social processes, but part of the social process.
Thus, in the first instance I would take a Foucaultian perspective on the question of giving professionals such power over daily life. We can interpret such moves as the extension of surveillance and regulation, in the name of

liberal, professional benevolence. It is precisely such forms of control that community groups active in the domains of health, ecology, education and planning are increasingly struggling against. Such liberal benevolence can be seen as profoundly anti-democratic. In the second instance, I would argue most strenuously that law is a social process, like other social processes. It does not float above the throng in an uncontaminated fashion. Law is as much part of the problem as part of the solution. Just as we have come to recognise that medicine does not simply 'cure' disease, but also creates disease states and the conditions under which disease changes, but is never eradicated, so we must recognise that law is not an instrument but a social relationship. If we do this we can reposition law in our understanding of social change. This will not prevent us from positing legal changes and using legal strategies where they are suitable, but it will mean that we need also to think beyond legal strategies and interventions, especially if legal strategies tend to harmonise and homogenise a society which we must increasingly recognise as being diverse and multi-cultural.

References

Barrett, M. & McIntosh, M. (1982). *The anti-social family*, London: Verso.

Brophy, J. & Smart, C. (Eds.) (1985). *Women in law*. London: Routledge and Kegan Paul.

Clarke, J., Cochrane, A. & Smart, C. (1987). *Ideologies of welfare*. London: Hutchinson.

Dennis, N. & Erdos, G. (1993). *Families without fatherhood* (2nd Ed.). London: Institute of Economic Affairs.

Department of Social Security (1985). *Improving child support*. London: DSS.

Donzelot, J. (1979). *The policing of families*. London: Hutchinson.

Norton, C. (1982). *Caroline Norton's defence.*Chicago: Academy. Originally 1854.

Smart, C. (1995). *Law, crime and sexuality*. London: SAGE.

Young, M. & Willmott, P. (1957). *Family and Kinship in East London*. London: Routledge and Kegan Paul.

Young, M. & Willmott, P. (1973). *The symmetrical family*. London: Routledge and Kegan Paul.

6

Paternal influences on child development

Michael Lamb

Over the last forty years, a considerable number of researchers have studied paternal influences on child development. Because this paper appears in the context of a number of reports by sociologists and demographers concerned with the changing nature of fatherhood in modern industrialised societies, however, my review of the evidence is intentionally brief and incomplete. Instead of reviewing the design, results, and flaws of specific studies, my goal is to summarise in broad strokes the results of these studies and the emergent portrait of paternal influences they have helped us paint. More thorough reviews of the literature are currently being compiled for the third edition of *The role of the father in child development* (Lamb, in press) to which readers are referred for the most recent and complete information. Several earlier books may also prove useful (Adams, Milner & Schrepf, 1984; Biller, 1993; Bozett & Hanson, 1991; Bronstein & Cowan, 1988; Lamb, 1976, 1981c, 1986, 1987).

In summarising and synthesising the research on paternal influences, I find it helpful to distinguish among five genres or research traditions, each of which has contributed in important ways to our understanding of paternal influences. I will discuss these five research paradigms roughly in the chronological sequence in which each achieved prominence. In so doing, I do not wish to imply that any of these genres has become old-fashioned or outdated. Rather, I have grouped the studies in this fashion primarily as a means of facilitating the presentation of the most important findings and insights they have spawned.

Correlational studies

I first consider studies concerned with the search for correlations between paternal and filial characteristics. This strategy was adopted in many of the earliest studies of paternal influences, the vast majority of which were focused on sex-role development, especially in sons (for reviews see Biller, 1971, 1993; Lamb, 1976, 1981b). This is understandable, since many of these studies were conducted in the years between the 1940s and the early 1960s when the father's role as a sex-role model was considered most important. The design of these early studies was quite simple: The researchers assessed masculinity in fathers and in sons, and then determined how strongly the two sets of scores were correlated. To the great surprise of most researchers, there was no consistent correlation between the two constructs, a puzzling finding because it seemed to violate a guiding assumption about the crucial function served by fathers. If fathers did not make their boys into men, what role did they really serve?

It took a while for psychologists to realise that their guiding assumption might be the problem, for they had failed to ask: Why should boys *want to be like* their fathers? Presumably they should only want to resemble fathers whom they liked and respected, and with whom their relationships were warm and positive. In fact, the quality of father-son relationships proved to be a crucial mediating variable: When the relationships between masculine fathers and their sons was good, the boys were indeed more masculine. Subsequent research suggested that, so far as the development of filial masculinity was concerned, the quality of the father-child relationships was most important, whereas the masculinity of the father was rather unimportant (Mussen & Rutherford, 1963; Payne & Mussen, 1956; Sears, Maccoby & Levin, 1957). Boys seemed to conform to the sex-role standards of their culture when their relationships with their fathers were warm, regardless of how 'masculine' the fathers were. We might thus expect that the effects of close father-son relationships have changed over the last 25 years, during which cultural preferences for and expectations of male behaviour have changed also. Since androgyny seems to be the contemporary goal, for example, we might expect warm fathers who have close relationships with their children to have more androgynous sons that other fathers today (Baruch & Barnett, 1983; Radin, 1978; Radin & Sagi, 1982) just as similarly close relationships potentiated the development of masculine sons in times and cultures which value traditional masculinity.

As far as paternal influences on sex-role development are concerned, it appears that the father's masculinity is much less important than his warmth and the closeness and nature of the father-son relationship. This is an interesting and important finding because warmth and intimacy have traditionally been seen as feminine characteristics. Thus 'feminine' characteristics of the father — his warmth and nurturance — seem to be associated with better adjustment in sons, at least to the extent that adjustment is defined in terms of sex role[1]. A similar conclusion is

---

1   This is a questionable assumption, particularly given the ways in which sex roles are usually operationalized in the research literature. Readers are referred to Pleck (1981) and Lamb et al. (1985) for further discussion of these issues, which are not critical to the

suggested by research on other aspects of psychosocial adjustment: Paternal warmth or closeness is advantageous, whereas paternal masculinity appears to be irrelevant (Biller, 1971; Lamb, 1981b).

Similar findings have been obtained in studies concerned with paternal influences on achievement (Radin, 1981). Initially, the assumption was that highly achieving fathers would foster achievement motivation in their sons; fathers were the family members who exemplified achievement in the real world and their sons would surely want to emulate them in this regard. Once more, it soon became clear that the fathers' warmth, closeness, and involvement were more important than their professional success or achievement motivation; fathers who were warm tended to have competent and achievement-oriented sons (Radin, 1981). The same characteristics are important with regard to maternal influences on children's achievement, again implying that fathers influence children not by virtue of 'male' characteristics (like masculinity) but by virtue of nurturant personal and social characteristics.

In sum, across these three areas of development — sex-role development, achievement, and psychosocial adjustment — children seem better off when relationships with their fathers are close and warm. In general, the same is true in the case of mothers, and children who have close relationships with both parents benefit greatly. As far as influences on children are concerned, very little about the gender of the parent seems to be distinctly important. The characteristics of the father as a parent rather than the characteristics of the father as a man appear to be most significant.

Studies of father absence

While the whole body of research that is here termed 'correlational' was burgeoning in the 1950s, another body of literature was developing in parallel. This involved investigations in which researchers tried to understand the father's role by studying families without fathers. The assumption was that, by comparing the behaviour and personalities of children raised with and without fathers, one could -essentially by a process of subtraction- estimate what sort of influence fathers typically had on children's development. The early father-absence and correlational studies were conducted in roughly the same era; not surprisingly, the outcomes studied were very similar and the results were similar in many ways as well. In the case of the father-absence studies, the results also appeared consistent with popular assumptions, although this was and remains a voluminous and

---

argument being developed here.

controversial literature (see Adams et al., 1984; Biller, 1974, 1993; Herzog & Sudia, 1973; Whitehead, 1993 for reviews). In the present context, suffice it to say that boys growing up without fathers seemed to have 'problems' in the areas of sex-role and gender-identity development, school performance, psychosocial adjustment, and perhaps in the control of aggression.

Two related issues arising from father-absence research must be addressed, however. First, even when researchers accept the conclusion that there are differences between children raised in families with the father present and those raised in families with the father absent, they must ask *why* those differences exist and how they should be interpreted. Second, it is important to remember that the existence of group differences between, say, 100 boys growing up without fathers and 100 boys growing up with fathers does not mean that every child growing up without a father has problems in at least some of the areas just mentioned, or that all boys whose fathers live at home develop normatively. One cannot reach conclusions about the status of individuals from data concerning groups simply because there is great within-group heterogeneity. This forces us to ask why such heterogeneity exists among children in father-absent families: Why do some boys appear to suffer deleterious consequences as a result of father absence, while others do not? More broadly, the question is: What is it about the father-absence context that makes for group differences between children in father-absent and father-present contexts, and what accounts for the impressive within-group variance?

Researchers and theorists first sought to explain the effects of father absence by noting the absence of male sex-role models in single-parent families. In the absence of a masculine parental model, it was assumed that boys could not acquire strong masculine identities or sex roles and would not have models of achievement with which to identify (Biller, 1974, 1993). The validity of this interpretation is weakened by the fact that many boys without fathers seem to develop quite normally so far as sex-role development and achievement are concerned. Clearly, some factors other than the absence of a male sex-role model may be at least as important as (if not much more important than) the availability of a sex-role model in mediating the effects of father absence on child development. What might these factors be?

First, there is the absence of a coparent — someone to help out with child care, and to take over when one parent needs a break from the incessant demands of the children (Maccoby, 1977). In single-parent families, children consistently do better when they are able to maintain meaningful relationships with both parents (e.g., Emery, 1982; Guidubaldi & Perry, 1985; Hess & Camara, 1979; Hetherington, Cox & Cox, 1982, 1985; Kurdek, 1988; Wallerstein & Kelly, 1980). Second, there is the economic stress that frequently accompanies single motherhood (Pearson & Thoennes, 1990). The median and mean incomes of single women who head households are significantly lower than in any other group of families, and the disparity is even larger when one considers per capita income rather than household income (Glick & Norton, 1979). Third, the tremendous economic stress experienced by single mothers is accompanied by emotional stress occasioned by a degree of social isolation and continuing (though diminished) social disapproval of single or divorced mothers and children (Hetherington et al., 1982). Lastly, there are the cancerous effects of predivorce and postdivorce marital conflict. This may be an especially important issue because there can be little doubt that children suffer when there is hostility or conflict in the family (Amato, 1993; Amato & Keith, 1991; Lamb, 1981b; Rutter, 1973, 1979). Since most single parent families are produced by divorce and since divorce is often preceded and accompanied by periods of overt and covert spousal hostility, parental conflict may play a major role in explaining the problems of fatherless children. By contrast, fatherless children who have good relationships with both parents before and after divorce tend to be better adjusted than those who do not, even when there is conflict between the parents (Hess & Camara, 1979).

In sum, the evidence suggests that father absence may be harmful not necessarily because a sex-role model is absent, but because many aspects of the father's role — economic, social, emotional — go unfilled or inappropriately filled. Recognition of the father's multiple roles as breadwinner, parent, and emotional partner is essential in understanding how fathers influence children's development.

Descriptive studies of fathers and children

Partly in reaction to research designed to describe fathers' influences by studying what happens in their absence, a number of researchers initiated research in the mid-1970s designed to describe, often by detailed observation and sometimes also by detailed maternal and paternal reports, the nature and extent of paternal involvement with children. These studies have consistently shown that fathers spend much less time with their children then mothers do. In two-parent families in which the mother is unemployed, fathers spend about 20 to 25 percent as much time as mothers do in direct interaction or engagement with their children, and about a third as much time being accessible to their children (Lamb, Pleck, Charnov & Levine, 1987; Pleck, 1983). The largest discrepancy between paternal and maternal involvement is in the area of responsibility. Many studies show that fathers assume essentially no responsibility (as defined by participation in key decisions, availability at short notice, involvement in the care of sick children, management and selection of alternative child care, etc.) for their children's care or rearing. In two-parent families with employed mothers, the levels of paternal engagement and accessibility are both substantially higher than in families with unemployed mothers (Lamb et al., 1987; Pleck, 1983). In such families, paternal involvement in direct interaction and accessibility averages 33 percent and 65 percent of the relevant figures for mothers, respectively. As far as responsibility is concerned, however, there is no evidence that maternal employment has any effect on the level of paternal involvement. Even when both mothers and fathers are employed 30 or more hours per week, the amount of responsibility assumed by fathers appears as negligible as when mothers are unemployed.

In light of the controversies that have arisen on this score, it is worth noting that fathers do not spend more time interacting with their children when mothers are employed; rather the proportions just cited go up because mothers are doing less. Thus, fathers are *proportionally* more involved when mothers are employed, even though the extent of their involvement, in absolute terms, does not change to any meaningful extent. The unfortunate controversies in this area appear attributable to a confusion between proportional figures and absolute figures.

Both observational and survey data also suggest that mothers and fathers engage in rather different types of interaction with their children (Goldman & Goldman, 1983; Lamb, 1981a, 1981b). These studies have consistently shown that fathers tend to specialise in play, while mothers 'specialise' in caretaking and nurturance, especially (but not only) in relation to infants. Although such findings have been repeated on multiple occasions and thus seem quite reliable, the results have often been misrepresented. Compared with mothers, fathers indeed spend a greater proportion of their time with children engaged in play, but they still spend a small proportion of their time in play. In absolute terms, most studies suggest that mothers play with their children more than fathers do, but because play is more prominent in father-child interaction (particularly boisterous, stimulating, emotionally-arousing play), paternal playfulness and relative novelty may help make fathers especially salient to their children. This enhanced salience may increase fathers' influence beyond what would be expected based on the amount of time they spend with their children.

Increased paternal involvement

We must now consider several studies concerned with the effects of increased paternal involvement on children. In these studies, researchers have compared the status of children in 'traditional' families with that of children whose fathers either share in or take primary responsibility for child care (Lamb, Pleck & Levine, 1985; Russell, 1983, 1986). The effects of increased paternal involvement have been addressed in several major studies, and the results have been remarkable consistent with respect to infants and preschool-aged children whose fathers are responsible for at least 40 percent to 45 percent of the within family child care. Children with highly involved fathers are characterised by increased cognitive competence, increased empathy, less sex-stereotyped beliefs and a more internal locus of control (Pruett, 1983, 1985; Radin, 1982; Radin & Sagi, 1982; Sagi, 1982). Again the question that has to be asked is "*Why* do these sorts of differences occur?"

Three factors are probably important in this regard (Lamb et al., 1985). First, when parents assume less sex-stereotyped roles, their children have less sex-stereotyped attitudes themselves about male and female roles. Second, particularly in the area of cognitive competence, these children may benefit from having two highly involved parents rather than just one. This assures them the diversity of stimulation that comes from interacting with people who have different behavioural styles. A third important issue has to do with the family context in which these children are raised. In each of the studies cited above, a high degree of paternal involvement made it possible for both parents to do what was rewarding and fulfilling for them. It allowed fathers to satisfy their desires for closeness to their children while permitting mothers to have adequately close relationships with their children and to pursue career goals. In other words, increased paternal involvement may have made both parents feel much more fulfilled. As a result, the relationships were probably much warmer and richer than might otherwise have been the case. One can speculate that the benefits obtained by children with highly involved fathers is largely attributable to the fact that the high levels of paternal involvement created family contexts in which the parents felt good about their marriage and the child care arrangements they had been able to work out.

In all of these studies, fathers were highly involved in child care because both they and their partners desired this. The effects on children appear quite different when fathers are forced to become involved, perhaps by being laid off from work while their partners are able to obtain or maintain their employment (Johnson & Abramovitch, 1985). In such circumstances, wives might resent the fact that their husbands cannot support their families while husbands resent having to do 'women's work' with the children when they really want to be 'out there' earning a living and supporting their families (see Johnson & Abramovitch, 1988; Russell, 1983). Not surprisingly, this constellation of factors appears to have adverse effects on children, just as the same degree of involvement has positive effects when the circumstances are more benign. The key point is that the extent of paternal involvement may be much less significant (so far as the effects on children are concerned) than are the reasons for high involvement and the parents' evaluation of that level of involvement. In sum, the effects of increased involvement may have more to do with the context than with father involvement per se. I suspect that it matters less who is at home than how that person feels about being at home, for the person's feelings will colour the way he or she behaves with the children. Parental behaviour is also influenced by the partner's feelings about the arrangement: Both parents' emotional states affect the family dynamics.

Children of divorce

In a conceptual and empirical extension of research on the effects of father absence, many researchers initiated studies in the early 1980s designed to explore more carefully the ways in which divorce and the transition to fatherlessness might influence children's development. These studies have underscored the many ways in which paternal absence influences children. As noted earlier, children of divorce are affected by the conflict that often precedes the marital separation, they are affected by the declining economic circumstances that often follow the divorce, they are affected by the social and emotional isolation and psychosocial distress of their single mothers, and they are affected by the perceived, and often actual, abandonment by one of their parents (see Thompson, 1986, 1994 for reviews). They also lack male sex role models, of course, and this was once viewed as the most important of the factors involved in explaining the effects of divorce on children. Most of the research conducted to date, however, would suggest that the absence of a male gender model is much less important in explaining the effects of divorce than are these other broader implications of paternal absence. Such findings underscore the diverse roles that fathers play in the family and in their children's lives.

Conclusion

The five genres and waves of research described here together paint a remarkably consistent picture. In addition, the results of each of these research paradigms contribute one or more important insights to our understanding of paternal influences. In this section, I briefly summarise the five that I consider to be the most important.

First, by and large fathers and mothers seem to influence their children in similar rather than dissimilar ways. Contrary to the expectations of many psychologists, including myself, who have studied paternal influences on children, the differences between mothers and fathers appear much less important than the similarities. Not only does the anatomy or description of mothering largely resemble the description of fathering (particularly the version of involved fathering that has become increasingly prominent in the late 20th century) but the mechanisms and means by which fathers influence their children appear very similar to those that mediate maternal influences on children. Stated differently, students of socialisation have consistently found that parental warmth, nurturance, and closeness are associated with positive child outcomes regardless of whether the parent or adult involved is a mother or a father. The important dimensions of parental influence are those that have to do with parental characteristics rather than gender-related characteristics.

Second, as research has unfolded, psychologists have been forced to conclude that the characteristics of individual fathers-such as their masculinity, intellect, and even their warmth — are much less important, formatively speaking, than are the characteristics of the relationships that they have established with their children. Children who have secure, supportive, reciprocal, and sensitive relationships with their parents are much more likely to be well-adjusted psychologically than individuals whose relationships with their parents — mothers or fathers — are less satisfying. Likewise, the amount of time that fathers and children spend together is probably much less important than what they do with that time and how fathers, mothers, children, and other important people in their lives perceive and evaluate the father-child relationship.

Third, we have come to see that individual relationships are in fact less influential than the family context. Fathers must thus be viewed in the broader familial context; positive paternal influences are more likely to occur not only when there are supportive father-child relationships, but when the fathers' relationships with their partners, and presumably other children, establish a positive familial context. The absence of familial hostility is the most consistent correlate of child adjustment, whereas marital conflict is the most consistent and reliable correlate of child maladjustment.

Fourth, these factors all underscore the fact that fathers play multiple roles in the family and that their success in these diverse roles all influence the way in which they affect their children's development and adjustment. Fathers have beneficial effects on their children when they have supportive and nurturant relationships with them, as well as with their siblings, when they are competent and feel fulfilled as breadwinners, when they are successful and supportive partners, and so on.

Fifth, the nature of paternal influences may vary substantially depending on individual and cultural values. A classic example of this can be found in the literature on sex-role development. As a result of cultural changes, the assumed sex-role goals for boys and girls have changed, and this has produced changes in the effects of father involvement on children. In the 1950s, gender-appropriate masculinity or femininity was the desired goal; today androgyny or sex-role flexibility is desired. And whereas father involvement in the 1950s seemed to be associated with greater masculinity in boys, it is associated today with less sex-stereotyped sex-role standards in both boys and girls. Influence patterns also vary substantially depending on social factors that define the meaning of father involvement for children in particular families in particular social milieus. More generally, this underscores the relative importance of the different paternal functions or roles varies across familial, subcultural, cultural, and, of course, historical contexts. There is no single 'father's role' to which all fathers should aspire.

Rather, a successful father, as defined in terms of his children's development, is one whose role performance matches the demands and prescriptions of his sociocultural and familial context. This means that high paternal involvement may have positive effects in some circumstances and negative effects in others. The same is true of low paternal involvement.

References

Adams, P.L., Milner, J.R. & Schrepf, N.A. (1984). *Fatherless children*. New York: Wiley.

Amato, P.R. (1993). Children's adjustment to divorce: Theories, hypotheses, and empirical support. *Journal of Marriage and the Family, 55*, 23-38.

Amato, P.R. & Keith, B. (1991). Parental divorce and the wellbeing of children: A meta-analysis. *Psychological Bulletin, 110*, 26-46.

Baruch, G.K. & Barnett, R.C. (1983). *Correlates of fathers' participation in family work: A technical report*. Wellesley, MA: Wellesley College Center for Research on Women.

Biller, H.B. (1971). *Father child, and sex role*. Lexington, MA: Heath.

Biller, H.B. (1974). *Paternal deprivation: Family, school, sexuality, and society*. Lexington, MA: Heath.

Biller, H.B. (1981). Father absence, divorce, and personality development. In M.E. Lamb (Ed.), *The role of the father in child development* (Second edition, pp. 489-552). New York: Wiley.

Biller, H.B. (1993). *Fathers and families*. Westport, CT: Auburn House.

Bozett, F.W. & Hanson, S.M.H. (Eds.) (1991). *Fatherhood and families in cultural context*. New York: Springer.

Bronstein, P. & Cowan, C.P. (Eds.) (1988). *Fatherhood today*. New York: Wiley.

Emery, R.E. (1982). Interparental conflict and the children of discord and divorce. *Psychological Bulletin, 92*, 310-330.

Glick, P.C. & Norton, A.J. (1979). Marrying, divorcing, and living together in the U.S. today. *Population Bulletin, 32*(5, whole issue).

Goldman, J.D.G. & Goldman, R.J. (1983). Children's perceptions of parents and their roles: A cross-national study in Australia, England, North America, and Sweden. *Sex Roles, 9*, 791-812.

Guidubaldi, J. & Perry, J.D. (1985). Divorce and mental health sequelae for children: A two-year follow-up of a nationwide sample. *Journal of the American Academy of Child Psychiatry, 24,* 531-537.

Herzog, R. & Sudia, C.E. (1973). Children in fatherless families. In B.M. Caldwell & H.N. Ricciuti (Eds.), *Review of child development research* (Vol. 3, pp. 141-232). Chicago: University of Chicago Press.

Hess, R.D. & Camara, K.A. (1979). Post-divorce family relationships as mediating factors in the consequences of divorce for children. *Journal of Social Issues, 35,* 79-96.

Hetherington, E.M., Cox, M. & Cox, R. (1982). Effects of divorce on parents and children. In M.E. Lamb (Ed.), *Nontraditional families* (pp. 233-288). Hillsdale, NJ: Erlbaum.

Hetherington, E.M., Cox, M. & Cox, R. (1985). Long-term effects of divorce and remarriage on the adjustment of children. *Journal of the American Academy of Child Psychiatry, 24,* 518-530.

Johnson, L.C. & Abramovitch, R. (1985). *Unemployed fathers: Parenting in a changing labour market.* Toronto: Social Planning Council.

Johnson, L.C. & Abramovitch, R. (1988). Parental unemployment and family life. In A. Pence (Ed.), *Ecological research with children and families: From concepts to methodology* (pp. 49-75). New York: Teachers College Press.

Kurdek, L.A. (1988). Custodial mothers' perceptions of visitation and payment for child support by noncustodial fathers in families with low and high levels of preseparation interparent conflict. *Journal of Applied Developmental Psychology.*

Lamb, M.E. (Ed.) (1976). *The role of the father in child development.* New York: Wiley.

Lamb, M.E. (1981a). The development of father-infant relationships. In M.E. Lamb (Ed.), *The role of the father in child development* (Revised edition, pp. 459-488). New York: Wiley.

Lamb, M.E. (1981b). Fathers and child development: An integrative overview. In M.E. Lamb (Ed.), *The role of the father in child development* (Revised edition, pp. 1-70). New York: Wiley.

Lamb, M.E. (Ed.) (1981c). *The role of the father in child development* (Revised edition). New York: Wiley.

Lamb, M.E. (Ed.) (1986). *The father's role: Applied perspectives.* New York: Wiley.

Lamb, M.E. (Ed.) (1987). *The father's role: Cross-cultural perspectives.* Hillsdale, NJ: Erlbaum.

Lamb, M.E. (in press). *The role of the father in child development* (3rd ed.). New York: Wiley.

Lamb, M.E., Pleck, J.H. & Levine, J.A. (1985). The role of the father in child development: The effects of increased paternal involvement. In B.B. Lahey

& A.E. Kazdin (Eds.), *Advances in clinical child psychology* (Vol. 8, pp. 229-266). New York: Plenum.

Lamb, M.E., Pleck, J.H., Charnov, E.L. & Levine, J.A. (1987). A biosocial perspective on paternal behavior and involvement. In J.B. Lancaster, J. Altmann, A.S. Rossi & L.R. Sherrod (Eds.), *Parenting across the lifespan: Biosocial perspectives* (pp. 111-142). Hawthorne, NY: Aldine.

Maccoby, E.E. (1977, September). *Current changes in the family and their impact upon the socialization of children.* Paper presented to American Sociological Association, Chicago.

Mussen, P.H. & Rutherford, E. (1963). Parent-child relations and parental personality in relation to young children's sex-role preferences. *Child Development, 34,* 589-607.

Payne, D.E. & Mussen, P.H. (1956). Parent-child relations and father identification among adolescent boys. *Journal of Abnormal and Social Psychology, 52,* 358-362.

Pearsson, J. & Theonnes, N. (1990). Custody after divorce: Demographic and attitudinal patterns. *American Journal of Orthopsychiatry, 60,* 233-249.

Pleck, J.H. (1981). *The myth of masculinity.* Cambridge, MA: MIT Press.

Pleck, J.H. (1983). Husbands' paid work and family roles: Current research issues. In H. Lopata & J.H. Pleck (Eds.), *Research in the interweave of social roles (Vol. 3), Families and jobs.* Greenwich, CT: JAI Press.

Popenoe, D. (1989). The family transformed. *Family Affairs, 2* (23), 1-5.

Pruett, K.D. (1983). Infants of primary nurturing fathers. *Psychoanalytic Study of the Child, 38,* 257-277.8

Pruett, K.D. (1985). Children of the fathermothers: Infants of primary nurturing fathers. In J.D. Call, E. Galenson & R.L. Tyson (Eds.), *Frontiers of infant psychiatry* (Vol. II, pp. 375-380). New York: Basic Books.

Radin, N. (1981). The role of the father in cognitive, academic, and intellectual development. In M.E. Lamb (Ed.), *The role of the father in child development* (Revised edition, pp. 379-428). New York: Wiley.

Radin, N. (1982). Primary caregiving and role-sharing fathers. In M.E. Lamb (Ed.), *Nontraditional families: Parenting and child development* (pp. 173-204). Hillsdale, NJ: Erlbaum.

Radin, N. & Sagi, A. (1982). Childrearing fathers in intact families in Israel and the U.S.A. *Merrill-Palmer Ouarterly, 28,* 111-136.

Russell, G. (1983). *The changing roles of fathers?* St Lucia, Queensland: University of Queensland Press.

Russell, G. (1986). Primary caretaking and role-sharing fathers. In M.E. Lamb (Ed.), *The father's role: Applied perspectives* (pp. 29-57). New York: Wiley.

Rutter, M. (1973). Why are London children so disturbed? *Proceedings of the Royal Society of Medicine, 66,* 1221-1225.

Rutter, M. (1979). Maternal deprivation, 1972-1978: New findings, new concepts, new approaches. *Child Development, 50*, 283-305.

Sagi, A. (1982). Antecedents and consequences of various degrees of paternal involvement in child rearing: The Israeli project. In M.E. Lamb (Ed.), *Nontraditional families: Parenting and child development* (pp. 205-232). Hillsdale, NJ: Erlbaum.

Sears, R.R., Maccoby, E.E. & Levin, H. (1957). *Patterns of child rearing.* Evanston, IL: Peterson.

Thompson, R.A. (1986). Fathers and the child's "best interests": Judicial decision making in custody disputes. In M.E. Lamb (Ed.), *The father's role: Applied perspectives* (pp. 61-102). New York: Wiley.

Thompson, R.A. (1994). Fatherhood and divorce. In *The future of children.* Palo Alto, CA: Packard Foundation.

Wallerstein, J.S. & Kelly, J.B. (1980). *Surviving the breakup: How children and parents cope with divorce.* New York: Basic Books.

Whitehead, B.D. (1993). Dan Quayle was right. *The Atlantic Monthly*, April, 47-84.

Artificial reproduction and paternity testing
Implications for fathers

William Marsiglio

Introduction

Relatively recent medical, technological, and biosocial developments in the reproductive field have raised new and fascinating questions for scholars and health care providers interested in fertility issues (Delaisi de Parseval & Hurstel, 1987; Edwards, 1991; Issacs & Holt, 1987; McNeil, Varcoe, and Yearley, 1990; Tripp-Reimer & Wilson, 1991). The medicalisation and increased use of artificial insemination (AI)[1], technological developments such as in vitro fertilisation (IVF), embryo transfer (ET)[2], and the DNA fingerprinting technique that tests for genetic associations between parents

---

1   Artificial insemination has been practiced in human beings since 1799 and can be accomplished without medical intervention. I have chosen to discuss this noncoital form of reproduction along side the more recent technological innovations in assisted reproduction because the medical community gradually gained control over this practice during the mid- and late 20th century. Moreover, the procedures have been perfected during this time and artificial insemination has increased dramatically during the middle and late 20th century (Curie-Cohen, Luttrell, & Shapiro, 1979; Issacs & Holt, 1987; McNeil, Varcoe, & Yearley, 1990; Office of Technology Assessment, 1988; Shalev, 1989; Stolcke, 1988). There are three forms of artificial insemination: (AIH) artificial insemination by husband (or partner), (AID) artificial insemination by donor, and (AIC) which represents a combination of the first two types.

2   Many authors refer to this technology as 'ovum transfer (OT)', but technically the ovum is fertilized outside the woman's body and a five-day-old embryo is then transferred to the woman. Another technology, 'gamete intrafallopian transfer' (GIFT) enables fertility specialists to place through laparoscopy a sperm and eggs directly into one or both fallopian tubes of the gestational mother-the normal cite of human fertilization. A third variation 'Zygote intrafallopian transfer' ZIFT is a hybrid of IVF and GIFT and involves egg retrieval and the incubation of the eggs and sperm. After fertilisation has taken place the Zygotes are transferred to the fallopian tube(s) (see Edwards, 1991; Issacs & Holt, 1987; Partridge-Brown, 1993; Serono Symposia, 1992). Finally, intra-cytoplasmatic sperm injection (ICSI) is a new and very promising technique that enables a single sperm to be injected into one ovum. This technique could have profound implications because it will enable men with extremely poor sperm qualities to experience biological paternity and thereby reduce the proportion of children conceived with donor sperm (Velde, 1994).

and children[3], in combination with biosocial innovations, most notably sperm banks and the practice of surrogacy[4], have prompted challenges to the basic assumptions about the reproductive process, definitions of family, and the link between biological and social fatherhood in industrialised countries.

While noncoital reproductive technologies are responsible for only a small proportion of all conceptions and births, their use has increased steadily since their development. It has been estimated that there are currently about 300 IVF clinics in the United States (SART, 1994 May, personal communication) and there are hundreds of other clinics around the world. The number of children born through this technique is thought to be doubling each year (Laborie, 1988). As of 1994, SART estimates that roughly 28,000 babies have been born in the U.S. using one of the 'assisted reproductive technologies'. Even more impressive is the number of women who make use of AI technology. During a twelve month period in 1986-87, it was estimated that 172,000 women in the U.S. were artificially inseminated resulting in 65,000 births (35,000 by AIH and 30,00 by AID) and the practice is common in other industrialised countries as well (Office of Technology Assessment, 1988). Edwards (1991) speculates that interest in this technique will continue to grow around the world. It provides a viable option to persons with various needs including those who have become less fertile or infertile due to exposure to hazardous environmental materials or medications, as well as those persons who want to have input in the genetic makeup of their child.

My major objective in this article is to assess how noncoital reproductive technologies affect the social (legal) fathers responsible for children conceived in this manner. I develop my analysis by first noting how these reproductive innovations, in conjunction with behavioural and attitudinal trends, are shaping an important moment in the history of fatherhood in Western, industrialised societies. Next, I discuss several timely issues related to fatherhood and the 20th century developments I noted above. I place my discussion within a larger framework for conceptualising men's experiences in the reproductive realm (Marsiglio, 1991). The first set of issues pertain to

---

3   Unlike the DNA fingerprinting test, earlier tests (ABO blood-typing system, Human Leukocyte Antigen (HLA) tissue-tying test) can only be used to exclude an alleged male from being identified as a particular child's father (Howe, 1993; Jackson, 1989). I will restrict my comments to the DNA fingerprinting test.
4   While I list the practice of surrogacy as a biosocial innovation, and in the process implicitly acknowledge that its practice is typically associated with the medical community, this process (in combination with self-insemination) can and has at times been used by individual women without the assistance of the medical community (Issacs & Holt, 1987; McNeil, 1990; Ragone, 1994; Whitehead, 1989).

those technologies that enable a woman to bear a child without having sexual intercourse with a man. I then briefly discuss the social significance of the new DNA fingerprinting technology that provides health care specialists with the means to identify biologically associated parent-child pairs.

Reproductive innovations: another significant historical moment?

To understand the impact these reproductive innovations and DNA technologies may have on fathers and others in industrialised societies, it is useful to place them in perspective by discussing how they represent a significant development in the history of fatherhood. In prehistoric times, male Homo sapiens did not recognise that they were in some cases the genetic father of children born to females with whom they had coitus — they were essentially oblivious to their role in the pregnancy process. Reiss (1986) has speculated that the physiologically gratifying experience of copulation, not knowledge of one's paternity, first lead some males to bond with a female partner and to develop feelings toward their partner's offspring. Early forms of social kinship may have evolved because of this process even though males did not comprehend the technical details of the reproductive process. It is also possible that they may have extended their protective services and nurturing care to children born to their favourite partner(s) even though, unbeknownst to them, the children may have actually been sired by another male. Unfortunately, we can only conjecture about these processes and how males came to develop conscious perceptions about their 'paternal' roles. One reasonable explanation suggests that knowledge of paternity coincided with the domestication of animals around 9000 B.C. when people began to watch more closely the sexual and reproductive experiences of specific animals over a period of time (Tannahill, 1980).

It is clear that men (and women) eventually developed a more accurate understanding of the reproductive process at some point. The discovery of biological paternity by persons who could subjectively evaluate its significance was a remarkable moment in the history of humankind, the reproductive process, and the social construction of fatherhood (O'Brien, 1981). O'Brien (1981) has argued that these early men experienced a dilemma because they had a crude sense that babies were created through coitus but they were physiologically detached from the gestation and labour process, which in turn made the establishment of paternity problematic. They had no way of being absolutely certain that a child was in fact their child. Documenting one's paternity was an act of personal faith reinforced by community cooperation. O'Brien goes on to assert that men's efforts to develop an ideology of continuity that linked fathers to their offspring necessitated that they develop social and legal institutions such as marriage in order for them to lay legal claim to their children. This practice connected the biological paternity of children and social fatherhood with men's marital relationships. Men were in a sense indirectly appropriating 'their' children by asserting their paternal rights vis à vis their legal relationship with, and ownership of, 'their' children's mother.

Today, we are in the midst of another important moment in the social construction of fatherhood even though it is unlikely to have the same type of revolutionary consequences. The distinctive nature of this period is based on several interrelated behavioural, cultural, and technological developments. Many societies, especially Western industrialised ones, have experienced significant changes in their childbearing, marriage, divorce, and remarriage patterns (Ahlburg & De Vita, 1992; Da Vanzo & Rahman, 1993). One consequence of these patterns relevant to the present discussion is that growing numbers of men at some point in their life are assuming father-like roles to children who are not biologically related to them (Larson, 1992). The cultural scenarios pertinent to fatherhood in general, or the stockpile of ideas related to how persons should and do express particular paternal roles, have become more varied. As a result, there is a greater diversity of paternal roles and the general definition of fatherhood has become more expansive (Marsiglio, in press; Gerson, 1993; Griswold, 1993; LaRossa, 1988).

These sociodemographic and cultural trends have prompted a series of lively academic and public debates that explore the definition and nature of 'family' and kinship as well as the meaning of 'fatherhood' (see Beutler, Burr, Bahr & Herrin, 1989; Delaisi de Parseval & Hurstel, 1987; Edwards, 1989; Griswold, 1993; Jurich, 1989; Menaghan, 1989; Seligman, 1990; Scanzoni & Marsiglio, 1991; 1993; Scanzoni, Polonko, Teachman & Thompson, 1989). Laypersons are slowly changing their perceptions about the meaning of 'family' in industrialised countries. Consequently, questions that explore whether socially constructed relationships, including those produced through reproductive technologies using donor semen and/or ova, can be as thick or thicker than 'blood' take on new meaning in this type of cultural climate.

These contemporary discourses are occurring alongside another remarkable shift in the nature of the reproductive process. The medicalisation of artificial insemination procedures, and the development of the more sophisticated, artificially assisted reproductive technologies have, in effect, helped to underscore the notion that biological paternity can be separated from sexual intercourse[5]. These patterns also contribute to the mix

---

5   The development and increasing use of innovations in reproductive technology overlaps the recent development of contraceptive technology--the second major moment in the history of reproduction according to O'brien (1981). These earlier (and ongoing)

of shifting cultural images and legal rulings that interpret the significance of differentiating biological paternity from social fatherhood. The contemporary use of reproductive technologies is thus blurring the traditional images of 'father', 'mother', and 'family relations' in some cases (Delaisi de Parseval & Hurstel, 1987; Edwards, 1991). Moreover, the once privileged position of paternal claims based on biological relations is being challenged by those who feel that genetic fathers must demonstrate some threshold level of responsibility toward their children to retain their formal or informal rights. It should also come as no surprise that the practical value of social fatherhood is being accentuated in an era marked by relatively high rates of divorce, single parenthood, and cohabitation. At the same time, biological paternity is being highlighted in a new way due to recent developments in the DNA fingerprinting technique that can now establish with near certainty the shared genetic heritage of fathers and their children. This innovation is particularly useful for documenting paternity in an effort to hold biological fathers accountable for the financial support of their children.

Procreative issues and reproductive innovations

In discussing how reproductive innovations are likely to affect fathers and children today and in the foreseeable future, it is instructive to place men's involvement in the reproductive realm into, not only a historical context, but a theoretical one as well. I have defined this domain elsewhere as "the variety of physiological, social-psychological, and interpersonal phenomena that are associated with fertility regulation, gestation, and procreation broadly defined. This comprehensive definition takes into account a male's perception of his responsibility to his offspring prior to and after their birth, as well as the symbolic meaning that fathering and raising children has for him" (Marsiglio, 1991: 285). I have attempted to conceptualise men's experiences in this life sphere by developing two distinct and abstract social psychological concepts: *procreative consciousness* and *procreative responsibility*.

The procreative consciousness concept takes into account the fact that men experientially relate to and perceive particular aspects of the reproductive realm. These experiences include a combination of mental activity and emotions, but they are largely distinct from men's beliefs about their obligations or their actual demonstration of the same in specific areas. Men's emotional and psychological experiences, as well as their self-images, will be associated with their self-concept as it is shaped by their sexual partner,

---

technological developments have provided women (and men) a greater opportunity to exert control over their reproductive potential without abstaining from coitus.

father, and gender role identities, respectively. In its broadest sense, typical research questions of interest related to the procreative consciousness theme would include the following: How do men feel about their ability or inability to procreate? To what extent do men associate their procreative potential with their masculinity? How do men experience seeing a visual image of their foetus/child in the mother's womb? In what ways, if any, do men feel differently about their 'social' child when he/she is conceived with donor sperm rather than their own sperm? What factors contribute to fathers' sense that their 'social child' is an extension of themselves? To what extent, and how, do men vicariously develop aspects of their procreative consciousness through their association with their partner during her pregnancy and after their social child is born?

The second concept, procreative responsibility, emphasises men's involvement and sense of obligation in the areas of contraception, pregnancy resolution, fertility testing, gestation, and child support/child care, respectively. It deals with both the practical aspects of these reproductive areas (e.g. going for a fertility test, using a condom) as well as men's perceptions about obligations they associate with the social roles of fatherhood (e.g. child support). Questions of interest would include: When do men feel compelled to accompany and support their partner during a pregnancy exam, an abortion procedure, check-ups during gestation, or fertility consultation? Why are some men more willing than others to assume responsibility for initiating or at least undergoing fertility testing? Do men feel differently about their level of obligation to help financially support and provide practical care for children depending upon their genetic relationship to them?

An important feature of the larger conceptual framework that incorporates these concepts is that men's views about reproductive issues, in conjunction with the interpersonal relationships they maintain, enable men to express their role identities (Stryker, 1980) as partner, father, and more generally as a masculine male. Men often attempt to manage their presentation of self so that others will perceive them to be a particular type of partner, father, or masculine male. While men express their role identities and experience the reproductive domain at the micro-level, larger social forces, including public policies and cultural/subcultural norms, can affect men's everyday life experiences in this realm.

Men frequently develop perceptions and feelings about their role identities and reproductive issues independent of a particular partner and relationship. However, their orientation towards aspects of the reproductive realm can also be shaped by their involvement with a specific partner. Men may reassess their perceptions of specific reproductive issues in response to particular partners who successfully persuade or 'force' them to reconsider their views.

This pattern underscores the dynamic and negotiated nature to men's feelings and thoughts about procreative issues. Men are apt to change their views in subtle and sometimes dramatic ways throughout their life course although they will not necessarily develop a specific level of awareness of, or sensitivity to, their specific procreative experiences. Moreover, some men will never develop an integrated view of themselves in terms of their procreative beliefs and experiences at any given point in time. There are two basic processes at work here.

The first deals with how men experience specific episodes in which they are involved in the reproductive realm. Men will vary in the way and extent to which they think and feel about these specific episodes. For example, men will probably differ in their emotional responses to their partner being impregnated with donor sperm. In addition, men will go through different periods of their lives where many or all of the aspects of the reproductive realm are not relevant to them. Consequently, they may spend little time thinking about aspects of the reproductive realm. However, men who are actively participating in the process of exploring some form of artificially assisted reproductive technology will probably be quite conscious of their procreative self.

The second issue addresses men's more general view of themselves in terms of the procreative dimensions to their life. Many men will not experience their procreative feelings and perceptions in an integrated fashion with a heightened sense of self-awareness. Instead, they may experience them in a fleeting and unstructured manner. Thus, my social psychological perspective suggests that the way men experience their procreative consciousness and sense of responsibility is likely to be more dynamic and fragmented in character than, say, their level of health awareness or their sense that they are a Fundamentalist Christian.

Noncoital reproduction (AI and IVF)

Men's procreative consciousness and sense of responsibility are likely to affect how they view reproductive innovations and their willingness to use them. For instance, men who view paternity as an ideal opportunity to demonstrate their masculinity may be reluctant to become a social father by using donor sperm. On the other hand, those men who want to become a social father in order to experience the developmental phase of generativity, the interest in creating and guiding younger generations (Erikson, 1982; Hawkins, Christiansen, Sargent & Hill, 1993), or to share in the childrearing experience with their partner, may be more willing to become a social father using whatever means necessary (Humphrey & Humphrey, 1988).

Technologies associated with AI and IVF can also affect how fatherhood is culturally constructed, to some degree, and how individual fathers perceive their paternal roles. If technologies using donor sperm were to receive even wider public acceptance they could enhance the legitimacy of social fatherhood and thereby expand the definition of fatherhood. These innovations can therefore influence aspects of fathers' procreative consciousness and sense of responsibility as well as provide them with opportunities for experiencing their relationship to the reproductive realm in novel ways. Numerous factors will affect how these technologies affect fathers. The outcomes will be based in part on some combination of individuals' perceptions (these may vary over the course of the pregnancy and the child's life), interpersonal dynamics, and the specific fertility circumstances associated with the application of the respective technology.

There are various ways of distinguishing between the different methods of artificial, noncoital reproduction. From the social or nurturing father's perspective, he could establish a paternal relationship to a child through AI (AIH or AID) or IVF in at least eight different ways (see Figure 1). While some of these eight combinations are much more prevalent than others, I will discuss each of them in turn. It is also possible that the absolute and relative frequency of some of these permutations may increase in the future (e.g. those involving surrogacy). Note that scenarios 1 and 2 preserve the genetic relations of both social parents to the child, 3 and 4 preserve only the social father's genetic ties, 5 and 6 preserve only the mother's genetic relations, and 7 and 8 preserve neither social parent's genetic ties (however, the mother's direct contribution during gestation is preserved in 7).

For simplicity sake, my discussion assumes that the partners comprise a heterosexual couple even though more lesbian and perhaps gay men may attempt to overcome stiff political resistance and avail themselves in the future to these alternative means of reproducing children. I also assume that the social father knows that his partner is experimenting with an alternative form of reproduction even though in rare cases a woman might attempt to deceive her male partner and covertly use one of these technologies. I discuss how men are likely to differ in the way they experience aspects of their procreative consciousness and sense of responsibility due to the unique combination of fertility circumstances they encounter by using one of the reproductive innovations. Their experiences will probably affect, as well as be affected by their tendency to develop a commitment to a paternal identity.

The first four scenarios outlined in Figure 1 refer to social fathers who use their own sperm to procreate. The use of one's own sperm can be an important issue for some men. Biological paternity may be a critical factor that shapes their perception of their role as a prospective father during gestation and as a social father after their child's birth as well (see Crowe, 1985; Overall, 1987). Snowden, Mitchell & Snowden's (1983) qualitative study

Case Scenario	Sperm[+]		Ovum[++]		Gestation Body	
	Own	Donor	Partner	Donor	Partner	Surrogate
1	*		*		*	
2	*		*			*
3	*			*	*	
4	*			*		*
5		*	*		*	
6		*	*			*
7		*		*	*	
8		*		*		*

Male's Own Sperm
1. Own sperm, partner's ovum, partner's gestation body
2. Own sperm, partner's ovum, surrogate mother's gestation body
3. Own sperm, donor's ovum, partner's gestation body
4. Own sperm, donor's ovum, surrogate mother's gestation body

Donor's Sperm
5. Donor's sperm, partner's ovum, partner's gestation body
6. Donor's sperm, partner's ovum, surrogate mother's gestation body
7. Donor's sperm, donor's ovum, partner's gestation body
8. Donor's sperm, donor's ovum, surrogate mother's gestation body

[+]   In some cases a semen specimen includes both the social father's sperm and sperm from a donor. I have excluded this variable from the table because it rarely occurs and its inclusion would make the conceptualisation less manageable.

[++] In many cases of IVF, more than one ovum will be used during any given treatment.

Figure 7.1.   Eight permutations of noncoital reproduction among heterosexual couples

of 57 couples who received AID between 1940 and 1980 at one clinic in the United Kingdom revealed that many fathers were concerned about whether they would be related to their child genetically. Many equated their fertility potential with their level of masculinity, a position reinforced by others' tendencies to stigmatise infertile men. As one husband in Snowden et al.'s study expressed: "I know a chap at work — he and his wife they've been trying for two or three years, and the amount of stick that that chap takes — virtually everyone that knows him has offered to go and do the job for him." (p. 128). Meanwhile, research on infertile couples suggests that middle class men are less likely than comparable women to feel devastated by their (couple's) inability to reproduce a child (Greil, 1991; Balen & Trimbos-Kemper, 1993). Thus, compared to women, men may place greater weight on having a genetic connection with their child, but they seem to become less upset about their own infertility, or the prospects of being a part of an infertile couple.

It seems reasonable to argue that men will probably feel the fullest psychological and emotional intensity of being a genetic father in the first case. This set of fertility circumstances most closely resembles the natural reproduction process because men use their own sperm to impregnate their partner who also uses her own ovum and carries the pregnancy to term.

Those social fathers using their own sperm who are represented by the second and third scenarios are probably very similar to each other and may have experiences comparable to men in the first category. In the seconnd scenario a man becomes a social father by using his partner's ovum, and a surrogate mother's body, whereas in the thirdrd scenario he uses a donor's ovum and his partner carries the pregnancy to term herself. If men experience the second and third scenarios differently it would probably result from them feeling as though the use of their partner's ovum was more or less important than the opportunity to experience the gestation process with her. The symbolic significance of these options may be quite different (Snowden et al., 1983). In either case, the man's partner would be making some type of physiological contribution to the eventual birth of the man's genetically related child.

It is also possible that if men do experience these two scenarios differently, the difference may subside over time or dissipate entirely. The way a man develops and experiences his procreative consciousness and sense of responsibility during a pregnancy initiated by AI or IVF may differ from his post-natal experiences at some point after the child is born. The degree of similarity in the child's and mother's appearance may be one meaningful factor that comes into play in this respect. While it may be of little consequence to prospective fathers during the prenatal period whether their partner contributes her ovum, it may be more meaningful after the child is born if the father's daughter or son physically resembles his partner.

Concerns about the partner's genetic or gestational contribution will affect a father's procreative consciousness or procreative responsibility only if his paternity experiences are shaped vicariously, at least in part, through his association with a partner. Fathers will also have to confront the reality that their child's appearance will be affected by the ovum donor's DNA, a fact that may or may not affect fathers' perceptions and experiences.

The circumstances that identify the highly unlikely, though possible, fourth case scenario where the man uses his own sperm but his partner plays no biological role in the child's conception or birth, are likely to foster different feelings and perceptions among men than either of the first three permutations. These distinctions will be accentuated during the gestation period to the extent that men's procreative consciousness is affected by their association with their partner when she assumes the gestational mother role. As with the first three cases, this distinction may dissipate once the child is born. On the other hand, some fathers may have a very active procreative consciousness and a strong sense of responsibility for their child under these circumstances because they have a direct link to their child whereas their partner does not. Much will probably still depend, though, on how the father and social mother develop and express their parental roles.

Case scenarios 5-8 represent examples of AI and IVF that involve donor's sperm. While it is beyond the scope of my discussion to address sperm donors' possible motivations and concerns about their paternity contribution (see, Kanter, 1994; Kovacs, Clayton & McGovern, 1983; Nichols & Tyler, 1983), donating sperm may influence some men's procreative consciousness in unique ways. Those men who assume the social responsibilities of fatherhood when donor sperm is used are likely to experience their prenatal procreative consciousness differently than those men who contribute their own sperm. A variety of factors will shape these differences. While these differences may be most pronounced when prospective social fathers are compared during the prenatal period, differences between these two categories of social fathers may persist sometimes even after a child's birth.

I suspect that men who experience the combination of fertility circumstances listed in the fifth scenario will be most likely, among those men using donor sperm, to have a strong sense of their paternal identity. In this instance their partner will use her own ovum and also carry the pregnancy to term. Thus, men will be able to draw upon their bond with their partner and her contribution to the conception, gestation, and actual birth process to reinforce their own pre and post-natal paternal identity and actual involvement with their child once the child is born (Humphrey & Humphrey, 1988; Snowden et al., 1983). Their partner's expectations for them to be a supportive partner during gestation will help remind them of their emerging father roles.

Those men included among the sixth scenario of cases may tend to feel somewhat alienated during gestation because they have not contributed their own sperm and have probably been unable to play an active part in the pregnancy process because their partner has not gone through a pregnancy (rare exceptions to this pattern probably occur when family or friends serve as surrogate mothers). It is possible that the symbolic significance to social fathers of having their partner carry the pregnancy to term versus using a donor's ovum may be very different for those men who rely on a donor's sperm compared to those who use their own. Men may place greater weight on their partner's genetic contribution when they are unable to make a similar contribution themselves (Snowden et al., 1983). Some men facing these fertility circumstances will probably have to struggle to develop a paternal identity during gestation.

Social fathers categorised according to the criteria for the seventh scenario may tend to have a stronger sense of their paternal identity, especially during the prenatal period, than men depicted by the sixth scenario. While men in the seventh scenario depend upon a donor's sperm and a donor's ovum, their partner is responsible for carrying the fertilised egg to term. Consequently, the man is able to be a daily witness to the pregnancy process and may even have the opportunity to visualise the foetus using ultrasonography. Aspects of the man's procreative consciousness are likely to be reinforced repeatedly as he and his partner experience the daily interaction rituals (including lamaze classes) that usually attend the pregnancy process when shared by two people who have actively tried to have a child and have access to modern prenatal care. Many of these men will also have an opportunity to be with their partner throughout the labour and delivery process.

Of the eight permutations, the final one most closely resembles the dynamics of parenthood through adoption. Those extremely rare cases where men depend on donated sperm, a donated ovum, and a surrogate carrier for the pregnancy, will typically include men with the least well-developed paternal identity. This should be especially true during the pregnancy. Men who become social fathers under these circumstances may still be quite committed to their father roles. However, they will have a greater chance to feel unsettled about their paternal identity than those who are genetically related to their child, or were at least indirectly involved in their child's birth due to their association with a partner who made a genetic and/or gestational contribution.

DNA fingerprinting and paternity establishment

While technological and biosocial innovations have made it possible for many individuals to have children in a variety of novel ways, modern technology has recently also made its mark on the reproductive realm in another way. It is now possible, thanks to DNA fingerprinting techniques, to determine whether two people are related genetically. Although this technology has been used rather sparingly, it is widely available and has become a political asset for those who wish to increase the rate of establishing paternity for children born to single women, especially in the United States. Their major objective is to increase the chances for these children to receive adequate financial child support (Wattenberg, 1993).

The primary use of DNA testing thus far has been to determine the validity of a mother's claim that a particular man is the biological father of her child. The threat of being forced to take such a test can prompt some men to acknowledge their paternity without contesting the matter further. In order for this technology to be used in those cases where a man does not voluntarily acknowledge his paternity, a woman must willingly identify a particular man (or several men) as the genetic (or probable genetic) father to the proper authorities. It is far less common, though not unheard of, for a man to use DNA testing as a means of establishing his biological and legal relationship to a child. Older children, sometimes adults, may also request that a paternity test be performed if they are curious about their origins[6].

This technology, when viewed from a sociohistorical perspective, offers the possibility of eliminating the time-honoured custom whereby men have chosen to trust women not to deceive them about their paternity status. While men in theory will no longer have to accept their partner's word, and women need not rely simply on normative pressure to persuade a former sexual partner to acknowledge his paternity and accept the accompanying obligations, the practical reality is that trust is likely to remain an essential feature of the social customs surrounding the reproductive process. The vast majority of males are not going to question their paternity status, and only a very small proportion of women who have multiple sexual partners, but are in an established relationship, will request that several men take a paternity test to determine the child's progenitor. Other women will be reluctant to use DNA fingerprinting to establish paternity because they want

---

6 I am familiar personally with one case in which a man in his late 20s is currently thinking about taking this test in order to establish whether a man he suspects may be his biological father is in fact related to him. The man's mother apparently has never been certain which of two men were responsible for her son's conception and she only recently informed him of this dilemma.

to preserve their control over their child and minimise their own involvement with the child's father. Notwithstanding these limiting factors, this technology opens up new possibilities for how men in the late 20th century might experience different aspects of the reproductive realm.

Summary and conclusion

It appears that a small but growing proportion of men living in industrialised societies will be directly affected by the increased availability and use of reproductive technologies, biosocial innovations, and DNA tests. While financially comfortable middle-class men are likely to remain the principle users of IVF technology (sometimes in combination with surrogacy), increasing numbers of middle-class and less affluent men may experiment with the relatively less expensive AI procedure without surrogacy (Issacs & Holt, 1987)[7]. In some countries, such as the Netherlands, access to expensive reproductive technologies may be greater than in countries like the United States because individuals are eligible for a limited number of IVF treatments that are reimbursed by the state or private insurance companies (Velde, 1994).

I have commented briefly on how these innovations and their increased use may help to shape a significant moment in the history and definition of fatherhood and 'family' in industrialised societies. In the absence of data, I applied my social psychological framework that broadly conceptualises men's relationship to the reproductive realm to speculate about the nature of men's experiences with these reproductive innovations. Men's orientation toward reproductive issues will affect the way they perceive and experience each of the eight permutations I outlined that are based on the multiple options individuals have for combining the genetic and gestational contributions needed to reproduce a child without sexual intercourse. Likewise, men's actual involvement with one of the techniques and the accompanying fertility circumstances they encounter may affect their procreative consciousness and sense of responsibility during the pre- and post-natal periods.

---

7   IVF technology in countries like the U.S. is extremely expensive and can involve tens of
    thousands of dollars in some cases (Beck, 1994). In comparison, the AI procedures, though
    expensive, are much more affordable. It was estimated, on average, that women in the U.S.
    had to spend $953 in 1986-87 to become pregnant through artificial insemination.
    Physicians reported that 51% of these women had insurance to cover this procedure, and
    insurance defrayed about 48% of the total cost (Office of Technology and Assessment,
    1988). Insurance coverage of IVF treatment procedures is typically not available in the U.S.
    (Serono Symposia, 1993).

At the heart of this discussion are questions related to men's beliefs and attitudes about biological procreation and social fatherhood. As Meerabeau (1991) notes, it has typically been the case that the phrase 'to father' has meant to procreate whereas 'to mother' has been associated with a longer term, nurturing image (see also Rothman, 1986). To the extent this image resonates with particular men, they will probably feel significantly different about their paternal identity when they are able to contribute their own sperm rather than using donor sperm.

Another issue central to my discussion involves the indirect route fathers take in defining their commitment to their paternal identity by linking it to their involvement with a romantic partner (Furstenberg, 1988; Marsiglio, 1993). Partners may often play a role in affecting fathers' procreative consciousness and sense of responsibility. Thus some men who use artificial reproductive techniques to become social fathers, not unlike fathers who reproduce children through natural means, may tend to experience their paternal identity by drawing on their association with their partner and her pregnancy experiences. This discussion raises a key question: To what extent do men's views about reproductive technologies and their paternal identity stem from their negotiated interactions with their partner rather than their own more general orientation toward procreation?

In some instances these reproductive innovations will provide men with their only opportunity to experience biological paternity, or at least to be a genetic father with a particular partner serving as the social mother. When any of the eight permutations are used successfully they will also give all male participants a chance to experience their social roles as fathers. As more men adopt alternative forms of reproduction, especially those that depart most radically from the natural reproductive process, the need for researchers to understand men's relationship to this aspect of the reproductive realm will grow accordingly.

Several interrelated research questions come to mind when contemplating the social and psychological implications for men who experience one of the eight specific forms of artificial, noncoital reproduction (for related questions see Edwards, 1991). When are men most likely to feel financially and emotionally obligated to 'their' children who are conceived using reproductive technologies? How are fathers' relationships with their children and partners affected by whether reproduction occurs through sexual intercourse or one of the artificial methods? Are there particular combinations of circumstances for artificial reproduction that affect men's pre- and post-natal perceptions and feelings about the reproductive process and their procreative experiences in particular? What factors affect men's perceptions of their noncoitally conceived child and their own paternal roles when their relationship with the child's mother dissolves? On a more theoretical level: Does an examination of men's responses to innovations facilitating noncoital reproduction reveal connections between aspects of men's procreative consciousness and their sense of procreative responsibility?

Although this essay has focused on fathers' perceptions and experiences, reproductive innovations may also have consequences for their children's development. A smaller proportion of children than fathers will be affected directly, though, because many more children than fathers will be unaware that alternative reproductive techniques played a role in their conception and birth[8].

To date, these children (and their families) have not been subjected to careful study so it is only possible to speculate about their socioemotional development (see Snowden et al., 1983; Iizuka, Swada, Nishina & Ohi, 1968). Noncoitally conceived children, especially those involving the use of donated sperm and/or ova, might have different familial experiences and self-perceptions if they were compared to children who have been reproduced naturally. This would be consistent with evidence that shows that adoptive and foster families often have different familial dynamics than those traditional families where a husband and wife live with their naturally conceived children (Humphrey & Humphrey, 1988). However, while it might be possible to draw some conclusions about these children's feelings by extrapolating from studies using adopted children, the comparison is confounded by the fact that adopted children will probably have a greater tendency to feel that they were abandoned as infants by a genetic and gestational mother, as well as by a genetic father in many cases. Children born with the aid of noncoital reproductive technologies will not experience this anxiety and may even feel special because their parents went to such great lengths to have them (Snowden et al, 1983). Snowden et al. concluded, based on their small, non-representative study of AI couples using donor semen, that all of the spouses:

> ... appeared to have accepted the children willingly and happily; indeed some of the fathers had a particularly close relationship with their children and appeared to be deeply involved in child care and family life. Because their children had been achieved after considerable heartache, and after much effort, they were particularly valued and loved and the

---

8   An important factor that needs to be taken into account when discussing the development of these children is whether or not they are aware of the circumstances surrounding their conception. The types of questions that researchers can address will obviously vary depending upon whether children have been informed of the nature of their conception and birth.

couples tended to find parenting particularly rewarding and satisfying (p. 81).

In sum, research with men who become social fathers by using noncoital strategies, though fraught with methodological difficulties in some cases, will enable researchers to assess how men define fatherhood and relate to unique aspects of the reproductive realm. In particular, scholars will be able to examine the relationship between men's perceptions of biological paternity, social fatherhood, and their expression of their social roles as fathers. These issues, though significant in their own right, will take on greater importance if they are found to be related to children's well-being.

References

Ahlburg, D.A. & De Vita, C.J. (1992). New realities of the American family. *Population Bulletin, 47,* 2. Washington, DC: Population Reference Bureau, Inc.

Balen, F. van & Trimbos-Kemper, T.C.M. (1993). Long-term infertile couples: A study of their well-being. *J. Psychosom. Obstet. Gynaecol. 14,* 53-60.

Beck, M. (1994). Making Babies. *Newsweek, January 17,* 54-57.

Beutler, I.F., Burr, W.R., Bahr, K.S. & Herrin, D.A. (1989). The family realm: Theoretical contributions for understanding its uniqueness. *Journal of Marriage and the Family, 51,* 805-816.

Crowe, C.. (1985). Women want it: In vitro fertilization and women's motivation for participation. *Women's Studies International Forum, 8,* 47-52.

Curie-Cohen, M., Luttrell, L. & Shapiro, S. (1979). Current practice of artificial insemination by donor in the United States. *New England Journal of Medicine, 300,* 585-590.

Da Vanzo, J. & Rahman, M.O. (1993). American families: Trends and correlates. *Population Index, 59,* 3, 350-386.

Delaisi de Parseval, G. & Hurstel, F. (1987). Paternity "A la Francaise". In M.E. Lamb (Ed.), *The father's role: Cross-cultural perspectives* (pp. 59-87). Hillsdale, NJ: Lawrence Erlbaum Associates.

Edwards, J.N. (1991). New conceptions: Biosocial innovations and the family. *Journal of Marriage and the Family, 53,* 349-360.

Edwards, J.N. (1989). The family realm: A future paradigm or failed nostalgia? *Journal of Marriage and the Family, 51,* 816-818.

Erikson, E. (1982). *The life cycle completed: A review.* New York: Norton.

Furstenberg, F.F. Jr. (1988). Good dads-bad dads: Two faces of fatherhood. In A. Cherlin (Ed.), *The changing American family and public policy* (pp. 193-217). Washington, DC: Urban Institute.

Gerson, K. (1993). *No man's land: Men's changing commitments to family and work*. New York, NY: Basic Books.

Greil, A.L. (1991). *Not yet pregnant: Infertile couples in contemporary America*. New Brunswick: Rutgers University Press.

Griswold, R.L. (1993). *Fatherhood in American: A history*. New York: Basic Books.

Howe, R-A.W. (1993). Legal rights and obligations: An uneven evolution. In R.I. Lerman & T.J. Ooms (Eds.), *Young unwed fathers: Changing roles and emerging policies* (pp. 141-169). Philadelphia: Temple University Press.

Hawkins, A.J., Christiansen, S.L., Sargent, K.P. & Hill, E.J. (1993). Rethinking fathers' involvement in child care. *Journal of Family Issues, 14*, 531-549.

Humphrey, M. & Humphrey, H. (1988). *Families with a difference: Varieties of surrogate parenthood*. London: Routledge.

Iizuka, R., Sawada, Y., Nishina, N. & Ohi, M. (1968). The physical and mental development of children born following artificial insemination. *International Journal of Fertility, 13*, 24-32.

Isaacs, S. & Holt, R.J. (1987). Redefining procreation: Facing the issues. *Population Bulletin, 42*, 3-37.

Jackson, D. (1989). DNA fingerprinting and proof of paternity. *Family Law Reporter, 15(28), May 16*, 3007-3013.

Jurich, J.A. (1989). The family realm: Expanding its parameters. *Journal of Marriage and the Family, 51*, 819-822.

Kanter, R. de (1994). *Psychic consequences of artificial insemination and the consequences on the experience of parenthood*. Paper presented at the Conference for Changing Fatherhood, Tilburg University, May.

Kovacs, G.T., Clayton, C.E. & McGovern, P. (1983). The attitudes of semen donors. *Clinical reproduction and fertility*, 73-75.

Laborie, F. (1988). New reproductive technologies: News from France and elsewhere. *Issues in Reproductive and Genetic Engineering, 1*, 77-85. Government Printing Office.

LaRossa, R. (1988). Fatherhood and social change. *Family Relations, 37*, 451-457.

Larson, J. (1992). Understanding stepfamilies. *American Demographics (July)*, 3-40.

Marsiglio, W. (in press). Fathers' diverse life course patterns and roles: Theory and social interventions. In W. Marsiglio (Ed.), *Fatherhood: Contemporary theory, research, and social policy*. Newbury Park: SAGE.

Marsiglio, W. (1993). Contemporary scholarship on fatherhood: Culture, identity, and conduct. *Journal of Family Issues, 14*, 484-509.

Marsiglio, W. (1991). Male procreative consciousness and responsibility: A conceptual analysis and research agenda. *Journal of Family Issues, 12*, 268-290.

McNeil, M. (1990). Reproductive technologies: A new terrain for the sociology of technology. In M. McNeil, I. Varcoe & S. Yearley (Eds.), *The new reproductive technologies* (pp. 1-26). MacMillan.

McNeil, M., Varcoe, I. & Yearley, S. (1990). *The new reproductive technologies.*

MacMillan Meerabeau, Liz. (1991). Husbands' participation in fertility treatment: They also serve who only stand and wait. *Sociology of Health & Illness, 11*, 396-410.

Menaghan, E.G. (1989). Escaping from the family realm: Reasons to resist claims for its uniqueness. *Journal of Marriage and the Family, 51*, 822-825.

Nichols, M.K. & Tyler, J.J.P. (1983). Characteristics, attitudes and personalities of AI donors. *Clinical reproduction and fertility, 2*, 47-64.

O'Brien, M. (1981). *The politics of reproduction.* Boston. Routledge & Kegan Paul.

Office of Technology Assessment. (1988). *Artificial insemination practice in the United States: Summary of a 1987 survey.* Washington DC: U.S.

Overall, C. (1987). *Ethics and human reproduction: A feminist analysis.* Boston: Allen & Unwin.

Partridge-Brown, M. (1993). *In Vitro Fertilization clinics: A North American directory of programs and services.* Jefferson, N.C.: McFarland & Company, Inc.

Ragone, H. (1994). *Surrogate motherhood: Conception in the heart.* Boulder, CO: Westview Press.

Reiss, I. (1986). *Journey into sexuality: An exploratory voyage.* Englewood Cliffs, NJ: Prentice-Hall.

Rothman, B.K. (1986). *The tentative pregnancy: Prenatal diagnosis and the future of motherhood.* New York: Viking/Penguin.

SART (personal communication, May 16, 1994). Society For Assisted Reproductive Technology. Birmingham, AL.

Scanzoni, J.H. & Marsiglio, W. (1993). New action theory and contemporary families. *Journal of Family Issues, 14*, 105-132.

Scanzoni, J.H. & Marsiglio, W. (1991). Wider families and primary relationships. In M. Sussman & T.D. Marciano (Eds.), *Marriage and the Family Review, 17 (1/2)*, 117-133.

Scanzoni, J.H., Polonko, K., Teachman, J. & Thompson, L. 1989. *The sexual bond: Rethinking families and close relationships.* Newbury Park, Sage.

Seligman, J. (1990). Variations on a theme. *Newsweek, Winter/Spring Special Issue*, 20-24.

Serono Symposia (1993). *Affording your infertility.* Norwell, MA: Serono Labortories, Inc.

Serono Symposia (1992). *ART: Assisted reproductive technologies.* Norwell, MA: Serono Labortories, Inc.

Shalev, C. (1989). *Birth power: The case of surrogacy*. New Haven, CN: Yale University Press.

Snowden, R., Mitchell, G.D. & Snowden, E.M. (1983). *Artificial reproduction: A social investigation*. London: Allen & Unwin.

Stolcke, V. (1988). New reproductive technologies: The old quest for fatherhood. *Issues in Reproductive and Genetic Engineering, 1*, 5-19.

Stryker, S. (1980). *Symbolic interactionism: A social structural version*. Menlo Park, CA: Benjamin/Cummings.

Tannahill, R. (1980). *Sex in history*. New York: Stein & Day.

Tripp-Reimer, T. & Wilson, S.E. (1991). Cross-cultural perspectives on fatherhood. In F.W. Bozett & S.M.H. Hanson (Eds.), *Fatherhood and families in cultural context* (pp. 1-27). New York: Springer.

Velde, E. te (1994). *The impact of some biomedical advances on reproduction and parenthood*. Paper presented at the Conference on Changing Fatherhood, Tilburg University, The Netherlands, May.

Wattenberg, E. (1993). Paternity actions and young fathers. In R.I. Lerman & T.J. Ooms (Eds.), *Young unwed fathers: Changing roles and emerging policies (pp. 213-234)*. Philadelphia: Temple University Press.

Whitehead, L.M. (1989). Commercial surrogacy: Social issues behind the controversy. In L.M. Whitehead & M.L. Poland (Eds.), *New approaches to human reproduction: Social and ethical dimensions* (pp. 145-169). Boulder, CO: Westview Press.

Gijs Beets

Marsiglio has written an interesting mainly methodological paper on aspects of reproduction which are always fascinating 'hot news' on the one hand but, many times, hardly (empirically) known on the other. Hardly known also because reproductive assistance is undergoing 'revolutionary' developments, and reproduction in general, whether assisted or not, is mostly shown from the woman's perspective. That is also the reason why the Conference on Changing Fatherhood was challenging to so many researchers interested in fertility issues. However, too many empirical facts are missing, so for the time being we have to work with hypotheses. Marsiglio develops several and does not provide (is probably not able to provide) the 'demographic' effects in figures, for example the shares of all eight scenarios (see his Figure 1) in the total current birth rate. That is not to blame Marsiglio as this exercise would probably also be practically impossible in the Netherlands. Moreover Marsiglio mentions "the absence of data".

As I had never questioned myself at what point in time male Homo sapiens recognised for the first time that he was the genetic father of children born to a woman with whom he had had sexual intercourse, it was revealing to learn that such knowledge of paternity coincided with the domestication of animals around 9000 BC, when people began to watch more closely the sexual and reproductive experiences of specific animals over a longer period of time. That sounds very reasonable, as does the 'second step': documenting one's paternity in social and legal institutions such as marriage in order to be "absolutely certain that a child was in fact their child". And nowadays we may be in the 'third step': revolutionary developments in childbearing, marriage, divorce and remarriage, giving rise to "a greater diversity of paternal roles", so that "the general definition of fatherhood has become more expansive". At the same time, however, the medicalisation of assisted reproduction underwent revolutionary developments giving rise to a society in which parenthood is completely separated from sexual intercourse. But, DNA fingerprinting is at reach to definitely prove genetic fatherhood.

As stated, most empirical fertility studies, whether studies in the medical or social sciences, are taken with females. Note that assisted reproduction is supplied by *gynae*cologists. However, if complaints that the father's perspective is not included in many of these female-oriented studies on reproduction were acted on, one might miss the woman's perspective in Marsiglio's social psychological paper. Although the author touches on that topic very shortly, I find the paper 'too narrow-minded' including the challenging final lines where Marsiglio hopes that the further examination of "relationships between men's perceptions of biological paternity, social fatherhood and their expression of their social roles as fathers (...) will take on greater importance if they are found to be related to children's well-being." How do female partners react to and handle men's feelings and obligations with respect to reproduction, and vice versa? It is only in the Summary that Marsiglio questions "to what extent do men's views about reproductive technologies and their paternal identity stem from their negotiated interactions with their partner rather than their own more general orientation toward procreation?"

Just as the majority of women will ultimately become a mother, the majority of males will ultimately become a father. They more (currently) or less (former days) deliberately choose, with their partners to become parents. Only a minority, although slowly increasing due to a rise in the age at marriage and consequently at first birth — basic background is a rise in educational level, i.e. quitting education at a higher age- is faced with in- or subfertility. Do males and females go around with involuntary childlessness in a similar way, or in a different way? How well are partners informed nowadays about the possible options open to them? What respect do partners have for their mutual feelings? And who makes ultimately the decision? What happens if the partners disagree? What is the influence of the gynaecologist trying to maybe softly push people to the most preferred or maybe even only solution for them? Are there special issues which males are concerned about, and how much do they differ from the maybe typical female concerns? From Marsiglio's paper I get the feeling that males can deliberately choose for themselves from eight different scenarios and that nearly all males are actually doing so (although Marsiglio states that "it appears that a *small but growing proportion* of men living in industrialised societies will be directly affected by the increased availability and use of reproductive technologies, biosocial innovations, and DNA tests").

With respect to the decision-making process at the couple-level I would like to state that there is enough evidence that couples are formed at the 'marriage market' via the principle of *Birds of a feather flock together*. So we still see that people with more or less the same background, whether age, religion, educational level etc., form a couple. Therefore I assume — and that has also been statistically documented — that the increase in the mother's age at first birth is also an indicator for the rise in the father's age at first birth. Moreover, there is quite some evidence that many males are initially rather vague about the possibility of fatherhood. Interviews about fertility intentions show that males are much vaguer than women are before becoming a parent. Quite a few males 'admit' that the ultimate decision will be made by their wives. As a consequence they do not state such exact and definite answers as women do. That is also the main reason, besides financial arguments, why many demographic fertility surveys are only conducted with female samples, as the 'value added' by also including males is limited. From such fertility studies you may also conclude that males think about having children in different terms than women do: women base fertility decisions more strongly on affective aspects, like how will the child grow up, be dressed, talk and play, and children are supposed to make all-day communication for women more enjoyable, while males base fertility decisions first of all on practical considerations of social status, the size of the dwelling, the size of the car, and the family income. And although things have changed of late, I support Te Velde's (1994) assumption that "fatherhood has changed dramatically, but not voluntarily, the woman forced her male partner to change, generally speaking". That means that, much more than Marsiglio suggests, males are most probably more or less forced into one of the reproductive scenarios if conceiving in the most natural way does not seem possible. Of course, Marsiglio is right in his suggestions that both the concepts of *procreative consciousness* as *procreative responsibility* are of utmost importance in such decision-making processes.

One of the points Marsiglio hardly touches on at all is the possibility that people may opt for one of the scenarios but regret their decision afterwards. What effect would that have on their biological or social fatherhood, and how do they themselves and their partners and children deal with such a sequential change? In this respect we will be confronted with completely new problems in the near future. There is, for example, already some judicial evidence in divorce cases where it was not at all clear what to do with the frozen embryos of the (ex)couple. Obviously, this couple had decided under more favourable circumstances to prepare embryos, although I do not know according to which of the eight scenarios. In court the male pleaded for destruction, the woman wanted a pregnancy. As women are more powerful in decision-making about a possible abortion than males are (males can hardly ever force females to have an abortion), the court decided to follow the woman's wish. And then the woman announced that she would certainly try to demand alimony from her ex-partner if she would become a mother. Maybe the only 'power' males have left is to use a condom!

Anyhow, I think that Marsiglio presents an interesting contribution, raises many new questions in the social psychological realm from a specific male viewpoint. His paper is interesting from a methodological perspective, but too narrow for practical application. However, I must admit that Marsiglio touches very briefly on the topics of:
- males having non-coitally conceived children and the possibility of their relationship with the child's mother dissolving;
- the father's perceptions on his children's socio-emotional developments.

Other points that I am missing are:
- the possible concern fathers (parents) may have about what their offspring, when grown up, might think about these scenarios themselves;
- the availability of all these scenarios for all layers of society, especially the poorest. Marsiglio only states in his Summary that "while financially comfortable middle-class men are likely to remain the principle users of IVF technology, increasing numbers of middle-class and less affluent men may experiment with the relatively less expensive AI procedure without surrogacy." Moreover, Marsiglio indicates that access and prices may differ from country to country. Stemming from rather liberal and tolerant Dutch roots I often wonder why the loud moralising voices and low levels of state intervention in the United States create so many poor population layers, i.e. I assume that many more US than, for example, Dutch couples — ceteris paribus — will face a dark future with respect to creating offspring in whatever way when sub- or infertility occurs.

References

Velde, E. te (1994). *The impact of some biomedical advances on reproduction and parenthood*. Paper presented at the Conference on Changing Fatherhood. Tilburg University, The Netherlands, May 1994.

New fathers
Changes in the family and emerging policy issues

Rosella Palomba

Family policies... Women and children first

It is common knowledge that in most Western countries women, as mothers, benefitted from forms of social protection before men and before their rights as citizens, such as the right to vote, were recognised. In Italy, for example, women gained the right to vote after the Second World War but they had benefitted since 1902 from laws aimed at safeguarding motherhood, even if these laws were mainly an attempt to keep women out of the labour market rather than to help them retain their jobs.

In legislation, a man's body is viewed as almost extraneous to the reproductive process, with the exception of legal proceedings to determine paternity, and the father is protected mainly on the basis of economic criteria. The new 'reproduction technologies', for example, have revolutionised the reproductive scenario of procreation and new rules and new laws are being established, not always to the advantage of the father's role. In this paper, the implications of the new reproduction technologies for the concept of fatherhood will also be examined.

Furthermore, the system of family and social policies that has evolved in Europe has established — and to a large extent maintained — a gender-related model of family roles, entrusting the mother with the tasks of raising and caring for children. This means that directly or indirectly the state has defined different obligations for men and for women as regards the care of family members (children, spouses, dependent parents, etc.). For example, in many countries, the availability of a place at a child care centre or a kindergarten depends on the mother's work, and so the mother is implicitly recognised as being the only person who can care for the children. Another obvious case of the low importance given to the male role as a caregiver in the family is seen in the different treatment of men and women as regards obtaining assistance in the home in the case of serious illness. In many countries, this assistance is denied to anyone with a wife or a daughter living at home, whilst the case of the presence of a husband or father or son is not even contemplated (Finch, 1989; Saraceno, 1992).

I would like to make it clear that it is certainly not my intention here to consider the injustices and discrimination suffered by men, ignoring the fact that quite different forms of discrimination and injustices have been and are enacted by men towards women. It is no coincidence that the author has on more than one occasion written about and debated the subject of the rights denied to women. However, there is a cultural and political area from which men are excluded and which specifically concerns fatherhood. Fathers, in fact, are a social group which does not count for much socially and fathers find it difficult to have their paternal role recognised in the context of social and family policies and the organisation of day-to-day living.

The state and the gender-related view of parenthood
The changes to existing legislation in recent years have tended to promote the image of women and mothers as being more autonomous, more independent of their husbands and better-off in terms of rights and legislative recognition. However, a less well-defined model of men and fathers has emerged; they seldom figure at all in family policies, recognised mainly as women's deputies. There are, however, some marked differences between the various countries as regards the way in which gender is institutionalised and defined at the level of social policies. My hypothesis is that the state is never neutral as regards the problems of parenthood and that the female model is usually placed before that of the male but that on the part of some men and fathers there is no clear desire for this social discrimination to come to an end. While in some cases fathers see themselves as a socially disadvantaged group, they have not yet found a politically effective way of demonstrating their desires.

In addition to this, increased marital instability has reinforced the ties between mothers and children from a legal point of view. In fact, in the event of divorce, in the large majority of cases, the man acquires the role of the non-custodial or absentee father and his relationship with his children — when he keeps it up — is often reduced to merely an economic contribution towards their upkeep. Besides this, recent data show that men do not seem to be very willing to continue to maintain their former families following a divorce, and in this way they also forego their traditional role as providers (OECD, 1990).

Fatherhood has therefore been diminished both in terms of its social value and as the central issue in the definition of a new male identity. "Men become fathers later, just over one in ten have no children,... an ever increasing percentage of fathers do not live with their own children... and a significant percentage live in families with children with whom there is no blood relation." (Jansen, 1992). It should be noted that this last point could be interpreted as an extension and not necessarily as a reduction of paternal responsibilities, but in the context of this extended fatherhood, men often find little institutional or legal recognition. While one might expect that fathers would be economically and emotionally responsible for the children of the women they live with, their relationships with these children are not legally defined and often the law considers these men as outsiders.

The questions I will try and answer in this chapter are therefore the following: Do mothers and fathers have the same rights under current legislation? Do fathers know how to take advantage of the social gains of which they are the protagonists, such as parental leave for example? What is the right way to go about gaining recognition for the social value of fatherhood?

My approach is not to denounce the non-recognition of fatherhood in family and social policies. Nor do I consider it useful to make recriminations in a sterile, non-constructive way as regards the discrimination suffered by women, and so it is a waste of time to do the same for men. My analysis will therefore be concerned with clearly explaining what is happening in Europe today as regards family policies, trying to identify any possible ways of making changes.

A brief look at the fathers under consideration
At the end of the 1980s, there were about 49 million fathers in the European Community countries living as part of a married or unmarried couple; there were 1,623,000 custodial fathers, 1,173,000 of whom were lone fathers and 453,000 custodial fathers living with someone else.

There are less data available for men in reconstituted families but we know that men are more likely to remarry than women and that women remain single for longer periods of time (Menniti & Palomba, 1992; Le Galle & Martin, 1992). From the point of view of children, in France for example 37 out of every 1,000 children live with their mothers and a stepfather as against 7 who live with their fathers and a stepmother (Leridon & Villeneuve-Golkap, 1988). In Italy, 329,000 men live in reconstituted families; in 66% of these cases, they are living with their own and their partners' children. In the U.K., it is estimated that in the year 2000 about 2.5 million children will be living in stepfamilies. Therefore, the phenomenon of reconstituted families is on the increase and above all, blood ties are becoming weaker within families: mothers and fathers are bringing up the children of other men and women whilst their own children are being raised in other families.

European statistics are not yet organised in such a way as to supply reliable and global data on these phenomena and many methodological problems have still to be resolved as regards data collection. What is more, the difficulties are probably not only methodological in nature but also cultural since the current statistical data do not make it easy to extract data on the father-children relationship in addition to the mother-children one. Demographic statistics on fertility and families always have a strongly gender-related starting point when evaluating the reproductive process which is sometimes too limited in light of recent changes in the family.

Fathers: part-time caregivers?

Fathers have low visibility in European social and family policies and countries that have benefits and policies, explicitly supporting fatherhood are few and far between. And yet for some time now we have seen that if men become more involved in the care of children this could lead to greater equality between the sexes in the distribution of the family workload and it could have beneficial effects on the mental and physical development of children, enriching the father's role with new aspects and stimulating new behaviour patterns as a result of their day-to-day contact with their children (Jalmert, 1990).

The reason why the social value of fatherhood is not recognised in the laws of almost any country in terms of the possibility for fathers to temporarily put their work to one side in order to dedicate themselves to their children, is undoubtedly to be found in the difficulty that fathers have in making the leap from being a social group to becoming a political group and thus being able to make politically valid demands. In fact, in those countries where fathers have made their views known, the legislature has listened to them and produced more favourable measures to allow men to stop work during the period around the birth of their children. These opportunities offered to fathers are a political response to changes which have emerged in the behaviour of men towards children and in the daily lives of families; this is an ongoing process.

Paternity leave
In Sweden fathers enjoy 10 days paternity leave and in Denmark they have two weeks of paid leave. This paternity leave was granted when it was noted that fathers in these countries were increasingly trying to find jobs which were less rigid from the point of view of working hours in order to be able to stay at home with their young children. The time spent at work was decreasing and that spent at home was increasing proportionally (Näman, 1992). As a result, this new male behaviour pattern induced the legislature in these countries (which are very sensitive to the needs of their citizens) to introduce at least a few days' paid leave for new fathers. In other countries where these changes in paternal behaviour have not yet been clearly demonstrated or where the traditionally asymmetrical family model is stronger, the birth of a child does not give the right to any leave at all.

With the exception of France, where new fathers may take three days' leave, the only way new fathers can stay off work in other countries is to take one or two days' leave for 'personal reasons' and therefore this is not directly linked to fatherhood.

Why is it so difficult to recognise the father's function at home when a child is born? It has already been mentioned that the state has a gender-related outlook towards parenthood which is linked to sexual divisions in the social role of men and women and to the physical and biological side of reproduction which centres on the female body both during pregnancy and during the breast- or bottle-feeding period. Furthermore, society defines what is male and what is female as regards the tasks and abilities of men and women, through the world of work and its organisation, and in this way the traditional division of family roles is maintained.

By ensuring that the mother stays beside her newborn baby through special types of leave and provisions to safeguard motherhood, society protects a woman's health and guarantees the well-being of the baby but it has also, indirectly, established that the mother alone can carry out this task. Therefore the baby has two parents one of whom is essential and the other is secondary and complementary to the first. This point of view is internalised by men and women, fathers and mothers and influences the way in which fathers make important choices as regards the possibility of taking advantage of the benefits to which they are entitled.

Parental leave and career breaks
The country with the best parental leave scheme in the world today is undoubtedly Sweden: 540 days' leave on the occasion of the birth of a child, 450 of which are paid. The leave can be freely divided between the father and mother, it can be divided into half or even quarter days and the entitlement lasts until the child is eight years of age (Näsman, 1991). In other countries, leave is more limited and is paid at a lower rate or not at all (see Table 8.1).

In some states, such as Italy the beneficiary of parental leave is the mother who can transfer the right to the father. Obviously if the mother does not work, the father cannot take parental leave. In other countries, like Belgium, parental leave as such does not exist but parents are given the chance to take a career break.

Across Europe men seldom avail themselves of the right to take parental leave. A recent survey carried out in some European countries shows that following the birth of a child, fathers usually return to work immediately

Table 8.1.   Parental leave in some European countries by duration, person who is entitled to it, and salary

	Duration	Person	Payment
Denmark	10 weeks	parents	90% of salary
Germany	18 months	workers	Cheque reversely related to family income
Greece	3 months 6 divorced	each parent	not paid
Spain	36 months	workers	unpaid
France	33 months	parents	Unpaid under 3 children; cheque
Italy	6 months	mother	30% of salary
Netherlands	6 months	both	unpaid
Portugal	24 months	workers	unpaid
Sweden	540 days	parents	90% of salary for 450 days

with no reduction in hours (particularly in Spain, Italy and the Czech Republic). Other fathers choose to take extra holidays (The Netherlands and Switzerland), and some choose to work part-time (see Table 2). It should be noted that a high percentage of women give up work entirely, a sign that children and the family are more important to women than work outside the home in their personal scale of priorities in life.

In Sweden, the advantageous conditions have meant that 24.5% of fathers take parental leave (although 75.5% do not), but only for a limited period of time (on average one and a half months) and in any case for a shorter period of time than their wives do (Näsman, 1990).

Fathers and parental leave: the self-denial mechanism

Few men actually take parental leave even when they are entitled to it. If we ask ourselves why this is the case, we find that the reasons are manifold. First of all, a man usually earns more than his wife and so if parental leave is unpaid or only partly paid, the loss of the husband's income is too heavy a burden for the family. The financial factor is therefore important but it does not explain why so few men take parental leave even in countries where such leave is paid (although the fact that the amount the state pays

Table 8.2.   Behaviour concerning work participation of parents after the birth of children (percentages)

	Part-time work		Extra holidays		Parental leave		Resumed work		Sick leave		Resigned
	M	F	M	F	M	F	M	F	M	F	F
Belgium	1.1	16.5	12.1	2.1	0.7[a]	5.7[a]	65.1	44.8	20.8	1.7	9.9
Czech Rep	2.7	12.5	4.1	8.9	1.0	23.9	91.7	37.7	..	..	25.1
Italy	..	..	10.3	5.7	3.4	..	86.2	68.6	..	..	25.7
Netherl	..	8.0	32.1	4.0	..	1.0	67.8	12.0	..	8.0	64.0
Spain	..	6.4	2.2	4.8	..	..	97.8	58.0	..	..	30.6
Switzerl	8.3	11.6	39.4	3.7	..	8.6	52.3	8.6	..	2.2	65.3

[a]   In Belgium parental leave does not exist, but career breaks for parents do exist.

Source: *PPA National Surveys* carried out by: CBGS (Belgium, 1991), Charles University (Szech Rep., 1991); IRP (Italy, 1991); NIDI (The Netherlands, 1990); CIS (Spain, 1992) and University of Zurich (Switzerland, 1992).

is related to income may discourage men from taking parental leave). This problem could perhaps be overcome by specific 'attendance' allowances to be granted to individuals who care for other family members at home.

The work environment is strongly anchored in a traditional view of family roles. If a father wants to experience fatherhood to the full, to be in close contact with his children from the moment they are born and to express his feelings by helping to care for them on a day-to-day basis, he is still viewed as behaving in too feminine a manner, in a way too far removed from the objectives of company profit and production and from the characteristics of the male sex.

The social and work context in which fathers find themselves may therefore discourage them from requesting any leave. In fact, in has been noted that men who work in places where there is a high proportion of female staff — and where taking parental leave is considered more 'normal' — men are much more willing to apply for it (Näsman, 1991). From an early age men are encouraged to control their emotions and they often find it difficult to demonstrate publicly their desire to take parental leave. They therefore deny themselves the right to stay at home. However, it is probably also true that many fathers still share the view that parental leave is mainly for the mother and they do not think it opportune to go beyond their role as secondary support to their wives as regards caring for their children.

Nevertheless, it has been noted that almost all fathers take paternity leave where it exists. The low level of demand on the part of men to take parental leave may therefore depend on the neutrality of this measure which is not specifically a benefit to fathers alone, as in the case of paternity leave, but to the advantage of the mother or the father. In this way, the idea is implicitly communicated that the father should take parental leave only if the mother is unable to do so. This is very evident in countries like Italy where parental leave can be requested by the father if the mother gives up her right to stay at home in his favour and, in any case, only if the mother is actually entitled to parental leave (Palomba & Menniti, 1992). It is clear that in this case, parental leave is not a right for men but for women who may extend it to their partners if they do not intend to make use of it themselves. The philosophy of the law is subtle but clear and, above all, men are aware of the message that by taking parental leave they are enjoying a benefit envisaged for women.

Custodial fathers

The regulations governing the custody of children in the event of a marriage breakdown have changed since separation and divorce became available in Europe. From a historical point of view, until the mid-1800s, children were usually entrusted to the father but with the passage of time this state of affairs has radically changed (Barbagli, 1990). Today, at the moment of separation or divorce, with only a few exceptions, the children are entrusted to the mother. Basically therefore, increased matrimonial instability has produced a growing number of mothers living alone with their children, thus revolutionising traditional life models. It seems that society openly refuses to recognise that the father is capable of bringing up and educating his children.

The proportion of one-parent families headed by women in European Union countries is very high, reaching 84.1% in the case of parents living alone with their children, and a little lower (66.5%) if the parent is living with another person (partner, relation, friend, etc.). The high proportion of lone mothers is the result of the dominant cultural models which see the mother as the principal caregiver, besides the fact that women tend to live longer. In Sweden, too, only 8% of fathers have custody of the children under 18 years of age.

The reasons for there being so few custodial fathers are many, and in part are to be found in cultural and social difficulties besides the psychological difficulty a mother has in giving up her custodial role. There is a deep-rooted conviction that only a mother can invest the necessary time and energy in the job of educator, only she is able to give the right amount of love and affection. In short, she is essential to the balanced growth of her children. Everyone seems convinced of this — mothers, fathers and the judges who rule on the custody of minors.

Furthermore, whilst the fathers who apply for sole custody are in the minority the world over, those who apply for joint custody are on the increase. Joint custody is a way for fathers to retain their place alongside their wives in the raising of their children and to participate in decisions concerning them. The presence of the father is, in any case, supported and completed by the mother's presence and the responsibilities for men are fewer than in the case of sole custody. But it is clear that both parents must be in agreement in order to make a success of this type of custody and so it applies only in the case of 'civilised' separations in which the husband and wife are still willing to work together for the sake of their children.

Table 8.3.   Lone father families[a] in some European countries, 1987 (percentages)

	Total	% lone father with children	families[b] with children and others
Belgium	21.0	17.9	45.4
Denmark	10.3	10.3	--
France	14.5	12.7	28.7
Germany	16.3	14.4	29.2
Greece	17.8	15.4	29.1
Ireland	28.6	15.7	30.1
Italy	22.8	20.0	42.9
Luxembourg	20.6	17.8	30.4
Netherlands	24.3	14.5	81.4
Portugal	16.7	15.1	19.8
Spain	18.3	15.6	24.9
United Kingdom	20.6	16.7	38.6
EU	18.6	15.9	33.5

a   Children of all ages
b   % inside each family typology
Source: Livraghi (1993).

Men are increasingly prepared to fight for the custody of their children when their marriages break up and this is a sign of greater paternal responsibility and an increased awareness of the fact that a father has his own important role to play in the upbringing of his children. Unfortunately, this positive fact is counteracted by an increase in the number of separated or divorced fathers who abandon wife and children, paying no maintenance at all. The signs are therefore contradictory and in light of the data on families following divorce, future trends as regards opinions on the social value of fatherhood and on the new male identity seem rather unclear at present.

Fathering another man's children: stepfamilies

When explaining the behaviour of fathers who do not pay maintenance to their ex-wives and children, judges often take into consideration the fact that the man has remarried or is living with another woman, or that the ex-wife has formed a new family. In fact, the moral and material ties and obligations towards the previous family on the part of a man who has remarried are weakened: firstly he has to fulfill the role of provider for his new family, and secondly if his ex-wife remarries or has a stable partner, the ex-husband — in many cases with the support of the law — believes that it is up to the new partner to maintain what used to be his family (Barbagli, 1990).

In Italy, for example, if a lone mother remarries or has a stable partner, the ex-husband can ask for a reduction in the maintenance payments to be made to his wife and children. A man, if he remarries or starts to live with another woman, can ask for a reduction in the financial support to be given to his former family on the grounds that he now has to take on new family and economic responsibilities (Menniti & Palomba, 1992).

In the U.K. the stepfather is jointly responsible, with the biological father for his wife's children, but only during her lifetime. Basically, responsibility for the stepchildren on the part of the stepfather derives from the fact that he is living with the mother and not from any matrimonial tie. If the two get divorced, his obligation towards the stepchildren ends. Under the new Child Support System, parental obligations towards children are shared by the biological parents and the income of the stepfather does not influence any possible benefits to which the lone mother is entitled (Maclean, 1992).

In general, legislation on the subject does not give any clear indications for stepfamilies and the relationships created between stepfathers/mothers and stepchildren are not well defined. There are some regulations — which do not go far enough — which try to find a balance between the economic obligations of the biological father and the stepfather so as to ensure the well-being of the child. In all cases, however, no tie is recognised between a man and his stepchildren. In the eyes of the law, a family composed of two adults plus children is never the same as a family of two parents plus children and the role of the man who fathers any children that are not his own has no legal definition.

Some plain speaking

Fathers find it difficult to enjoy rights which would allow them to spend more time with their children. This is due to various factors linked both to sexist stereotypes to be found in the social and, above all, in work environment, and to the difficulty that men have in identifying themselves as caregivers — a difficulty that derives from male psychology and the way in which boys are brought up.

However, the identity of a man today seems to be influenced by the greater — or at least potentially greater — interchangeability of maternal and paternal tasks, even though the family framework is still typified by a marked asymmetry in the roles of men and women. In fact, it is the woman who still does most of the daily domestic work and who organises family life. Therefore, fathers seem to be seeking equality with the mother in the sphere of love for and emotional closeness to the children — but this takes place within a context of fundamental inequality between the sexes. Men do not do the laundry, they do not do the ironing or make beds but they will happily play with their children, they take them out for walks and they scrupulously follow the doctor's health and dietary rules (Bimbi, 1990; Sabbadini & Palomba, 1994).

How much do men want to feel equal to their wives? What are the real limits of these demands for equality at the level of love and affection and family closeness which are in contrast with the usual desire to uphold the two different family roles? And, above all, is the low male profile in the field of family policies really a question of a lack of equality between the sexes?

The behaviour of fathers is certainly very contradictory. Their desire to take on traditional mother roles seems to mask a difficulty in finding new growth paths and different identities for men and women within the family. Men have recently been complaining about the lack of equality between mothers and fathers but this is in contrast to the fact that not many fathers choose to benefit from their rights as fathers, for example as regards taking parental leave. Basically, if their wives are at home, men feel it is less necessary to personally take care of their children; when their wives are no longer at home, they begin to worry about the lack of equality between the sexes because they feel excluded from contact with their children.

Regulations existing under social policies give rise to discrimination in favour of mothers, but this discrimination is more formal than substantial. For example, lone mothers continue to give the care that they gave in the past, even if they are economically worse off but it is only following a separation or divorce that men feel that they are being denied the right to daily contact with their children although they probably did not actually spend much time with them previously.

In terms of rights, it is desirable for men to apply for and be granted the right to be able to stay at home with their children. In doing so, fatherhood is given a social value. It is also a good thing that the state abandon its mother-centred view of the parent/child relationship. It should recognise that either parent is able to raise the children. In this way, the cliche that men are incapable of being caregivers could be put to an end. It should be remembered that policy actions in the field of the family also have an educational role in that they can stimulate the growth of a greater symmetry in family roles and so it is right to introduce measures to allow and encourage men to spend more time with their children. Lastly, it is also a good thing that mothers put a brake on their monopoly in the area of family care and organisation by recognising that a man has the same potential. Even if the woman's monopoly is sometimes necessary because of the refusal of the man to participate, on other occasions it is the result of the mother's excessive possessiveness towards her children and their care.

Men and fathers still have a long way to go before they become a social group able to make political demands based on firm principles that are nevertheless practicable in day-to-day life. The road towards equality for men and women is one which leads to the recognition of the fact that both maternal and paternal roles are essential for children and their well-being. There are no short-cuts along this road. Men cannot ignore the question of the symmetry of roles within the family and they must be prepared to share the family workload in order to achieve equality in the right to love and to raise their children. Therefore, in all ways possible and, above all, through policy measures explicitly and exclusively designed for fathers. The state must stop seeing men and women as vastly different in terms of roles within the couple and the family, and must try to encourage men to find a new identity as males and fathers based on companionship rather than authority.

References

Barbagli, M. (1990). *Provando e riprovando*. Bologna: Il Mulino.
Bertoia C. & Drakich J. (1993). The fathers' rights movement. *Journal of Family issues, 14*, 4, 592-616.
Castellano, B.F. (1992). *Madri e padri*. Milano: Franco Angeli.
Finch, J. (1989). *Family obligations and social change*. Cambridge: Polity Press.

Furstenberg, F.F. & Harris, K. (1992). The disappearing american father? Divorce and the waning signficance of biological parenthood. In S.S. South & S.E. Tolnay (Eds.), *The changing American family: Sociological and demographic perspective.* Boulder, CO: Westview.

Jalmert, L. (1990). Increasing father participation to children care. *Men and Children Care*, EEC, V/1731/90-EN.

Jansen A.M. (1992). *Changing gender roles as reflected in children's families.* Paper presented at IUSSP Seminar on Gender and Family change in industrialized societies, Rome, 26-30 January

Le Galle, D. & Martin C. (1992). *Reconstituted families in France: The process of new family transition and production of norms.* Paper presented to the International Workshop on 'Reconstituted families in Europe', CBGS-EAPS, Brussels 26-28 November.

Leridon H. & Villeneuve-Golkap, C. (1988). Entre père et mère. *Population et Société, 220.*

Livraghi, R. (1993). Famiglia e problematica femminile. *Tutela, VIII,* 4.

Maclean, M. (1992). *Resource allocation between first and second families in U.K.* Paper presented to the International Workshop on 'Reconstituted families in Europe', CBGS-EAPS, Brussels, 26-28 November.

Menniti A. & Palomba R. (1992). *Reconstituted families in Italy.* Paper presented to the International Workshop on 'Reconstituted families in Europe', CBGS-EAPS, Brussels 26-28 November.

Näsman, E. (1990). Importanza della politica per la famiglia perchè i padri si occupino dei figli. *Men and Children Care*, EEC, V/1731/90-EN

Näsman, E. (1991). The Swedish case. *AA.VV. Famiglia, Figli e società.* Torino: Fondazione Agnelli.

OECD (1990). *Lone parent families: The economic challange.* Paris.

Palomba, R. & Menniti A. (1994). Genitori e figli nelle politiche familiari. In A. Golini (Ed.), *Le politiche di popolazione.* Bologna: Il Mulino.

Sabbadini, L.L. & Palomba, R. (1994). *Tempi diversi, Poligrafico dello Stato,* Roma.

Saraceno, C. (1992). *Elementi per un'analisi delle trasformazioni di genere nella società contemporanea e loro conseguenze sociali.* Paper presented to the Seminar 'Generi, strutture sociali e stili di vita', Pisa, 28-31 october.

Marry Niphuis-Nell

The paper of Rosella Palomba brings many interesting questions to the fore. So, the preparation of my reaction has not been very difficult. Moreover, I was in luck because I don't agree with a central argument in the paper. Perhaps it is better to say that we are in luck, because disagreeing is far more stimulating for discussion than agreeing.

What do I disagree with? I disagree with the central thesis in Palomba's paper, namely that in European and social policies fatherhood is not recognised and has a low, or no, visibility.
Contrary to this central thesis I would like to posit
a. that fatherhood is just as visible in legislation and other government policies as motherhood, and that it receives as much recognition; and
b. that this statement is valid for the past and the present. However, the way fatherhood and motherhood are recognised in legislation and other government policies has changed, and is still changing.

To support my thesis some explanation is needed:
1. What kind of policies am I talking about?
2. In which shape and form can we find recognition of fatherhood and motherhood in legislation and other policies? and
3. What is needed to let a child grow up into a healthy and well-balanced adult?

Ad 1. *Kind of policies*
The policies that are at issue here relate to family law as well as legislation and policies with respect to paid labour, social security and taxes. Relevant policy measures can be taken within the scope of family policies, financial or labour policies, or equal opportunity policies. This context can vary greatly by country.

Ad 2.   *Shape and form of recognition in policies*
Visibility or recognition of fatherhood and motherhood in state policies may
vary from very direct forms which are easy to identify to more indirect and
implicit forms which can be more difficult to identify. Very direct forms of
visibility and recognition of fatherhood and motherhood can be found in
family law, because here the terms father and mother are explicitly used.
Whenever the term parents is used, without specification as to sex, it is still
a direct form of recognition. Examples can be found in legislation for
parental leave, at least in some countries.

   In indirect forms of visibility or recognition the terms father, mother or
parents are not used but the regulation under consideration has an influence
on alternatives for parental behaviour. Such regulations can be designed
with the position of parents in mind but this is not necessarily the case.
Examples of these indirect forms can be found in regulations for part-time
work.

Ad 3.   *Necessities to let a child grow up*
And then, what is needed to let a child grow up into a healthy and well-
balanced adult?

   Firstly, one needs a house, clothes and food; one needs labour input by
the parents, for instance, to keep the house clean and to prepare meals; and
one needs money to buy the house, furniture and clothes, to name but a few.
Secondly, the child needs care and attention from his or her parents, who
should take on responsibility for its well-being, but others also play an
important role in this respect, such as child minders, family and friends, and
school.

The answer to the question 'Which parent does what?' is but too well-
known. Fathers earn the money needed and maintain some discipline and
mothers perform the tasks of day-to-day care for the children and the
household. Even today, with an increasing and in some countries even high
labour force participation by women with children, these are still the
primary responsibilities for fathers and mothers, respectively.

Legislation and state policy two or three decades ago

I now come to the question what legislation and state policies were like
some two or three decades ago. By that time the division of tasks between
fathers and mothers had been explicitly incorporated in government policy.
In family law this was expressed in the rule that the married man was the
head of his family and that he had authority over the children. In social
security and the tax system it was explicitly the married man who was
treated as the breadwinner and as such he had certain advantages over

married women and unmarried persons. In some countries married women were even excluded from participation in the labour market or from some specific occupations, or were excluded from certain regulations in the social security system. In policies with respect to the labour market there was only one norm as to working time. Employees were expected to work full-time, 40 hours or more a week, during their entire lifetime and their legal position in the social security system was based on that situation.

So, all these regulations implied a recognition of the specific breadwinner-task of fathers. At the same time they implied a recognition of the specific tasks of mothers because through these regulations they had the opportunity — and obligation — to stay at home with their children.

This situation with regard to family law, social security, tax systems and labour market policy, was found in most European countries until the sixties. However, since that period there have been a lot of changes in government policies. In order to understand what has happened we must realise what societal developments lie behind these policy changes:
- the struggle for equal opportunities for women;
- changes in family relations as a result of increasing divorce rates, and increasing unmarried cohabitation and extramarital births;
- low birth rates.

Women's emancipation, especially the increasing labour force participation by women with children, has paved the way for the adoption and improvement of regulations for leave of absence — in some countries for mothers only, but in most countries for both parents. Also, the increasing proportion of women working part-time has prompted governments to improve the legal position of part-time workers.

Another consequence was the elimination or at least the decline of facilities for male breadwinners in social security and tax systems. The male breadwinner has lost his privileged position and has eventually been replaced by a breadwinner who is neutral by sex and only has very small prerogatives. This implies that as a rule prerogatives for dependent partners have diminished or disappeared; partners are expected to earn their own income and if they don't, the state no longer sees it as its duty to support the sole breadwinner. However, when a couple has children the situation is somewhat different. For the maintenance of children there are still several financial facilities, like family allowances and tax facilities. These financial facilities for children are increasingly formulated in a neutral way as to the sex of the parent who is entitled to it.

Changes in family relations through increasing divorce, unmarried cohabitation and extramarital births put fathers in a weak legal position with respect to their children. This was a result of the fact that, initially, family law was not adjusted to these new developments. At present we can say that this seems to be a temporary phenomenon. Family law as regards the position of fathers outside of marriage is in an obvious state of flux, in which fathers are reconquering their lost position. They are assisted in their struggle by the judge and by the government which is preparing and implementing new laws.

Low birth rates, finally, have stimulated the adoption or improvement of facilities for parents, such as regulations for leave, child care facilities and family allowances. In some countries low birth rates have functioned as a more direct incentive, in other countries they stimulated the improvement of facilities for parents in a more indirect way.

Conclusion

I would now like to come back to my disagreement with Palomba's central thesis that fatherhood is invisible and not recognised in family and social policies. In family law, fatherhood is in a state of flux, but it is still as visible and recognised as in former times and just as recognised as motherhood is. In social security, tax systems and labour policy, in former times, the father used to be a parent with a sex; nowadays he is a parent without a sex. Through that, perhaps, he seems to be invisible; but when one takes a closer look, one can see him shimmer through his neutrality.

This conclusion has to be accompanied by an important remark. The fact that the father is present in government policies does not by definiton imply that these policies are vigorous enough to create real new fatherhood, instead of only marginal new fatherhood. In general, the creation of policies on the domain of division of tasks in families follows societal developments; not the other way around. Government policies seldom take the lead.

9

Fathers, patriarchy, paternity

Yvonne Knibiehler

One should never oppose a stable and homogeneous 'former times' to a 'present' where everything is confused. In the past there were 'new fathers' at every turning-point in civilisation, because paternity is a socio-cultural institution which is incessantly transforming under the pressure of multiple factors. Becoming aware of these changes can help us to better understand and better accept what we are undergoing. We are creatures of memory and history. The trajectory of each individual prolongs and modifies that of the generations which preceded him.

Has this evolution destroyed what is called 'patriarchy'? It is more correct to say that patriarchy, the domination of fathers over mothers and children, has also been transformed, without disappearing.

To note a number of essential stages, to begin with the foundations of patriarchy in Roman and Christian antiquity are recalled; then the characteristics of the customary patriarchy as it has developed in the West from the 12th century to the French Revolution; then the new conditions which have been imposed on the father in the contemporary period will be looked at in more detail.

The ancient forms of patriarchy

It can be said that paternity is not a fact of nature but a human invention. Maternity has always been evident due to the fact of pregnancy and childbirth. But not paternity. When was the human male able to decipher the biological connection which united him to his progeny? We do not know. But anthropologists ascribe great importance to the prohibition of incest which they discover at the origins of all civilisation. Men in a group are forbidden to touch women who are near relatives, their daughters, their sisters, so that they can give them as virgins to men from another group, and likewise. It was necessary to impose this rule so that the generation of fathers governed that of sons and daughters. In the West this seizure of power produced the patriarchal family (dominated by the father); one can also call it patrilinear (the children bear the name of the paternal line) and patrilocal (the children are born in the father's house). We know that elsewhere in the world civilisations exist where the family is matrilineal and matrilocal, but they are not at all matriarchal: there it is the brother of the mother who protects and governs the children.

The pater familias

The patriarchy instituted by Roman law is a model of the type.

The pater familias possessed *la patria potestas*, which is an absolute power. It allows no rights as in principle it is unlimited. It is the origin and source of all power, and includes the political and religious: the senators are called patres, the aristocrats patricii, the emperor pater patriae, and the God who represents the ruling function is Jupiter (root: father). Paternity is a primordial and unitary idea which finds expression within the family through the intermediary of the pater familias, but also in the city through the intermediary of the magistrates.

Paternity is in itself a magistrature, in the sense that the father raises the children in the service of the city, outside of which he is nothing. It is therefore the service of the collective which justifies the father's power in the first place. He also raises them to serve his genes, the great family which descends from the same ancestor. The child will have to bear and transmit a name, a patrimony, the titles and the goods; he will have to continue the cult of the ancestors.

Roman paternity is like an adoption, as the man is only father by his own will, notwithstanding the fact that his wife brought the child into the world. He does not have to recognise this child, he may refuse to raise it. The midwife places it at his feet; if he picks it up it means he accepts it as his (for a girl it is enough to say: 'Feed it'). In the opposite case the newborn will be exposed in a place especially for this purpose (at the foot of the column Lactaria, at the foot of Mont Aventin, near the Velabre marshes). Exposure was the main means of avoiding the family burden, of getting rid of the undesirables: the equivalent of contraception. It was above all puny children and surplus girls who were rejected. Moreover, even if he has children from his wife the pater familias can adopt. In general he adopted a nephew, a relative, the son of a friend. The boy adopted is never a small child, but an adolescent who can give his consent. The adoption breaks all legal bonds between the adopted and his begetter, but not the emotional bonds. The adopted boy has two fathers, but his social father prevails over his biological father. Women are not involved in adoption, neither as adopting parties nor as the party adopted.

The authority of the father lasts as long as he lives. The idea of coming of age did not exist in Rome. The children, even adults, themselves married and parents, are subservient to the pater familias, (at least if he does not free them, which often happened.)

This absolute power which the Roman law ascribed to the father was perhaps intended to involve him more in the paternal function, in responsibilities of upbringing. As it was not biologically evident, paternity was made evident by the law, by the power over the child: it was established when maternity was not.

Two customs confirmed the absolute power of the father: one is related to divorce, the other to nursing. In contempt of the moralist, divorce became frequent in Rome in the last century before Christ of the Republic. In principle the two spouses are equal, each can take the initiative: but as the spouse who asks for divorce risks losing his or her marriage portion, the initiative came most often from the husband. The procedure is simple and rapid, a letter is enough. The man generally divorced his wife without complaint or bitterness against his wife (in Rome marriage was not based on Eros); usually he aspired to a more advantageous, more glittering alliance. If the couple had children they stayed in the house where they were born, that of the father, whatever their age. But the father awarded to his wife what we call visitation rights.

A surprising and frequent practice was divorcing a pregnant wife to marry her to a friend of the husband, a friend without offspring. This was like a gift between men. The child born in the house of the second husband belonged to him, but everyone knew who the begetter was. The best known example is that of Cato of Utica who was lucky enough to have a fertile wife, Marcia. He divorced her when pregnant, so that she could marry Hortensius, who had no offspring; Marcia also gave other children to Hortensius. When he died Cato remarried Marcia. There was nothing unusual about this behaviour. It is explained by the fact that there was a shortage of fertile wives in Rome.

The children were not raised directly by their parents. They were entrusted to nurses and then to teachers. The custom of wet-nurses continued in Western societies. We should try to understand its origins.

And anyway, who was the authority in this? Certain moralists accused the noble ladies of not wanting to damage their breasts, and of lightly casting off the labours of motherhood. But the omnipotence of the pater familias leads us to think that if he had demanded that his wife give breast-feeding, she would not have been able to escape it. The truth is undoubtedly complex. The wealthy Roman citizen could have had many reasons for refusing maternal suckling. In the first place the desire to beget as many children without delay. The Emperor Augustine, worried about the demographic decline, promulgated laws (9 and 17 AD) depriving the right of inheritance from anyone having less than three children. Nursing played the role of a rather effective contraceptive: the husband was able to avoid that obstacle. Another reason is that it was believed that milk, like blood, transmitted hereditary traits. He who wanted to lend preference to his own line perhaps considered it sufficient that his wife had nursed the child with his blood for the nine months of pregnancy; for the nursing, it was easy to call on slave girls who had given birth at the right time. Yet another reason was fear of the intimacy which nursing created between mother and child: powerful emotional ties could follow, ties judged detrimental particularly for sons, who one did not want to get too attached to their mothers. The doctors did not discourage a practice which they compared to grafting: to have a good crop the gardener sows and then transplants the young shoots.

The father according to Christianity

We now know from science that the functioning of the Roman family was not transformed by Christianity but that it was evolving before any conversion. The Romans had started to appreciate chastity and fidelity, they cut down the practice of divorce and that of homosexuality before encountering the Christian doctrine and morality. Christianity came to consolidate, confirm, diffuse a new familial system. Christian monotheism led to the gradual appearance of a 'new patriarchal' father.

This new father was simultaneously exalted in his prestige and limited in his powers. Exalted in his prestige? There were no more feminine gods, the one God had become a father. The God of Israel was already unique but he was never called Father. Thus the Christian God was designated father by Jesus himself. The mystery of the Incarnation introduced a strict communication between God and his creatures. When God became a father, the father became the 'image of God' (said the theologians). Yet the terrestrial father figure was removed: Joseph is only a foster-father.

Exalted in his prestige, the father is limited in his powers. The only true creator of children who come into the world is God: the rights of God prevail over those of the begetter. (There has never been any question of the rights of children in Christianity). The father only has the children 'in trust' says Paul: he has to secure their lives, assure their education, respect their freedom. Even though abandonment or exposure was never prohibited, the number of children exposed was reduced to special cases. The only Christian manner of lightening the burden of the family is chastity, which moreover is strongly recommended. The Church Fathers taught that Christianity and virginity, 'salutary' virtues par excellence, are infinitely superior to fecundity. It was all as if a pious elite rejected the destiny of procreation...

Marriage is only a concession made to those who could not resist concupiscence. Monogamous and indissoluble, it became a severely austere institution which took the Church some centuries to impose. Divorce also fell into disuse even in the case of sterility of the couple. And the same applies to adoption: a sterile couple had to respect the will of God, resign themselves to having no heirs and leave their goods to the Church for the benefit of the poor. The only means for a man to become a father is to found a family and get married.

Another specific aspect of Christianity was to introduce the spiritual parent. The true birth of the child is its baptism: the priest welcomes it in the house of God. It is the soul which matters, more than the body. The priest represents God and assumes a paternity according to the Spirit. In addition, in the course of the ceremony it is not the father who has a dialogue with the priest but the godfathers and godmothers, responsible for the Christian education of the child, also parents in spirit.

These are the paternal figures inherited from antiquity. The Roman pater familias and the Christian father were submerged for a while by the great invasions and the chaos which followed them. Roman law, rediscovered from the 12th century onwards, aroused the admiration of medieval jurists; it allowed the reconstruction everywhere of la patria potestas upon which absolute rulers have always tried to base themselves:
God, the King, the father of the family, such is the trinity which guaranteed order under the old system.

As far as Christian values are concerned, they are no longer subscribed to nowadays. Church teaching no longer has the same clarity, the same vigour. In this respect the flock has changed: after the Romanised people of the Mediterranean basin, it preached to the barbarian hordes with various customs, then the feudal societies, then the subjects of the absolute Kings. Diverse interests resisted its message or adapted it. On various occasions the idea of the family has become blurred. The violence and disruption imposed tight, complex binds between men and individual autonomy practically ceased to exist; paternity seemed to dissolve into the group or the lineage. Even patrilinearity was lost: it was only after the 12th century that 'the name of the father' once again imposed itself everywhere.

Customary paternity

It was under the effect of such factors that what we can call customary paternity came into being. The society which was emerging after the 11th century was hierarchical, unequal: there were many models of fathers according to social milieu. This variety derives from the fact that the father's role, under the old regime, consisted above all of transmitting a patrimony, and it is the diversity of patrimonies on which the diversity of paternal figures is based.

The aristocratic model ascribed very great importance to lineage. The ancestors built up a patrimony fundamentally symbolic, composed of titles, privileges, honour, glory and power. Their role in education is of equal importance to that of the father: their portraits ornament the walls of the chateau and their brilliant history is put forward as the model for each descendant. The noble child, furnished with strong roots, is launched into the future only because of his inheritance: the father effortlessly inserts his children into a story which transcends both him and them. They are only the links in a chain, which the hereditary forename well expresses.

The aristocratic model imposes a distance. Like the Roman pater familias, the nobleman delegated the child-rearing tasks. The use of wet-nurses found new justifications. A taboo came to rest on sexual relations during nursing: they said that the sperm spoiled the milk. Sexual relations were supposed to cause periods to return thus making fertilisation possible, dangerous to the health of the mother and that of the infant at the breast. But the Christian father could not commit adultery. If he cannot stay away from his wife, he is led to reject the child.

In principle it was he who decided: all the wet-nurse contracts preserved (notably in Italy) are signed by two men, the begetter and the foster-father. The women have no say in the matter. The foster-father is invited to see himself in the role of Saint Joseph: in practice he sells his wife's milk as he sells that of a cow...

As titled families stayed in the countryside, the parents were not far from their offspring and the nursing industry created bonds between nobles and peasants: every noble child had a 'maman teton', a foster-father, brothers and sisters 'in milk' to whom he showed affection. But in the course of the classical age, titled families increasingly came to live in the cities. The cities were very unhealthy (without sewers, narrow streets, refuse) and epidemics developed rapidly. It was a reason for placing small children in the countryside. But then the separation between parents and children was complete.

More especially as the education of the young then increasingly took place in a college or boarding school. This formula was successfully proposed by the new religious orders of the Counter Reformation (Jesuits, Oratorians, Ursulines, Order of the Visitation). These religious wanted to reestablish Catholic influence after the religious wars; they were able to win the confidence of parents by coming up with programmes of education and training which corresponded perfectly to the needs of the ruling classes. In these institutions the essential role was restored to the confessor, the 'spiritual director'; he it was, rather than the begetter, who guided the infant soul. He was addressed as 'Father'. The religious, while they took a vow of chastity, did not at all believe themselves excluded from paternity, on the contrary, they felt they had received the best part, which is spiritual. That share relieved simultaneously the responsibility of the parents and also the burden of their authority over the children.

The children returned to their parental home around the age of 15 or 16, all the crises of adolescence behind them. They then established relations with their begetter founded on respect rather than on tenderness. This aristocratic model did not scandalise anyone: far from criticising them, those who aspired to rise in the social ladder adopted or imitated the behaviour of titled families.

The peasant model is numerically the most widespread. Here, patrimony is the land, a vast estate or a simple plot. The peasant is particularly attached to what he has won with such difficulty. For a long time he was a serf in fief to his lord; it was only after the 11th century that the 'tenures' became free. This became the symbol of liberty, of dignity. The cult rather than the culture of the land, shaped the paternal soul. The peasant bred less out of fatalism than to compensate in advance for infant mortality which always threatened to deprive him of an heir. But he was caught in a bind: if death does not take enough, the number of children could form a destructive burden. That is why infanticide has lasted in the countryside (despite the prohibition of the Church), often camouflaged as an accident. And in periods of misery deserted children multiplied. The poorest peasants sometimes put their children into domestic service from the age of 10.

Educational tasks were divided according to sex. The father did not concern himself with infants, who depend on the mother. He paid little attention to daughters: they had to learn the feminine tasks and roles which the father could not show them. But he took charge of the boys as soon as they were able to help him: he subjected them to the demands of the farm animals, to the whims of the weather, to the rhythm of the seasons. It was an education through work, by example, not very verbal and often rough. 'Work, do your best, it's the best basis' says the labourer in La Fontaine. Violence was part of a virile identity, the child was not spared shouts and blows. But that was rarely reduced to a face-to-face confrontation with his begetter; it was other men who contributed to his education: an uncle, an elder brother, the godfather, the neighbor. And from his fifteenth year the young man joined a 'youth society' where he achieved socialisation far from the paternal gaze. The equivalent existed on the female side.

The third model is that of the city dweller: artisan, tradesman, those who practice liberal professions or have purchased offices. What they transmit is essentially a state, a trade. Labour is not enough, you need savoir-faire, knowledge, talent. The father who wants his son to succeed him is not only a master but also a teacher: the relationship gets richer, more complex. And the daughter is annexed. As the father often works at home, close to his own, he wants to marry his daughter to a colleague, to a disciple, and he educates her to this end. All the historians agree in thinking that it was in the urban middle classes that family intimacy ripened, that the bond between father and children retrenched. There, familiarity is practiced before the Revolution, emotions begin to be expressed. Rousseau, who came from this milieu, expressed this sensibility in the Nouvelle Heloise and in Emile. As did Diderot in the theatre.

One can object that Rousseau abandoned the five children he had with his companion, something which draws attention to the father as abandoner, an ancient figure as we have seen. In the classical age one can distinguish two categories of abandoning fathers:

a   the poor ones: Tom Thumb's father loses his children in the forest so as not to see them dying of hunger. In the cities, in hard times, many children were abandoned. There were institutions to accommodate the children from the 14th century onward, but almost always in pitiful conditions. Mortality was appalling. These institutions looked for foster families, offering payment, without much success. Nevertheless there were always foster families who were prepared to take in the foundlings 'for the honour of God'; that is, for free. They raised them like their own children and left them some assets: it was an adoption of the heart, for lack of legal adoption.

b   The other category of the deserting father is the illegitimate father. It was not always like that. In the Middle Ages, and even in the 16th and 17th centuries, the great lords accepted their illegitimate offspring, raised them and made settlements on them. But after the Counter Reformation, the Church became increasingly strict about this, with the support of the King. Little by little, having bastards became shameful and men no longer recognised them. To begin with judges did their utmost to find the absconding fathers; but at the end of the 18th century, the scourge got worse and the judges gave up. It was then that the expression 'girl-mother' made its appearance: the language admitted that an unmarried girl could have a child, that a child has a mother, but no father. Some hospices acquired 'turn-boxes' in which the fatherless infant could be placed anonymously; the 'girl mother' could forget it and return to the path of righteousness. Henceforth the abandonment would be attributed to the mother, no longer to the father.

Preindustrial societies thus show diverse models of paternity. But the shared, fundamental trait which must be insisted upon is the preponderance of the father's responsibility. The public authorities only recognise him. The child's destiny depends on who its father is, its social status is that of its father. The father keeps 'the patria potestas'.

If customs vary from one region to another, the law of the father is hard everywhere. His power of punishment allows him to throw his sons in prison, his daughter in the convent, by simply asking the judge (a letter with seal is enough). The son under 30 and the daughter under 25 cannot enter into a contract: they can neither get married, not enter religious orders, nor use their own assets. It is the father who decides the future of each one, sometimes even without notification; it is he who negotiates favourable alliances where interest prevails over feelings; it is he who fixes the amount of a dowry, or an inheritance; it is he who directs his younger children into the Church. He demands not only respect and obedience from all, but also love and recognition, as he gave them life and supported them in their early years. Freud found the law of the father still intact at the end of the 19th century.

The law of the father is hard for the father too. In order to protect the patrimony he has to favour the eldest at the expense of the younger, the boy at the expense of the girl, the legitimate at the expense of the bastard, occasionally reluctantly. He does not allow himself the right to show feelings. Tenderness would be a sign of weakness: it would reveal their power to the child (or to the woman).

The advent of the Oedipal family

The decline of the 'traditional' family is also above all characterised by a slow and progressive withdrawal of the presence and the power of the father, and by an affirmation of the mother. This counterbalancing movement leads to the threshold of the Oedipal family.
The factors of change are political and economic.

Political factors
Locke, Puffendorf, Rousseau, the Encyclopedia, are the philosophical bases of a rationalism which in the 18th century undermined all the foundations of absolute power. The authority of the father, said the philosophers and the jurists, is only justified by the needs of the child; it must cease when the child leaves his care. The State can, and must, regulate the rights of the father and transform them into educational duties. In this manner, on the eve of the French Revolution an awareness began to take shape of the rights of the child, which is no longer the property of its begetter. And in this new perspective, even the rights of God are called into question.

In France, for example, the revolutionary legislation brought about a reversal of values. La Constituante, while abolishing the letters with seal in 1790, limited the paternal right to punish. La Legislative defined the age of majority at 21 years (law of 20-25 September 92): the father lost all power over the child, boy or girl, when they reached that age. La Convention (law 7-11 March 93) imposed the equal division of inheritances, which deprived the father of the free disposal of patrimonial assets (a means of pressuring rebellious children). In addition the patriots increased the projects of public instruction which created State schools and national programmes. And the Convention wanted to make the schools of the Republic compulsory for all children, including girls. Balzac saw the execution of Louis XVI (21 January 1793) as the symbol of the 'murder of the father'. It is true that the Napoleonic Code partially reestablished paternal power with regard to the right of punishment and inheritances. But it retained the fundamentals.

Economic factors
The economic factors worked against the father. The first industrial revolution reduced salaries, which sometimes compelled the mother and children to go and work in the factory. Child labour was soon a scandal: it was ruining the health of the race, the vital force of the nation. But the protection of children was confined to the father's authority over them. It was timidly that the French lawmakers in 1841 decided to promulgate a law regulating child labour, a law which was badly applied. Compulsory schooling in 1882 met the same fate. Finally, in 1889, after 9 years of

passionate discussions, a law was passed authorising the judge to strip a man of his paternal authority. Indeed the police deplored the worsening of child 'vagrancy', and juvenile delinquency; in certain cases it was established that the father himself pushed his children into theft and prostitution. Paternal authority then appeared to be guilty of an abuse which menaced the social order. The power of the father ceased to be a thing untouchable in itself, it was subject to the criteria of public safety and placed under the control of the community. Patriarchy was shaken to its very foundations. In fact the law was only seldom applied and only affected those on the margins of society.

But even in the middle and upper strata, economic evolution tended to reduce paternal authority.

The rise of capitalism gradually ruined family businesses. People no longer produced at home. To feed their offspring the father was thus forced to leave his home. This had several consequences. In the first place the man disassociated his professional life from his family life, and he tended to ascribe more and more importance to the former, which promised him, or at least suggested to him, new chances of success, of repute, of social climbing, of personal valorisation. The novels of Balzac are peopled with young ambitious men beside which le Pere Goriot, devoured by paternal love, inspires more pity than envy. Many men delayed or even rejected marriage, to indulge in this new liberty which was called the 'boy's life'. They did have illegitimate children, but unlike the nobles of the classical age they did not recognise them, they left them with the 'girl-mother', doomed to public contempt and to misery. Married men restricted their offspring. Procreation lost much prestige in masculine consciousness (the 'rabbitism' of some was even ridiculed) and the burdens of child-rearing began to seem heavy.

At the same time, as he worked outside the home the father's work became invisible, and his children could no longer measure its excellence, nor the results, nor its worth. Suddenly his authority was void of all justification, its only function was repressive, and then it triggered the child's rebellion, or else it met with his indifference.

Another separating factor was study: the possible success of the children seemed increasingly their personal doing. They owed much less to the patrimony passed on by the father, much more to the knowledge which the father did not possess.

Let us add the catastrophic effects of the First World War. Not only were the fathers absent for far too long, but in addition they were demoralised by a terrible slaughter, whose justification was no longer at all obvious. Returning to the home they looked for emotional consolation.

During those times the centre of gravity in the family shifted toward the mother. As the father went to work outside the mother established herself in the home ('the mother at home'), assuming an increasing educational responsibility, even with regard to the boys. Furthermore, they were bringing fewer children into the world which allowed them to have more individual relations with each one. They got used to the idea that their children belonged to them, that they knew them better than their father could know them. It was then that maternal love became the object of a lyrical exaltation. Moreover, after the restoration of divorce (1884 in France), it was almost always the mother to whom the Judge entrusted the children of the divorcing couple. The female worker was much more highly esteemed than the male: she was counted upon to preserve and transmit family virtues and Christian faith, to prevent her sons going to the cabaret and listening to socialists. The First World War which left so many orphans confirmed that women could raise their children alone, without any major risk to the latter.

This evolution of parental roles was very slow and for a long time was invisible to the father. It was only between 1965 and 1975 (in France) that the decisive laws on parental authority, on the decriminalisation of contraception and abortion made the powers of the mother clear.

Nevertheless, to appreciate the father's new situation, it is necessary to take into account another very decisive element, that is, the invasion of private life by public powers. Those who prophesy matriarchy are mistaken. Certainly, the mother and child are less and less under the control of the father, but they have come under the control of social workers, doctors, the shrink, the judge. And the laws which determine their lot are developed and promulgated by men. Patriarchy no longer functions inside the family, but it remains powerful in society.

As far as the educator or the child-carer is concerned, one can see a professionalisation, the parental function becoming technical, with training and diplomas; to such an extent that one may well wonder whether someday it will be necessary to study and pass an exam to become a parent. At the same time, a woman declares her pregnancy to the father if she so desires, but she is obliged to declare it to those responsible for public health; she is obliged to spend the pregnancy under medical supervision; she brings the child into the world outside the father's house; she subjects the child to compulsory visits. The father is not excluded from the process, but he is of no use whatsoever. And in addition, since Freud psychoanalysis has strongly desanctified the patriarchal family: the mother-child, father-child relationship has become a scientific subject. One specialised researcher studies the divorced father, another the violent father; one questions the applicant for vasectomy, another the sperm donor etc.. The last invaders are the jurists. The ancient right of the family is currently submerged by the right of the child: axiomatic and precious certainly, but it postulates a possible incompetence on the part of the parents. There are children's judges — but also judges for family matters, and children's lawyers.

All these intermediaries are becoming indispensable since the unstable, 'uncertain' (says Louis Roussel) family is coming together, decomposing, recomposing, ad infinitum, and the adult male assumes in his home the education of children begotten by others. The doctor, the shrink, the judge, these are the new fathers. Why would the 'old' father not be at a loss? The figure of the father, formerly a reflection of divine majesty, has been detached once and for all from the sacred. What is called the crisis of paternity, is the awareness of these phenomena; it has been slow and belated. Currently, a dual reaction by the fathers can be observed:

a   one is violent, is the act of angry men who cannot accept the loss of their ancient supremacy. They are regrouping in societies to defend the 'paternal condition', and to seek recognition of their rights which they consider to be flouted. They occasionally find redress. In France the law has granted parental authority to the biological father not married to the mother if he has recognised the child (with the consent of the mother).

b   the other reaction tries to be constructive. It is the act of psychologists or psycho-sociologists who want to help men build new relations with their children. A flood of works since 1945 have had as title something roughly approximating 'The vocation of father'. The term vocation is interesting, this shows that paternity is no longer a power: it has become a service and a relationship. These books insist on the emotional contentment which paternity brings, even if adoptive. From whence comes the behaviour of these 'new fathers' who want so much to be nurturing, but who always avoid the servile tasks, (giving the meal, but not washing the plate...)

What would appear to be the newest thing in this definition of the vocation of father, is the perpetual movement which characterises our culture: everything is evolving too quickly. The father can no longer help his child at school because the knowledge and method are continuously mutating; he can no longer impose a profession, nor even a morality, for analogous reasons. And as the masculine and feminine roles are tending to flow together, he can no longer prepare his son for a virility resembling his own.

Here we touch upon the core of the problem. Wondering how to be a father is also wondering how to be a man.

The fathers of the younger generations should know that from now on they will have three sorts of relationships to manage, and to begin with, to construct: with a woman-mother, with the public authorities, and with the children who are no longer, and undoubtedly never again will be, uniquely theirs.

Note:
This chapter summarises the work by Yvonne Knibiehler, *Les pères aussi ont une histoire*, Hachette, 1987.

Tamara Hareven

The article of Yvonne Knibiehler represents a summary of her book, *Les pères aussi ont une histoire*. In the article, the author argues that the evolution of the role of the father from antiquity to the present did not destroy the patriarchate, but rather transformed it, and that many of the historic characters of the patriarchate have survived, but in a modified form. She outlines several stages in the evolution of the role of the father from antiquity to the present. The first stage is the patriarchy in the roman period; the second is the emergence of the patriarchy in medieval Christianity along lines already developed in the Roman period prior to Christianity; and the third encompasses an undifferentiated long phase stretching from the French Revolution to the present, which the author defines as 'La Famille Oedipienne'. Because of the absence of empirical supportive data in this paper, it is difficult to comment in detail on the author's arguments. I shall address my more general comments specifically to her interpretation of the last period involving the emergence of the 'Oedipal Family'.

Knibiehler outlines linear changes that emerged in this period stretching from the French Revolution to the present, without differentiating between more specific important historical transitions that may have occurred since the late eighteenth century. She sketches the evolution and transformation of the father's role and status as one from an omnipotent patriarchy, involvingthe father's control over his family and his children to a weaker and more distant father role; and from one of the father's exclusive economic, educational and legal control over the children, to one where the father's functions have been taken over by public institutions and agencies. Viewing the emergence of the mother's monopoly over child-nurture as a main cause, she depicts the role of the father in contemporary society as distant and ambiguous. She argues that in our times, fatherhood has become a kind of profession — *metier*.

The author explains these changes as resulting from several historical developments: The idealogy of the Philosophes about childhood; the legislation that established the rights of children during the French Revolution; the industrial revolution that undermined the father's authority as breadwinner; the further development of capitalism, that has led to the separation of the father's workplace from the family abode; and finally to educational reforms that transferred educational authority from the father to other institutions. These changes, she argues, were accompanied by the idealisation and sentimentalisation of maternal love and the monopoly that mothers developed over child nurture.

The model that Knibiehler is depicting here for France is also that of the bourgeois family as it emerged in Western Europe, as well as in the United States in the late eighteenth and early nineteenth centuries. This family type is characterised by the separation of the spheres between the home (mother) and the outside world (father), by the emergence of the family as a child-centered and private refuge, and of motherhood becoming a full-time career.

When interpreting the changes in father's role during this period, both as a consequence of industrialisation and in the context of the emergence of the 'domestic' family, Knibiehler oversimplifies the model. Recent research on the process of industrialisation has shown that factory work did not necessarily undermine the father's authority over his family members. In the early phases of industrialisation, entire families worked together and, in many cases, the father acted as a 'quasi foreman', supervising his children in the new factory. The transformation of the roles of both fathers and mothers across the society has been more gradual and uneven among various social classes. The separation of the workplace from the home following industrialisation as Knibiehler describes them and which led to the restructuring of familial roles occurred initially only in the middle class. Throughout the nineteenth century, rural and working-class families continued to maintain a collective family economy. In urban working-class families, wives often worked side-by-side with their husbands and their children. Even if they did not work together in the same establishment, working-class families continued to maintain a strong collective family economy, but one in which the father was still considered the main breadwinner.

Similarly, Knibiehler's emphasis on 'father absence' as a result of the separation of the spheres between home and work was limited to the middle class. Even among middle-class families, however, the father took on new roles such as a sharing of leisure activities with the family, and particularlywith the children. The author mentions World War I as a significant factor in promoting the father's absence from the family and in shifting the weight to the mother, but does not address the impact of World War II on gender roles and on the division of labour in the family.

When explaining changes in the role of the father, it would be worthwhile mentioning three additional significant developments that may have contributed to the changing role of the mother and the father, but which are absent from Knibiehler's explanations. These are: first, the demographic changes which had a significant impact both on fathers and mothers — the decline in age at marriage (since the nineteenth century), the decline in fertility and the resulting changes in the life course and in age configurations within the family. These changes had a significant impact on both parents. They have affected the time overlap between mother and father and parents and children over their life course. The decline in fertility has reduced the number of children in the family, and has thus affected the role of parenting; and finally, the decline in mortality and the extension of life in the later years has extended the period of parenting and has increased the opportunity for fathers' overlap with their adult children.

Secondly, the increase in mothers' labour force participation — which modified the role of the father as an exclusive breadwinner, and which also led, among certain social groups, to a renegotiation of gender roles within the family and to sharing of child-rearing tasks in the family.

The third is the increase in divorce, which has further removed the non-custodial fathers from their children. Remarriage following divorce, on the other hand, has expanded the identity of fathers from one that is not strictly dependent on biological paternity.

The main problem with the narrative of linear change which Knibiehler provides is in its simplification of the complexity of the process of change and of class differences. Furthermore, mothers and fathers act out and negotiate their roles within the family, as well as the social milieu. The changes that Knibiehler sketched here need to be understood, therefore, in the *context* of changes in the family. One needs to understand what transformations occurred within the family (as well as society) that have affected the respective roles of mothers and fathers, as well as their interactions with each other. Did the fact that some of the family's functions had been taken over by educators and judges really weaken the role of parents, or did it lead to greater specialisation in the family and to a greater concentration on emotional nurturing? In other words, does loss of power in certain areas of parenting provide empowerment in others?

10

Understanding the future of fatherhood
The 'daddy hierarchy' and beyond

Arlie Russell Hochschild

In her memoir, Sweet Summer, Bebe Moore Campbell describes a conversation between four African American girls growing up in the urban middle-class in the 1950's. Their fathers had divorced their mothers, but to varying degrees the girls were still 'daddies' girls'. Comparing their fathers to a prior image of a 'good dad' in a 'good family' in their time and place, they located them as higher or lower on a 'daddy hierarchy' (The children presumed the presence and involvement of their mothers and so declined to arrange a hierarchy of mothers.) At the top of the girls' list was the daddy of a little white girl who spent time with her and built her a beautiful doll's house. In the middle were daddies present but preoccupied with repairing broken cars, or daddies who loved their children but spanked them too hard. At the bottom were 'dead beat dads' who disappeared from their children's lives altogether[1].

Drawing on the American experience, I trace changes in both the ideals and reality of fatherhood. The older ideal of the father who commands authority and pays the bills has partly given way to the ideal of the nurturant new father who bonds with his child (but still pays some bills.) In addition, this new ideal of the nurturant father is born in a context of multiplying ideals and images of a good father and a good family.

As the ideals of fatherhood have changed and diversified, so too have the realities. Compared to their fathers and grandfathers, modern new fathers are more tightly bonded to their children, while dead beat dads and anonymous sperm donors in fertility clinics are far less so.

---

1   One purpose of the girls' conversation is to try to agree on the definition of a 'good daddy'. Is a good daddy one who does not buy a new car for himself before he buys necessities for his child? Is he one who visits and calls often? Is he one that negotiates reasonably with one's mother about one's welfare? Answers to such questions become the basis of their 'daddy hierarchy'.

Animating changes in both the ideal and reality of fatherhood, I shall argue, are two clusters of trends. One set of trends presses women to work outside the home, which in turn sets up pressures for men to do more at home. Doing more at home, men often strengthen bonds with their children. The second cluster of trends push in the opposite direction — namely, toward more labile bonds between men and women and weaker bonds between men and children. These two clusters of trends operate in a context of 'the capitalisation of emotions' and influence the degree to which men emotionally 'invest' in their children. Cultural ideals guide the way. The future of fatherhood will reflect the effect of theses two clusters of trends on behaviour and emotional life. How far these trends go in influencing fatherhood depends, in part, on the degree to which culture shields people against the rationalisation of emotional life[2].

Trends in ideals: the new father and the alternatives

Forty years ago it was socially acceptable for a father to come home after work, pick up the newspaper, wait for dinner, play with his children when he felt like it and enforce his authority as required. That was 'good enough'. Today, in addition to working for pay, a father is expected to attend the birth of his children, be an interested guide, an engaged friend and warm presence to his children at home (Cutright, 1986). As an ideal in Western culture, the 'new father' has come to challenge the older ideal of the breadwinner, even as it sometimes blends with it[3].

Ideals function differently in post industrial society than they have in earlier times. In an ever more rationalised capitalist culture, the principles of public life increasingly apply to private life as well. Just as capitalists invest and divest economic capital in more or less profitable enterprises, so fathers invest — and

---

2   Trends run on cultural soil. I take the rationalisation of emotional life to be a key aspect of that 'soil'. Drawing from the Frankfurt School of Sociology I focus here on rationalisation - a process that applies to four aspects: a) a mentality (the tendency to 'save' time, plan, divide life into means and ends); b) a norm (a value on the principle of efficiency; c) a set of social relations (time and purpose limited, based on the principle of exchange); and d) a set of wider social circumstances (availability of many services, commodification in advanced capitalism). Thus, the rationalisation of emotional life refers to the shaping and management of emotions to adapt individuals to life which has become rationalized in these four ways (e.g. to try to feel what it is useful to feel).

3   As a cultural image, the new father masculinizes a cultural turf formerly seen as the province of women. So in the film Kramer vs Kramer the nurturant dad who kisses his son goodnight is also shown as athletic and undomestic (e.g. eating from cans 'the way a man would'). Each cultural notion of a good father thus has differing relations to the image of a manly man.

tragically, divest — emotional capital in their children. Ideals guide 'investment strategies'. I do not mean by this that modern fathers are more detached from their children, only that emotional men increasingly live in a culture of emotion management, a culture that demands a capacity for attachment and detachment.

The modern mix of ideals of fatherhood thus point to a mixture of emotional strategies. Even as men are increasingly encouraged to invest more emotional capital in their children, they are also influenced by a culture of emotional 'deregulation' which frees them to 'divest' from their children and become dead beat dads. Much new age ideology of self discovery may correspond to new notions of 'moveable capital' applied to the emotional realm.

Any ideal of fathering corresponds to a certain transfer of resources from father to child. These resources can be seen as various forms of capital — for example, economic, cultural and emotional capital (Bourdieu, 1984). A father may pass on his farm to his son (economic capital). Or he may pass on occupational training (cultural capital). We can think of the 'new father' ideal as the promise to transfer a form of emotional cultural capital from father to child[4].

Some children are 'rich' and others 'poor' in emotional capital. That is what the 'daddy hierarchy' describes. Like material capital, paternal emotional involvement helps reproduce individual class standing. Insofar as social class is correlated to marital stability, and marital stability to fatherly involvement, emotional capital can become a means through which class reproduces itself. Insofar as social class is not related to marital stability or marital stability to a father's emotional investment in his children, emotional capital is its own thing. Whether 'emotional capital' is linked to, or independent of social class, the ideal of the involved father is an ideal sustaining the idea of emotional investment in one's progeny[5].

At the same time, the ideal of the 'new father' is a contested ideal. Perhaps most American children who grow up without strong emotional bonds with their

---

4   The current research on fatherhood provides material and guideposts for an as yet undeveloped structural theory of fathering. Currently two theories might be mentioned: a) interest theory, according to which women mainly rear children because it is in men's interest to leave it to women (Polatnick, 1974); b) psychoanalytic theory, according to which women mainly rear children because, for social reasons, they want to do so more than men do (Chodorow, 1980).

5   We know that the higher the class, the more stable the marriage in general, and the more stable the marriage, the more father-child contact. But we also know that some upper class marriages are unstable and some children of stable marriages have little real contact with their fathers.

fathers, like the girls of Sweet Summer, nonetheless accept the ideal of 'the new father' (Billingsley, 1993). But in addition, a growing minority have come to question the nuclear family to which the 'new father' is the latest adaptation. Other systems of transfer of emotional capital — by those who are not the biological father — are proposed as equally beneficial to a child. Lesbian mothers who conceive children through artificial insemination, heterosexual mothers single by choice or necessity, seek to legitimate alternatives to the 'new father'. The role and ideal of parent is transferred, as it is in some non-Western societies, to related or unrelated males, or to females. To escape the responsibilities of the new father, Barbara Ehrenreich has argued, some fathers themselves reject the ideal (Ehrenreich, 1983). Thus, on the cultural horizon are those who question both the indispensibility of a child's emotional tie to the biological father, and the principle of legitimacy. The daddy hierarchy is no longer a hierarchy with an up and a down, but a set of parallel ideals of parenting. In this view, neither kinship nor gender need guide the emotional investments in children that children need.

Trends in reality: diversity of fatherhoods

Parallel to the growing diversity in ideals of fatherhood is a diversity in the realities of it. The breadwinner/authority father has been marginalised by the new father on the one hand and the dead beat dad on the other (Gerson, 1993).

Two clusters of trends have fostered this spread of realities. On the one hand, inflation and the globalisation of capitalism have reduced male wages, creating a need for women to contribute to the family income. At the same time, a declining birth rate and higher rates of female education and the industrialisation of housework have created opportunities for women to work. Today, two out of three American mothers with preschool children work outside the home, and half the mothers of children aged one and under. As ideal and reality, the new father is partly a response to this new reality.

In my research on fifty 2-job couples in the San Francisco Bay Area, I found that one out of five working husbands were 'new men' in the sense of fully sharing the care of the children and home and fully identifying themselves as men through this sharing (Hochschild, 1989). In Michael Lamb's 1986 review of large-scale quantitative studies on fathering, he distinguishes between engagement (for example, feeding child, playing catch), accessibility (cooking in the kitchen while the child plays in the next room) and responsibility (being the one who makes sure the child gets what he or she needs). When wives go out to work, men become more engaged and accessible but not more responsible for their children (Lamb 1986, pp. 8, 11). In two out of three ways, men are doing more.

At the same time, another cluster of trends points in an opposite direction. The rising rate of divorce and unwed pregnancies is related to weakening bonds between fathers and children. The United States has the highest divorce rate in the world; half of all marriages now end in divorce (In the Netherlands in 1980, one in four marriages ended in divorce). Sixty percent of American divorces involve children. Of divorces involving children, roughly half of the fathers eventually lose touch with their children. In his large-scale study of children of divorce, Frank Furstenberg found that nearly half of the children had virtually no contact with the non-custodial parent (90 percent of whom were fathers) within the last year. One out of six had seen him as regularly as once a week (Furstenberg, 1983)[6]. The proportion of children living with two parents has declined from 85 percent in 1970 to 72 percent in 1991.

Fathers who lose touch with their children often retreat into what Judith Wallerstein so poignantly calls phantom relationships with their children, putting a photo of the child on an office desk, and thinking, "My child can call me any time he wants" (Wallerstein, 1989). Such fathers imagine a relationship at one end that a child does not feel at the other.

In addition, based on the National Survey of Children, James Peterson and Nicholas Zill were able to compare the relationship of children (aged 12 to 16) with their parents as this varied according to different types of family situations. Even among children living with both biological or adoptive parents, a scant 55 percent had positive relations with both parents. Of children living only with their mothers, 25 percent had good relations with both parents. Of children living with just their fathers, 36 percent had good relations with both parents perhaps because the mothers stay more involved (Peterson and Zill, 1986).

Parallel to the rise in divorce, is a rise in the rate of out-of-wedlock pregnancies largely (though not exclusively) associated with the growth of poverty. According to Dugger, the percentage of children born to unwed parents

---

6   In his study of sixty African American mothers and the fathers of their children, Frank Furstenberg found an "unambiguous and universal" norm that biological fathers are obliged to support their children materially and emotionally (Furstenberg, 1991, p.8). But most of these poor African American young fathers nonetheless gradually lose touch with their children. Men offered different accounts for why this occurred: "It's not my child; Someone else has taken my place; My support isn't going to the child; I don't have the money; She doesn't let me see my child" (1991, p. 12-14). For their part, the young mothers argue that "men are spoiled," or "selfish, indulges," or "men can't accept the responsibilities of parenthood," and "aren't ready to become fathers" (Ibid 15). Furstenberg found a high level of mistrust between men and women. At the same time, the father and (though this was less obvious) the mother needed to form what Furstenberg calls an umbrella contract between the pair in order to facilitate the father-child bond.

increased from 5 percent in 1958 to 18 percent in 1978 to 28 percent in 1988 (Dugger, 1992). The vast majority of unwed mothers know the identity of the father, and many cohabit with them, but the breakup rate is higher for cohabiting than for married couples, and fewer than a fifth of unwed mothers report receiving child support for the year prior to breakup (Furstenberg, 1991)[7]. These trends make children more vulnerable to emotional 'divestment'.

To sum up, one cluster of social trends lead men to become more involved in their children's lives than their fathers or grandfathers were. Another set of trends lead men to become less so while a diminishing number continue the tradition of their fathers as traditional breadwinners. The overall picture is thus one of increasing diversity.

Social contradictions and male identity making

To be sure, in the past, there were always many ways of being a father. Fathers deserted families under the guise of seeking work, migrating, or under no guise at all. Similarly many breadwinner fathers were very emotionally engaged with their children even when it was not their 'role' to be. But the sheer diversity within the realm of values and behaviour, and more important, the contradiction between the ideal of the new father and the reality of the disengaged dad are new, at least in scope[8].

---

7   In any society, some sub-groups become a bellwether for the rest of society. In the United States, African Americans of the 1950's and 1960's foretold the future for white Americans in the 1980's and 1990's. The trends that characterized African American families earlier spread to whites later. The tendency for mothers to work outside the home, for men to share the care of the home and childrearing (black men still do more than white men, though still less than black women), and the higher rate of non-marital pregnancy and divorce - increasingly describe white families in America today. Even the bifurcation of fatherhoods into new men and dead-beat dads occurred first for blacks, later for whites. The reason, I believe, has to do with the absence for blacks earlier - and for whites later - of the central breadwinner wage for men. In a sense, then, the new man is not so new.

8   The cultural context of fathering in the future is thus likely to remain plural. This means that each type of father becomes the cultural context for the other. Each type of father is likely to live in a fathering subculture congenial to himself, but different kinds of fathers also know about each other's subcultures. Active fathers see films, hear stories about, have friends who are - and perhaps themselves once were - dead-beat dads. For their part, dead-beat dads see films, hear stories about or have friends who are, or were once themselves, new fathers. They compare themselves to other kinds of fathers. They define themselves as more or less lucky, emotionally richer or poorer in relation to active fathers. Just as unionized companies set the context for non-union companies, and the communist world once set the context for the capitalist world, so different realities of fatherhood set the context for each other. This context-setting is as important as the diversity on which it is based.

As a consequence, fathers of all sorts have a more active relationship to culture. Fatherhood is increasingly that which one does, and less what one simply is. For example, a married father may come home from work and play ball in the back yard with his son. The boy is there. The yard is there. The ball is there. His father played with him when he was his son's age. The context, the cake of custom, tells him how to be a father. A divorced father, who takes a job in another city, must decide to call his child and may get his ex-wife on the phone instead. He must figure out whether talking to his child is more important to him than avoiding talking to his ex-wife. Will he be the kind of father who waits for his child to call him? Or the kind of father who calls no matter what? The culture provides examples of both kinds. The context, the cake of custom, does not make the key decision for him to quite the degree that it does for the ball-throwing father in an intact marriage. As the kin system weakens its controls on both men and women, fatherhood, like much else in life, becomes more a matter of active choice. As Anthony Giddens notes in Modernity and Self Identity, the modern individual does not so much receive an identity as make it (Giddens, 1991). One aspect of this bracing constructionist stance toward culture, for fathers, is the decision about how much emotional capital to invest in one's children. The cultural signals about this are mixed. More investment than ever before is recommended, but less investment than ever before is occurring.

The contradictions facing men are likely to differ according to social class. Here a certain irony unfolds. The cultural ideal of the new active father has changed much faster, especially in the middle classes, than the reality of the new father. In a reversal of Ogburn's theory of 'culture lag', we can say that for many middle-class men, there is a reality lag. Many middle-class men will want to be new fathers. They will fall in love with educated women who have or want professional careers, and be able to attract such a wife partly because they offer to be new fathers. But forced into an inhospitable career system, many will live with a contradiction between thinking new father but acting old father.

On the other hand, among working-class men, the reverse may occur. Working-class men (whose less educated wives are more likely to prefer to stay home, and who cannot afford paid help) often cherish a more traditional ideal but nonetheless do a great deal with home and children (Rubin, 1976; Lamphere et al., 1993). In both cases, men are living with ideals that do not fit the reality of their lives.

In the future, we may well see the middle-class ideal of the new active father spreading, as ideals often do, down the social class ladder. This has begun already. At the same time, the working-class reality of economic necessity for two incomes, and the availability of less desirable jobs may well be rising up the class ladder. In the end, for stable couples in both classes, reality and ideal may increasingly point together toward the new active father.

Three scenarios of the future

Given present trends, I can visualise three scenarios. In the first one, as more women work, the need for the new father increases as does the appeal of the ideal; the reality and the ideal go together. In the second scenario, family ties continue to loosen, and the ideal of the new father becomes more removed from the reality of life; indeed that ideal increases and develops a powerful life of its own. In the third scenario, family ties loosen, but in doing so, they weaken the ideal of the new father, following the logic: if dads are likely to divorce moms, and if moms go with children, maybe fathers should not get so involved to begin with. I expect the future of fatherhood to reflect the presence of — and a tension between — all three scenarios.

New father in what kind of culture?

The mix of family scenarios will vary depending on economic and political forces. But it will also be shaped by culture, and in particular by ideas about what children need. While the United States is a youth-oriented culture, it is not a child-oriented one. Many parents cherish their children but devalue the work of raising them. They focus on their children, privately, one by one, but largely ignore the social world in which they grow up.

Thus, even if more men become active fathers they may do so in a context of declining state subsidies for children, cuts in public school budgets, shortening of library hours, low wages for daycare teachers, and the absence of family-friendly reforms which would allow parents more time at home. The new father may be moving in the right direction while his society moves in the wrong one.

The new father may have to move against a deeper, more long term, cultural current as well. I would argue that the terms of understanding about time, appreciation, and honour that had previously been dominant at work are increasingly, if unwittingly, adopted at home. Perhaps this is an instance of what Jurgen Habermas has called the "colonisation of the life world". As a colonised sphere, the home has become less able to exert a magnetic draw on men or women, while the workplace has increased its draw. The social and cultural trends pushing both men and women into a highly valued formerly male public work culture — in which work is a major source of self appreciation, security and enjoyment — are stronger than the trends pushing men or women into active involvement with children at home, a relatively less valued, formerly female realm.

Thus, regardless of gender, in much of the American middle and even working classes, the draw of work seems to be increasing while the draw of family is decreasing and at the same time, for some, work becomes more like home (Hochschild, 1994). More than we have realised, work competes with family as a haven in a heartless world[9].

Conclusion

Fostering the new father will take both social programmes and a more basic shift in culture. Enlightened societies can foster three kinds of support to encourage active fathering. The first could reduce strains on existing families. Work sharing and company family-friendly policies could spread work, give parents more control over work time, more flexible and shorter hours. In the last fifteen years, many large American companies have instituted family-friendly policies. In 1993, President Bill Clinton also signed into law the Family and Medical Leave Act, which permits workers in companies with 50 workers or more twelve weeks of unpaid leave. By reducing the external strain on families, such policies can enable more fathers to live up to the ideals they already hold.

Second, while we can not, and probably should not, prevent all divorce among parents of small children, we can reduce the negative impact of divorce on children. We could expand mediation programmes and counselling services that could help fathers keep contact with children after divorce. Third, we can increase the supply of nurturant men for children who are estranged from their fathers. A number of projects throughout the US are reaching out to men through daycare father outreach programmes. Children who lack regular contact with their fathers can get contact with fatherly men who volunteer in nursery school or grade school. Thus, we can increase the supply of father substitutes or quasi-substitutes[10].

---

9   This is because the family has become more like a workplace; often the tired worker returns to unwashed dishes, unmet human needs, and no time to relax. Ironically, the emotional engineers of late capitalism have made the workplace for some people in certain ways more like home. One can chat and joke with co-workers, get help with problems, and feel appreciated for one's skills (Hochschild, 1994).

10 James Levine, head of the Fatherhood Project at the Families and Work Institute in New York City, notes, "often early childhood communication systems are designed - albeit unintentionally - to promote interaction between female parents and female staff" (Levine, 1993, p.12). In his activist booklet, Getting Men Involved: Strategies for Early Childhood Programs he describes various initiatives. At the Ounce of Prevention Fund in Chicago, which serves mainly minority families, organizers hire male involvement specialists who

Finally, we need to think out the chain of connections between the rationalisation of emotional life, the new mobility of emotional capital, and the important needs of small children. As a culture in which capitalism may have made the deepest inroads, the United States may prove to be the handwriting on the wall for countries like Holland, even as the fifties childhood of Sweet Summer foretold the future of many children in America. Or it may not. Either way, the future can be one of strengthening the trends that produce daddies children feel lucky to have.

References

Anderson, E. (1990). *StreetWise: Race, class and change in an urban community.* Chicago/London: University of Chicago Press.

Arendell, T. (1968). *Mothers and divorce.* Berkeley/Los Angeles: University of California Press.

Arendell, T. (1992). After divorce: Investigations into father absence. *Gender and Society 9,* 4, 562-86.

Billingsley, A. (1993). *Climbing Jacob's ladder: The enduring legacy of African American families.* New York: Simon and Schuster.

Bourdieu, P. (1984). *Distinction: A social critique of the judgement of taste.* Cambridge, MA: Harvard University Press.

Campbell, B.M. (1990). *Sweet summer: Growing up with and without my dad.* New York/London: Harper Collins.

Chodorow, N. (1980). *The reproduction of mothering.* Berkeley, CA: University of California Press.

Cutright, P. (1986). Child support and responsible male procreative behavior. *Sociological Focus, 19,* 1, 27-45.

Dugger, C.W. (1992). Establishing paternity earlier to gain child support later. *New York Times,* (Jan 3): A1-B6.

Ehrenreich, B. (1983). *The hearts of men: American dreams and the flight from commitment.* Garden City NY: Anchor Books.

---

recruit fathers and other male relatives to work with the children. Another programme combines parenting classes for men estranged from their children with adult education programmes, computer training and early childhood certification. Most remarkable of all is a programme created by the Texas Migrant Council which organizes daycare vans to follow the migratory pattern of fruit pickers, providing schooling for the children of migrant workers, and opportunities in daycare jobs to men.

Furstenberg, F. Jr., Nord, C., Peterson, P. & Zill, N. (1983). The Life Course of Children of Divorce: Marital Disruption and Parental Contact. *American Sociological Review, 48,* 656-668.

Furstenberg, F. Jr. (1991). *Daddies and fathers: Men who do for their children and men who don't.* Unpublished paper, Sociology Department, University of Pennsylvania.

Furstenberg, F. Jr. & Cherlin, A. (1991). *Divided families: What happens to children when parents part.* Cambridge, MA: Harvard University Press.

Gerson, K. (1993). *No man's land: Men's changing commitments to family.* New York: Basic Books.

Giddens, A. (1991). *Modernity and self-identity: Self and society in the late modern age.* Stanford, CA: Stanford University Press.

Goldscheider, F.K. & Waite, L.J. (1991). *New families, no families? The transformation of the American home.* Berkeley/Los Angeles: University of California Press.

Hareven, T. (1975). Family time and industrial time: Family and work in a planned corporation town, 1900-1924. *Journal of Urban History, 1,* 365-89.

Hertz, R. (1986). *More equal than others: women and men in dual career marriages.* Berkeley/Los Angeles: University of California Press.

Hochschild, A. & Machung, A. (1989) *The second shift: Working parents and the revolution at home.* New York: Avon Books.

Hochschild, A., Lydia Morris, L. & Lyon, S. (Ed.) (1994). Gender relations in public and private: Changing research perspectives. London: MacMillan Publishers (forthcoming).

Lamb, M.E. (Ed.) (1986). *The father's role: Applied perspectives.* New York: John Wiley & Sons.

Lamphere, L. et al. (1993). *Sunbelt working mothers.* Itaca, NY: Cornell University Press.

Levine, J.A. et al. (1993.) *Getting men involved: Strategies for early childhood programs.* New York: Scholastic Inc., Early Childhood Division.

Malinowski, B. (1930). The Principle of Legitimacy. In V.F. Calverton & S.D. Schmalhausen (Eds.), *The New Generation* (pp. 113-55). New York: Macauley Co.

Peterson, J. & Zill, N. (1986). Marital disruption, parent-child relationships, and behavior problems in children. *Journal of Marriage and the Family, 48,* 295-307.

Pleck, J.H. (1983). Husbands' paid work and family roles: current research issues. In H. Lopata & J.H. Pleck (Eds.), *Research in the interweave of social roles* (Vol 3). Families and jobs. Greenwich, CT: JAI Press.

Pleck, J.H. (1985). *Working wives, working husbands.* Beverly Hills/London/ New Delhi: SAGE.

Polatnick, M. (1974). Why men don't rear children: A power analysis. *Berkeley Journal of Sociology, 18*, 45-86.

Rodin, N. & Russell, A. (1982). Increased father participation and child development outcomes. In M.E. Lamb (Ed.), *Nontraditional families: Parenting and child development* (pp. 191-218). Hillsdale NJ: Enlbamm Publishers.

Rubin, L.B. (1976). *Worlds of pain: Life in the working-class family*. New York: Basic Books.

Sachs, A. (1994). Men, sex and parenthood in an overpopulating world. *World Watch, 7*, 2,12-19.

Schor, J. (1992). *The overworked American*. New York: Basic Books.

Segal, L. (1990). *Slow motion: changing masculinities, changing men*. New Brunswick, NH: Rutgers University Press.

Wallerstein, J.S. & Blakeslee, S. (1989). *Second changes: Men, women, and children a decade after divorce*. New York: Ticknor and Fields.

Weitzman, L. (1985). *The divorce revolution: The unexpected social and economic consequences for women and children in America*. New York: Free Press.

Tineke Willemsen

From typologies to diversities. A note on studying 'new fathers'

In her chapter on the future of fatherhood Arlie Hochschild describes how the ideals and realities of 'new fathers' have changed. She presents a number of trends that will shape the future of fatherhood in the USA. In this short comment I will mainly focus on the notion of the diversity of fatherhood that Hochschild has discussed, on the increasing pluriformity in the ways men shape their fatherhood. I will elaborate in particular on the consequences which this pluriformity should, in my opinion, have for research on 'new fathers'. Like many other authors present in this book Hochschild seems to subscribe to the ideal of the new father as an involved, available and responsible father (cf. Lamb, 1986). This is an ideal of fatherhood (and of motherhood, for that matter) anyone can easily share. However, there is less agreement on how new fathers should be studied. Towards the end of this paper I will present my ideal of how research on new fathers should be carried out. But first let me explain briefly how the new father forms part of another phenomenon: the new man.

The gender identity of 'new men'

New fatherhood is emerging in the context of new manhood. In my opinion the trend that fathers are changing and are becoming new types of fathers forms part of a trend that men in general are changing. At least, this seems to be the case in the Netherlands. According to my definition a 'new man' is a man who does not come up to the traditional masculine stereotype of dominance, rationality and independence and who describes himself also in terms that used to be characteristic of women, like caring, warm and sensitive. For instance, in 1992 a representative sample of more than 500 Dutch men between 18 and 45 years of age said their most characteristic personality traits were trustworthy, caring, considerate, comradely, sporty and understanding (R + M, 1992). Especially notable in this profile are the two stereotypic feminine traits *caring* and *understanding*. In the Netherlands these traits were, at the same time, considered to be very feminine (Willemsen, 1992). On the basis of this and similar studies one is tempted to conclude that men are becoming more androgynous as they combine traditionally masculine characteristics like trustworthiness and comradeship with traditionally feminine qualities such as consideration and understanding. In studies in which a unidimensional view of gender identity is used, i.e. in which gender identity is measured only in terms of personality traits, such a conclusion may be warranted. However, there is more to gender identity than just personality traits. Ashmore (1990) proposes a multiplicity model of gender identity in which biological characteristics, symbolic behaviour, interests and abilities, and social roles are included alongside personality traits. For the Netherlands we developed a measure of gender identity that includes self-descriptions of personality traits, appearance, interests, abilities, social relations and sex role behaviours (Willemsen & Fischer, 1995). Studies based on a multidimensional concept of gender identity show a more differentiated picture of new men. In the Willemsen & Fischer (1995) study two groups of respondents were compared, a 'young' group with a mean age of almost 19 years and an 'older' group with a mean age of around 45 years. In the older group we found all the traditional sex differences, i.e. men were more masculine than women and women more feminine than men, both on the subscales of the personality items and on the subscales composed of the other aspects (called 'behaviours' for the sake of convenience). For the younger group the differences between the sexes were much smaller, and not significant on the subscale of masculine personality traits; i.e., men and women did not differ in the amount of (self-ascribed) masculine personality traits. However, men scored substantially higher on the masculine behaviour subscale, and women scored higher in feminine behaviour. So, although differences in personality traits are becoming smaller, there are still differences in sex role behaviour. This is consistent with the fact that in the Netherlands in general men more often have jobs and work more hours than women, whereas women do most of the housework and fathers who spend a considerable amount of time on child care are few and far between. Most individuals still tend to assume traditional sex roles, especially when they are responsible for young children.

To take a more positive view, we found that younger men were generally more feminine than older ones. This may mean that men in general are becoming, at least according to their self descriptions, better at child care tasks than they used to be, as they possess more of the social-emotional characteristics needed for successful parenting. The trends we see in fatherhood may well be trends that we see in manhood in general, i.e. men are developing more and more of the qualities that were traditionally associated with women and motherhood, so that they are better able to do those tasks we used to call mothering. That is what we generally mean when we talk of 'new fathers': men who incorporate in their fatherhood the qualities and behaviour that we used to associate with mothers.

Studying new fathers: the daddy hierarchy in research

To study fatherhood at this moment means studying a phenomenon that is in a process of change. This is of course a difficult endeavour, since the descriptive results of these studies are likely to become obsolete in a relatively short time. It is also, on the other hand, a very challenging situation. We are now able, for the first time, to study the effects and consequences of new forms of fatherhood in real situations. However, researchers do not always know how to handle the different forms which fatherhood can take in their research projects. Between the workaholic who hardly sees his children and the full-time houseman there is a whole range of other forms of fathering. In women's studies there is a tradition of studying the diversity of women and mothers. Unfortunately, this tradition is not upheld in this relatively new field of studying fathers, especially new fathers. Hochschild, for instance, considers the diversity of fatherhood in general but discusses only two types of fathers in some detail: the 'new' father and the 'absent' father. In a number of recent Dutch studies of fathers we see a tendency to restrict the diversity of modern fatherhood by immediately pigeon-holing it.

From studies in the field of social psychology we know that categorising affects the way the categorised persons are perceived (Tajfel, 1981). Perceivers who think in terms of categories will experience *assimilation* within categories, i.e. they tend to overlook the differences betwen the members of a category and to emphasise the similarities between them. On the other hand there is a process of *contrast* between categories, i.e. differences between members of different categories are emphasised wheras similarities tend to be overlooked. Differences on dimensions that are highly valued by the perceiver tend to be exaggerated in this process that generally occurs unintentionally. Categorisation thus leads to a hierarchy, a division into groups that are valued to a greater or lesser extent. These differences in appreciation, combined with the assimilation effect, can in turn lead to discrimination, the attribution of all kinds of negatively valued characteristics to all members of a certain category and acting accordingly, without acknowledgement of the differences that exist between the members of the same category (Tajfel, 1981).

An example of such an unnecessary categorisation that almost elicits discrimination can be found in a study on 'new fathers' by Mozes-Philips and Wester (1993). To find out what exactly a caring father is these authors studied a group of fathers who all contributed, to varying degrees, to the care of their children. On the basis of twenty interviews the authors developed four categories based on the relative contribution the fathers made to household tasks and to child care tasks. Mozes-Philips and Wester named these categories: 'the new-style traditional father', 'the assisting father', 'the participating father' and 'the caring father'. The data they collected in the next part of their study are placed into these categories and interpreted in relation to them.

Of course, the popular media are only too keen to make use of such a typology when it is presented to them. All they have to do is copy these very appealing terms. And that is exactly what happened. A good example of the discrimination such a typology can lead to, was an article in a magazine geared to 'professional women with ambition' (called VBmagazine, where V stands for Vrouw, woman, and B for Bedrijf, company). The article, which described the results of the study by Mozes-Philips and Wester, seized the opportunity offered by these authors, and adopted the typology. However, in presenting these four categories the magazine added its own evaluation of each type of father. The new-style traditional father received the comment 'for professional women this type of father is of no use at all'. The assisting father was put down as 'nice but not really practical'. The participating father ended up somewhat higher in the hierarchy with the comment 'very useful, because he will generally stick to an agreement and you can really delegate some chores to him'. The caring father was the only one to get a positive comment: 'the only type of father who is really of some use for the division of tasks'.

These comments clearly show how counterproductive a system of categories can be. It almost inevitably leads to a hierarchy and as a result everyone who is not in the top category is put down without mercy. In Women's Studies processes like this one have often been described in connection with the oppression or discrimination of women due to the male-female categorisation. I think we should learn from this experience and not start on the wrong foot by inventing new typologies for fathers. There are more types of fathers than just old ones and new ones. Social scientists should not pretend to be able to assess the daddy hierarchy. Even within the same family, the preference for a certain type of fathering is not necessarily stable. Within families the need for a fathers' contribution can change over time, and fathers themselves change. Different women have different preferences which are, moreover, contingent on their own situation. A mother who has a satisfying and well-paid full-time job may want the father of her children to make a big effort towards taking on household and child care tasks. A mother who holds a low-paid, part-time job, however, may prefer the father to exploit his wage-earning capacities to the full, even if that detracts from his household and child care activities. A typology of fathers that does not consider the context, and which only acknowledges the time spent on one type of task is inadequate because it fails to take account of the considerations that may underlie the division of tasks. This is not made good by the fact that the tasks on which the typology is based are in the traditionally female domains of household and child care.

Towards studying parents

We can take the abolition of unnecessary categorisation in research one step further. Fathers can only be free to find out how they want to shape their fatherhood, and mothers can only be the mothers they want to be, if the context in which they live does not continuously confront them with expectations that fathers and mothers should do different things, or even that they are essentially different human beings. Social scientists also form part of the context in which fathers and mothers live. Why is our research divided into separate studies of fathers and separate studies of mothers, often performed from thoroughly different theoretical viewpoints?

A well-known example of research that focusses on the traditional role of the mother is the research tradition of studying the effects of 'maternal deprivation' that has resulted from Bowlby's (1958) publications. In this line of research the problem studied is whether children who do not receive sufficient attention from their mothers suffer from developmental disorders. The concept of 'paternal deprivation' does not even seem to exist in developmental psychology. In the introductory text by Hetherington and Parke (1986) used at many universities, the term 'maternal deprivation' is included in the glossary and the index; this is not the case for 'paternal deprivation'. An example of an opposite phenomenon, namely that women are overlooked, is to be found in research on the effects of unemployment on families. Leana and Feldman (1991) have noticed that in these studies the unemployment of fathers — who have lost their traditional role as a breadwinner — is almost always the exclusive focus of interest.

Many of the theories that take the differences between fathers and mothers for granted, especially psychoanalytical theories, stem from times when motherhood implied the full-time presence of a mother at home, while fatherhood was not much more than being a breadwinner for the whole family. I doubt whether such theories can still be applied to fathers and mothers who live in differently stuctured families in a different cultural context.

Of course, I do not want to remove gender from our studies of parenthood. Gender is the strongest structuring principle of the world we live in and will inevitably influence the way we think about parenthood and the way we study parenthood. However, it is precisely because men and women are beginning to abandon traditional gender roles within families that we are interested in studying them. So why would we do these studies using theories and methods based on traditional gender roles? It would be more useful to study 'new fathers' and 'new mothers' in their own right, instead of studying them in relation to old gender roles. This is often the case since in many studies traditional gender roles are used as the norm to which actual roles are compared. The whole concept of 'new fathers' is, of course, a comparative one. I think we should study parenthood and the influence of sex and gender on parenthood without including all kinds of stereotypic assumptions on how male parents are different from female parents in the problem definition and design of the study. Rather, our research should consider whether, and how, masculinity and femininity influence the phenomena we study.

References

Ashmore, R. (1990). Sex, gender, and the individual. In L.A. Pervin (Ed.), *Handbook of personality* (pp. 486-526). New York: Guilford.

Bowlby, J. (1958). The nature of the child's tie to his mother. *International Journal of Psychoanalysis, 39*, 350-373.

Hetherington, E.M. & Parke, R.D. (1986). *Child Psychology (3rd ed.)*. New York: McGraw-Hill.

Leana, C.R. & Feldman, D.C. (1991). Gender differences in responses to unemployment. *Journal of Vocational Behavior, 38*, 65-77.

Lamb, M.E. (1986). *The father's role. Applied Perspectives*. New York: Wiley.

Mozes-Philips, M. & Wester, F. (1993). *Zorgen voor de toekomst* [Caring for the future]. Den Haag (Netherlands): Ministerie van Sociale Zaken en Werkgelegenheid.

R + M, Research en Marketing (1992). *Onderzoeksresultaten in het kader van een onderzoek naar de rol van de man in deze tijd t.b.v. VNU Tijdschriftengroep bv te Amstelveen* [Results from a study on the role of the man in this time for VNU Magazinegroup at Amstelveen]. Heerlen (Netherlands), unpublished report.

Tajfel, H. (1981). *Human groups and social categories*. Cambridge: Cambridge University Press.

VB Magazine (april 1994). *De nieuwe vaders. Wat heb je er eigenlijk aan?* [The new fathers. Of what use are they, really?]. pp. 36-41.

Willemsen, T.M. (1992). Sekse als cognitieve categorie [Sex as a cognitive category]. In T. Top & J. Heesink (Eds.), *Psychologie en sekse* [Psychology and gender], (pp. 60-79). Houten (Netherlands): Bohn Stafleu Van Loghum.

Willemsen, T.M. & Fischer, A.H. (1995). *Femininiteit en masculiniteit* [Femininity and masculinity]. Manuscript submitted for publication.

Subject index